MYTHS
OF THE
NEW WORLD

MYTHS
OF THE
NEW WORLD

The Symbolism And
Mythology Of The Indians
Of The Americas

by Daniel G. Brinton, M.D.

Introduction by Paul M. Allen

Multimedia Publishing Corp.
Blauvelt, New York 10913 U.S.A.

Library of Congress Catalogue Card Number 72-81594

Printed in the United States of America

INTRODUCTION

Daniel Garrison Brinton, pioneer American archeologist and ethnologist, was born at Thornbury, Pennsylvania on May 13, 1837. After his graduation from Yale University in 1858 he studied for two years in Jefferson Medical College, becoming a qualified physician and surgeon in 1860. Wishing to supplement his medical training by study in Europe he went to Heidelberg for a short time and afterward to the Sorbonne.

The outbreak of the War Between the States brought him back to Pennsylvania and from 1862 to 1865 he served as surgeon for the Union Army, first on the battlefields where he was cited for his courage and bravery in carrying out his professional ministrations, often under heavy artillery fire, afterward as surgeon-in-charge of the United States Army General Hospital at Quincy, Illinois. A man of deep religious convictions, his quiet kindliness and evenness of temper won him the respect and gratitude of those under his care.

Following his wartime service Brinton practised medicine at Westchester, Pennsylvania for several years. At this time he became known widely in the profession as editor of a weekly periodical, The Medical and Surgical Reporter, a position he filled with marked ability from 1874-1887.

Meanwhile Dr. Brinton's interests had extended beyond the fields of medicine and surgery into archeology, ethnology and folklore, particularly concerned with the Indians of North America. His studies bore rich fruit, not only in the many volumes he wrote but in his activities in the scholastic field as well. In 1884 he was appointed professor of Ethnology and Archeology in the Academy of Natural Science in Philadelphia. Two years later he was elected to the chair of American Linguistics and Archeology in the University of Pennsylvania, a position he held with great distinction until his death at Philadelphia on July 31, 1899. He was a member of many learned societies in the United States and Europe and was president for several terms of the Antiquarian Society of Philadelphia, of the American Folklore Society, and of the American Society for the Advancement of Science.

Out of the wealth of essays, brochures, magazine articles and books Dr. Brinton wrote during the forty years between 1859 and his death, many remain of permanent value in the field of American Indian studies. These include his *American Hero Myths*, 1882, *Essays of an Americanist*, 1890, *Races and Peoples*, 1891, *Religions of Primitive Peoples*, 1897. Between 1882 and 1890 Dr. Brinton edited an important series of eight volumes under the general title, *A Library of American Aboriginal Literature*, considered one of the most valuable contributions ever made to the science of American anthropology. His deep interest in the mythology and customs of the Indians of North America led him to an extensive study of the various Indian languages, about which he wrote a number of important studies, including a *Grammar of the Choctaw Language*.

In April 1868 Brinton completed what is generally considered his most important, original contribution to an understanding and appreciation of the mythology of the Indians of North America, his *Myths of the New World*. The book excited widespread interest, and soon further editions were required. Today it remains what one eminent authority has described as a landmark in "the attempt to analyze and correlate, according to true scientific principles, the mythology of the American Indians."

Dr. Brinton himself described his object in writing the book in a brief preface which appeared in the first edition. There he said that "among the universally interesting questions which I attempt to solve in this book are: What are man's earliest ideas of his own origin and destiny? Why do we find certain myths, such as of a creation, a flood, an after-world; certain symbols, as the bird, the serpent, the cross; certain numbers, as the three, the four, the seven — intimately associated with these ideas by every race?..."

Today people in many countries — young people in particular — are markedly attracted to these "universally interesting questions," the esoteric secrets concerning man's origin and destiny, the true purpose and meaning of life, as these have been expressed from times immemorial in the mythologies of the various peoples of the earth, the Indians of the Americas in particular.

For extraordinarily significant reasons the wisdom of the Ancient American Indian Mystery Centers, preserved in folklore, language, customs and mythology, is stirring modern American consciousness in a quite new way, exerting a profound influence beneath the surface of contemporary events.

Like "voices from the dust" the figures of a long-forgotten past begin to speak to modern men, awakening in them a keen desire to understand the picture-language of the mythology of the ancient Americans. Daniel Brinton's book can be of greatest assistance to this understanding.

— Paul M. Allen.

Botton Hall,
Danby/Whitby,
Yorkshire, England.
Spring 1974.

CONTENTS.

CHAPTER I.

GENERAL CONSIDERATIONS ON THE RED RACE.

CHAPTER II.

THE IDEA OF GOD.

CHAPTER III.

THE SACRED NUMBER, ITS ORIGIN AND APPLICATIONS.

CHAPTER IV.

THE SYMBOLS OF THE BIRD AND THE SERPENT.

CHAPTER V.

THE MYTHS OF WATER, FIRE, AND THE THUNDER-STORM, AND THE RELIGION OF SEX.

CHAPTER VI.

THE SUPREME GODS OF THE RED RACE.

CHAPTER VII.

THE MYTHS OF THE CREATION, THE DELUGE, THE EPOCHS OF NATURE, AND THE LAST DAY.

CHAPTER VIII.

THE ORIGIN OF MAN.

CHAPTER IX.

THE SOUL AND ITS DESTINY.

CHAPTER X.

THE NATIVE PRIESTHOOD.

CHAPTER XI.

THE INFLUENCE OF THE NATIVE RELIGIONS ON THE MORAL AND SOCIAL LIFE OF THE RACE.

THE MYTHS OF THE NEW WORLD.

CHAPTER I.

GENERAL CONSIDERATIONS ON THE RED RACE.

Natural religions the unaided attempts of man to find out God, modified
by peculiarities of race and nation.—The peculiarities of the red race :
1. Its languages unfriendly to abstract ideas. Native modes of writing
by means of pictures, symbols, objects, and phonetic signs. These
various methods compared in their influence on the intellectual faculties. 2. Its isolation, unique in the history of the world. 3. Beyond
all others, a hunting race.—Principal linguistic subdivisions : 1. The
Eskimos. 2. The Athapascas. 3. The Algonkins and Iroquois. 4.
The Chahta-Muskokees. 5. The Dakotas. 6. The Aztecs. 7. The
Mayas. 8. The Muyscas. 9. The Quichuas. 10. The Caríbs and
Tupis. 11. The Araucanians.—General course of migrations.—Age of
man in America.—Unity of Type in the red race.

WHEN Paul, at the request of the populace of
Athens, explained to them his views on divine
things, he asserted, among other startling novelties,
that "God has made of one blood all nations of the
earth, that they should seek the Lord, if haply they
might feel after him and find him, though he is not
far from every one of us."

Here was an orator advocating the unity of the
human species, affirming that the chief end of man is
to develop an innate idea of God, and that all religions except the one he preached, were examples of

1

more or less unsuccessful attempts to do so. No wonder the Athenians, who acknowledged no kinship to barbarians, who looked dubiously at the doctrine of innate ideas, and were divided in opinion as to whether their mythology was a shrewd device of legislators to keep the populace in subjection, a veiled natural philosophy, or the celestial reflex of their own history, mocked at such a babbler and went their ways. The generations of philosophers that followed them partook of their doubts and approved their opinions, quite down to our own times. But now, after weighing the question maturely, we are compelled to admit that the Apostle was not so wide of the mark after all—that, in fact, the latest and best authorities, with no bias in his favor, support his position and may almost be said to paraphrase his words. For according to a writer who ranks second to none in the science of ethnology, the severest and most recent investigations show that in all that we can suppose to constitute specific unity, the human race is one, and that " this opinion is attended with fewer discrepancies, and has greater inner consistency than the opposite one of specific diversity." [1] While as to the religions of heathendom, the view of Saint Paul is but expressed with a more poetic turn by a distinguished living author when he calls them " not fables, but truths, though clothed in a garb woven by fancy, wherein the web is the notion of God, the ideal of reason in the soul of man, the thought of the Infinite." [2]

[1] Waitz, *Anthropologie der Naturvoelker*, i. p. 256.
[2] Carriere. *Die Kunst im Zusammenhang der Culturentwickelung*, i. p. 66.

Inspiration and science unite therefore to bid us dismiss, as effete, the prejudice that natural religions either arise as the ancient philosophies taught, or that they are, as the Dark Ages imagined, subtle nets of the devil spread to catch human souls. They are rather the unaided attempts of man to find out God; they are the efforts of the reason struggling to define the unknown, they are the expressions of that "yearning after the gods" which the earliest of poets discerned in the hearts of all men. Studied in this sense they are rich in teachings. Would we estimate the intellectual and æsthetic culture of a people, would we generalize the laws of progress, would we appreciate the sublimity of Christianity, and read the seals of its authenticity: the natural conceptions of divinity reveal them. No mythologies are so crude, therefore, none so barbarous, but deserve the attention of the philosophic mind, for they are never the empty fictions of an idle fancy, but rather the utterances, however inarticulate, of an intuition of reason.

These considerations embolden me to approach with some confidence even the aboriginal religions of America, so often stigmatized as incoherent fetichisms, so barren, it has been said, in grand or beautiful creations. The task bristles with difficulties. Carelessness, prepossessions, and ignorance have disfigured them with false colors and foreign additions without number. The first maxim, therefore, must be to sift and scrutinize authorities, and to reject whatever betrays the plastic hand of the European. For the religions developed by the red race, not those mixed creeds learned from foreign invaders, are to be the subjects of our study. Then will remain the formidable undertaking of reducing the authentic materials thus obtained to system and order, and this not by any preconceived theory of what they ought to conform to, but learning from them the very laws of religious growth they illustrate. The historian traces the birth of arts, science, and government to man's dependence on nature and his fellows for the means of self-preservation. Not that man receives these endowments from without, but that the stern stepmother, Nature, forces him by threats and stripes to develop his own inherent faculties. So with religion. The idea of God does not, and cannot proceed from the external world. but, nevertheless, it finds its *historical* origin also in the desperate struggle for life, in the satisfaction of the animal wants and passions, in those vulgar aims and motives which possessed the mind of the primitive man to the exclusion of everything else.

There is an ever present embarrassment in such inquiries. In dealing with these matters beyond the cognizance of the senses, the mind is forced to express its meaning in terms transferred from sensuous perceptions, or under symbols borrowed from the material world. These transfers must be understood, these symbols explained, before the real meaning of a myth can be reached. He who fails to guess the riddle of the sphynx, need not hope to gain admittance to the shrine. With delicate ear the faint whispers of thought must be apprehended which prompt the intellect when it names the immaterial from the material; when it chooses from the infinity of visible forms those meet to shadow forth Divinity.

Two lights will guide us on this venturesome path.

Mindful of the watchword of inductive science, to proceed from the known to the unknown, the inquiry will be put whether the aboriginal languages of America employ the same tropes to express such ideas as deity, spirit, and soul, as our own and kindred tongues. If the answer prove affirmative, then not only have we gained a firm foothold whence to survey the whole edifice of their mythology; but from it we may draw evidence of the unity of our species far weightier than any unity of anatomy, evidence of the oneness of emotion and thought. True, the science of American linguistics is still in its infancy, and a proper handling of the materials it even now offers involves a more critical acquaintance with its innumerable dialects than I possess; but though the gleaning be sparse, it is enough that I break the ground. Secondly, religious rites are unconscious commentaries on religious beliefs. Some are devices to cajole the gods, while others represent their supposed actions. The Indian rain-maker mounts to the roof of his hut, and rattling vigorously a dry gourd containing pebbles, to represent the thunder, scatters water through a reed on the ground beneath, as he imagines up above in the clouds do the spirits of the storm. Every spring in ancient Delphi was repeated in scenic ceremony the combat of Apollo and the Dragon, the victory of the lord of bright summer over the demon of chilling winter. Thus do forms and ceremonies reveal the meaning of mythology, and the origin of its fables.

Let it not be objected that this proposed method of analysis assumes that religions begin and develop under the operation of inflexible laws. The soul is shackled by no such fatalism. Formative influences there are, deep seated, far reaching, escaped by few, 'but like those which of yore, astrologers imputed to the stars, they do but potently incline, they do not coerce.

Language, pursuits, habits, geographical position, and those subtle mental traits which make up the characters of races and nations, all tend to deflect from a given standard the religious life of the indi vidual and the mass. It is essential to give these due weight, and a necessary preface, therefore, to an analysis of the myths of the red race is an enumeration of its peculiarities, and of its chief families as they were located when first known to the historian.

Of all such modifying circumstances none has greater importance than the means of expressing and transmitting intellectual action. The spoken and the written language of a nation reveal to us its prevailing, and to a certain degree its unavoidable mode of thought. Here the red race offers a striking phenomenon. There is no other trait that binds together its scattered clans, and brands them as members of one family, so unmistakably as this of language. From the Frozen Ocean to the Land of Fire, without a single exception, the native dialects, though varying infinitely in words, are marked by a peculiarity in construction which is found nowhere else on the globe. [1] and which is so foreign to the genius of *our* tongue that it is no easy matter to explain it. It is called by philologists the *polysynthetic* construction.

---

[1] It is said indeed that the Yebus, a people on the west coast of Africa, speak a polysynthetic language, and *per contra*, that the Otomis of Mexico have a monosyllabic one like the Chinese.

What it is will best appear by comparison. Every grammatical sentence conveys one leading idea with its modifications and relations. Now a Chinese would express these latter by unconnected syllables, the precise bearing of which could only be guessed by their position ; a Greek or a German would use independent words, indicating their relations by terminations meaningless in themselves; an Englishman gains the same end chiefly by the use of particles and by position. Very different from all these is the spirit of a polysynthetic language. It seeks to unite in the most intimate manner all relations and modifications with the leading idea, to merge one in the other by altering the forms of the words themselves and welding them together, to express the whole in one word, and to banish any conception except as it arises in relation to others. Thus in many American tongues there is, in fact, no word for father, mother, brother, but only for my, your, his father, etc. This has advantages and defects. It offers marvellous facilities for defining the perceptions of the senses with accu-

Max Mueller goes further, and asserts that what is called the process of agglutination in the Turanian languages is the same as what has been named polysynthesis in America. This is not to be conceded. In the former the root is unchangeable, the formative elements follow it, and prefixes are not used ; in the latter prefixes are common, and the formative elements are blended with the root, both undergoing changes of structure. Very important differences. Mr. J. H. Trumbull, in saying that the radicals of American languages " enter into composition without undergoing change of form " (*Trans. Am. Philol. Soc.*, 1869-70, p. 66), certainly goes too far ; when the root contains more than one phonetic element it changes *par voie d'intro-susception* (See *Jugement erroné sur les Langues Sauvages*, 2d Ed., p. 31).

racy; but regarding everything in the concrete, it is unfriendly to the nobler labors of the mind, to abstraction and generalization. In the numberless changes of these languages, their bewildering flexibility, their variable forms, and their rapid deterioration, they seem to betray a lack of individuality, and to resemble the vague and tumultuous history of the tribes who employ them. They exhibit an almost incredible laxity. It is nothing uncommon for the two sexes to use different names for the same object, and for nobles and vulgar, priests and people, the old and the young, nay, even the married and single, to observe what seem to the European ear quite different modes of expression. Families and whole villages suddenly drop words and manufacture others in their places out of mere caprice or superstition, and a few years' separation suffices to produce a marked dialectic difference. [1] In their copious forms and facility of reproduction they remind one of those anomalous animals, in whom, when a limb is lopped, it rapidly grows again, or even if cut in pieces each part will enter on a separate life quite unconcerned about his fellows. But as the naturalist is far from regarding this superabundant vitality as a characteristic of a high type, so the philologist justly assigns these tongues a low position in the linguistic scale. Fidelity to form, here as everywhere, is the test of superiority. At the outset, we divine there can be nothing very

[1] In a review of the first edition of this work Professor Steinthal, of Berlin, questions this statement. Mr. J. H. Trumbull expresses a modified belief in it (*Trans. Am. Philol. Soc.*, 1869–70, p. 61). After careful consideration I leave it unaltered, as I am still persuaded the picture is not overdrawn.

subtle in the mythologies of nations with such languages. Much there must be that will be obscure, much that is vague, an exhausting variety in repetition, and a strong tendency to lose the idea in the symbol.

What definiteness of outline might be´ preserved must depend on the care with which the old stories of the gods were passed from one person and one generation to another. The fundamental myths of a race have a surprising tenacity of life. How many centuries had elapsed between the period the Germanic hordes left their ancient homes in Central Asia, and when Tacitus listened to their wild songs on the banks of the Rhine? Yet we know that through those unnumbered ages of barbarism and aimless roving, these songs, " their only sort of history or annals," says the historian, had preserved intact the story of Mannus, the Sanscrit Manu, and his three sons, and of the great god Tuisco, the Indian Dyu. [1] So much the more do all means invented by the red race to record and transmit thought, merit our careful attention. Few and feeble they seem to us, mainly shifts to aid the memory. Of some such, perhaps, not a single tribe was destitute. The tattoo marks on the warrior's breast, his string of grisly scalps, the bear's claws around his neck, were not only trophies of his prowess, but records of his exploits, and to the contemplative mind contain the rudiments of the beneficent art of letters. Did he draw in rude outline on his skin tent figures of men transfixed with arrows as many as he had slain en-

---

[1] Grimm, *Geschichte der Deutschen Sprache,* p. 571.

emies, his education was rapidly advancing. He had mastered the elements of *picture writing*, beyond which hardly the wisest of his race progressed. Figures of the natural objects connected by symbols having fixed meanings make up the whole of this art. The relative frequency of the latter marks its advancement from a merely figurative to an ideographic notation. On what principle of mental association a given sign was adopted to express a certain idea, why, for instance, on the Chipeway scrolls a circle means *spirits*, and a horned snake *life*, it is often hard to guess. The difficulty grows when we find that to the initiated the same sign calls up quite different ideas, as the subject of the writer varies from war to love, or from the chase to religion. The connection is generally beyond the power of divination, and the key to ideographic writing once lost can never be recovered.

The number of such arbitrary characters in the Chipeway notation is said to be over two hundred, but if the distinction between a figure and a symbol were rigidly applied, it would be much reduced. This kind of writing, if it deserves the name, was common throughout the continent, and many specimens of it, scratched on the plane surfaces of stones, have been preserved to the present day. Such is the once celebrated inscription on Dighton Rock, Massachusetts, long supposed to be a record of the Northmen of Vineland; such those that mark the faces of the cliffs which overhang the waters of the Orinoco, and those which in Oregon, Peru, and La Plata have been the subject of much curious speculation. They are the mute epitaphs of vanished generations.

I would it could be said that in favorable contrast

to our ignorance of these inscriptions is our comprehension of the highly wrought pictography of the
Aztecs. No nation ever reduced it more to a system.
It was in constant use in the daily transactions of life.
They manufactured for writing purposes a thick,
coarse paper from the leaves of the agave plant, by a
process of maceration and pressure. An Aztec book
closely resembles one of our quarto volumes. It is
made of a single sheet, twelve to fifteen inches wide,
and often sixty or seventy feet long, and is not rolled,
but folded either in squares or zigzags in such a manner that on opening it there are two pages exposed to
view. Thin wooden boards are fastened to each of
the outer leaves, so that the whole presents as neat an
appearance, remarks Peter Martyr, as if it had come
from the shop of a skilful bookbinder. They also
covered buildings, tapestries, and scrolls of parchment
with these devices, and for trifling transactions were
familiar with the use of *slates* of soft stone, from which
the figures could readily be erased with water. [1]
What is still more astonishing, there is reason to believe, in some instances, their figures were not painted,
but actually *printed* with movable blocks of wood, on
which the symbols were carved in relief, though this
was probably confined to those intended for ornament
only.

In these records we discern something higher than
a mere symbolic notation. They contain the germ of
a phonetic alphabet, and represent sounds of spoken
language. The symbol is often not connected with
the *idea* but with the *word*. The mode in which this

[1] Peter Martyr, *De Insulis nuper Repertis*, p. 354 ; Colon. 1574.

is done corresponds precisely to that of the rebus. It is a simple method, readily suggesting itself. In the middle ages it was much in vogue in Europe for the same purpose for which it was chiefly employed in Mexico at the same time—the writing of proper names. For example, the English family Bolton was known in heraldry by a *tun* transfixed by a *bolt*. Precisely so the Mexican emperor Ixcoatl is mentioned in the Aztec manuscripts under the figure of a serpent *coatl*, pierced by obsidian knives *ixtli*, and Moquauhzoma by a mouse-trap *montli*, an eagle *quauhtli*, a lancet *zo*, and a hand *maitl*. As a syllable could be expressed by any object whose name commenced with it, as few words can be given the form of a rebus without some change, as the figures sometimes represent their full phonetic value, sometimes only that of their initial sound, and as universally the attention of the artist was directed less to the sound than to the idea, the didactic painting of the Mexicans, whatever it might have been to them, is a sealed book to us, and must remain so in great part. Moreover, it is entirely un-determined whether it should be read from the first to the last page, or *vice versa*, whether from right to left or from left to right, from bottom to top or from top to bottom, around the edges of the page toward the centre, or each line in the opposite direction from the preceding one. There are good authorities for all these methods, [1] and they may all be correct, for there is no evidence that any fixed rule had been laid down in this respect.

[1] They may be found in Waitz, *Anthrop. der Naturvoelker,* **iv.** p. 173.

Immense masses of such documents were stored in the imperial archives of ancient Mexico. Torquemada asserts that five cities alone yielded to the Spanish governor on one requisition no less than sixteen thousand volumes or scrolls ! Every leaf was destroyed. Indeed, so thorough and wholesale was the destruction of these memorials, now so precious in our eyes, that hardly enough remain to whet the wits of antiquaries. In the libraries of Paris, Dresden, Pesth, and the Vatican are, however, a sufficient number to make us despair of deciphering them had we for comparison all which the Spaniards destroyed.

Beyond all others the Mayas, resident on the peninsula of Yucatan, would seem to have approached nearest a true phonetic system. They had a regular and well understood alphabet of twenty-seven elementary sounds, the letters of which are totally different from those of any other nation, and evidently original with themselves. But besides these they used a large number of purely conventional symbols, and moreover were accustomed constantly to employ the ancient pictographic method in addition, as a sort of commentary on the sound represented. What is more curious, if the obscure explanation of an ancient writer can be depended upon, they not only aimed to employ an alphabet after the manner of ours, but to express the sound absolutely as our phonographic signs do. [1] With the aid of this alphabet, which has

---

[1] The only authority is Diego de Landa, *Relacion de las Cosas de Yucatan*, ed. Brasseur, Paris, 1864, p. 318. The explanation is extremely obscure in the original. I have given it in the only

fortunately been preserved, we are enabled to spell out a few words on the Yucatecan manuscripts and façades, but thus far with no positive results. The loss of the ancient pronunciation is especially in the way of such studies.

In South America, also, there is said to have been a nation who cultivated the art of picture writing, the Panos, on the river Ucayale. A missionary, Narcisso Gilbar by name, once penetrated, with great toil, to one of their villages. As he approached he beheld a venerable man seated under the shade of a palm-tree, with a great book open before him from which he was reading to an attentive circle of auditors the wars and wanderings of their forefathers. With difficulty the priest got a sight of the precious volume, and found it covered with figures and signs in marvellous symmetry and order. [1] No wonder such a romantic scene left a deep impression on his memory.

The Peruvians adopted a totally different and unique system of records, that by means of the *quipu.* This was a base cord, the thickness of the finger, of any required length, to which were attached numerous

sense in which the author's words seem to have any meaning. A useful *Bibliographic Paléographique Américaine* may be found in the *Archives Paléographique de l'Orient et de l'Amérique*, 1869. M. H. de Charencey has attempted several translations of the Palenque inscriptions and the *Manuscrit Troano.* A few years ago I reproduced the Maya alphabet in a pamphlet on " The ancient Phonetic Alphabet of Yucatan." A remarkable study of its pictorial derivation is given in Dr. Harrison Allen's work, *The Life Form in Art.* Phila. 1875.

[1] Humboldt, *Vues des Cordillères*, p. 72.

small strings of different colors, lengths, and textures, variously knotted and twisted one with another. Each of these peculiarities represented a certain number, a quality, quantity, or other idea, but *what*, not the most fluent *quipu* reader could tell unless he was acquainted with the general topic treated of. Therefore, whenever news was sent in this manner, a person accompanied the bearer to serve as verbal commentator, and to prevent confusion the *quipus* relating to the various departments of knowledge were placed in separate storehouses, one for war, another for taxes, a third for history, and so forth. On what principle of mnemotechnics the ideas were connected with the knots and colors we are very much in the dark; it has even been doubted whether they had any application beyond the art of numeration. [1] Each combination had, however, a fixed ideographic value in a certain branch of knowledge, and thus the *quipu* differed essentially from the Catholic rosary, the Jewish phylactery, or the knotted strings of the natives of North America and Siberia, to all of which it has at times been compared.

The *wampum* used by the tribes of the north Atlantic coast was, in many respects, analogous to the quipu. In early times it was composed chiefly of wood and shells of equal size but different colors. These were hung on strings which were woven into belts and bands, the hues, shapes, sizes, and combinations of the strings hinting their general significance. Thus the lighter shades were invariable harbingers

---

[1] Desjardins, *Le Pérou avant la Conquête Espagnole*, p. 122: Paris, 1858.

of peaceful or pleasant tidings, while the darker portended war and danger. The designs and figures had definite meanings, recognized over wide areas.

Besides these, various simpler mnemonic aids were employed, such as parcels of reeds of different lengths, notched sticks, knots in cords, strings of pebbles or fruit-stones, circular pieces of wood, "small wheels,"[1] or slabs pierced with different figures which the English liken to " cony holes," and at a victory, a treaty, or the founding of a village, sometimes a pillar or heap of stones was erected equalling in number the persons present at the occasion, or the number of the fallen.

This exhausts the list. All other methods of writing, the hieroglyphs of the Micmacs of Acadia, the syllabic alphabet of the Cherokees, the pretended traces of Greek, Hebrew, and Celtiberic letters which have from time to time been brought to the notice of the public, have been without exception the products of foreign civilization or simple frauds. Not a single coin, inscription, or memorial of any kind whatever, has been found on the American continent showing the existence, either generally or locally, of any other means of writing than those specified.

Poor as these substitutes for a developed phonetic system seem to us, they were of great value to the uncultivated man. In his legends their introduction is usually ascribed to some heaven-sent benefactor, the antique characters were jealously adhered to, and the pictured scroll of bark, the quipu ball, the belt of wampum, were treasured with provident care, and

---

[1] Reported of the Oenocks, an Algonkin tribe, by J. Lederer, *Discoveries*, p. 4.

their import minutely expounded to the most intelligent of the rising generation.   In all communities beyond the stage of barbarism, a class of persons was set apart for this duty and no other.   Thus, for example, in ancient Peru, one college of priests styled *amauta*, learned, had exclusive charge over the quipus containing the mythological and historical traditions ; a second, the *haravecs*, singers, devoted themselves to those referring to the national ballads and dramas ; while a third occupied their time solely with those pertaining to civil affairs.   Such custodians preserved and prepared the archives, learned by heart with their aid what their fathers knew, and in some countries, as, for instance, among the Panos mentioned above, and the Quiches of Guatemala,[1] repeated portions of them at times to the assembled populace.   It has even been averred by one of their converted chiefs, long a missionary to his fellows, that the Chipeways of Lake Superior have a college composed of ten " of the wisest and most venerable of their nation," who have in charge the pictured records containing the ancient history of their tribe.   These are kept in an underground chamber, and are disinterred every fifteen years by the assembled guardians, that they may be repaired, and their contents explained to new members of the society. [2]   Mr. Horatio Hale tells me that the Iroquois preserve a similar institution to keep up the interpretation of their wampum belts.

[1] An instance is given by Ximenes, *Origen de los Indios de Guatemala*, p. 186: Vienna, 1856.
[2] George Copway, *Traditional History of the Ojibway Nation*, p. 130: London, 1850.

2

In spite of these precautions, the end seems to have been very imperfectly attained. The most distinguished characters, the weightiest events in national history faded into oblivion after a few generations. The time and circumstances of the formation of the league of the Five Nations, the dispersion of the mound builders of the Ohio valley in the fifteenth century, the chronicles of Peru or Mexico beyond a century or two anterior to the conquest, are preserved in such a vague and contradictory manner that they have slight value as history. Their mythology fared somewhat better, for not only was it kept fresh in the memory by frequent repetition; but being itself founded in nature, it was constantly nourished by the truths which gave it birth. Nevertheless, we may profit by the warning to remember that their myths are myths only, and not the reflections of history or heroes.

Rising from these details to a general comparison of the symbolic and phonetic systems in their reactions on the mind, the most obvious are their contrasted effects on the faculty of memory. Letters represent elementary sounds, which are few in any language, while symbols stand for ideas, and they are numerically infinite. The transmission of knowledge by means of the latter is consequently attended with most disproportionate labor. It is almost as if we could quote nothing from an author unless we could recollect his exact words. We have a right to look for excellent memories where such a mode is in vogue, and in the present instance we are not disappointed. "These savages," exclaims La Hontan, "have the happiest memories in the world!" It was etiquette at their councils for each speaker to repeat verbatim all his predecessors had said, and the whites were often astonished and confused at the verbal fidelity with which the natives recalled the transactions of long past treaties. Their songs were inexhaustible. An instance is on record where an Indian sang two hundred on various subjects.[1] Such a fact reminds us of a beautiful expression of the elder Humboldt : " Man," he says, " regarded as an animal, belongs to one of the singing species ; but his notes are always associated with ideas." The youth who were educated at the public schools of ancient Mexico—for that realm, so far from neglecting the cause of popular education, established houses for gratuitous instruction, and to a certain extent made the attendance upon them obligatory—learned by rote, long orations, poems, and prayers with a facility astonishing to the conquerors, and surpassing anything they were accustomed to see in the universities of Old Spain. A phonetic system actually weakens the retentive powers of the mind by offering a more facile plan for preserving thought. " *Ce que je mets sur papier, je remets de ma mémoire*" is an expression of old Montaigne which he could never have used had he employed ideographic characters.

Memory, however, is of far less importance than a free activity of thought, untrammelled by forms or precedents, and ever alert to novel combinations of ideas. Give a race this and it will guide it to civilization as surely as the needle directs the ship to its haven. It is here that ideographic writing reveals

[1] Morse, *Report on the Indian Tribes*, App. p. 352.

its fatal inferiority. It is forever specifying, materializing, dealing in minutiæ. In the Egyptian symbolic alphabet there is a figure for a virgin, another
for a married woman, for a widow without offspring,
for a widow with one child, two children, and I
know not in how many other circumstances, but for
woman there is no sign. It must be so in the nature
of things, for the symbol represents the object as it
appears or is fancied to appear, and not as it is
thought. Furthermore, the constant learning by
heart infallibly leads to heedless repetition and
mental servility.

A symbol when understood is independent of sound,
and is as universally current as an Arabic numeral.
But this divorce of spoken and written language is of
questionable advantage. It at once destroys all permanent improvement in a tongue through elegance
of style, sonorous periods, or delicacy of expression,
and the life of the language itself is weakened when
its forms are left to fluctuate uncontrolled. Written
poetry, grammar, rhetoric, all are impossible to the
student who draws his knowledge from such a source.

Finally, it has been justly observed by the young-
er Humboldt that the painful fidelity to the antique
figures transmitted from barbarous to polished generations is' injurious to the æsthetic sense, and dulls
the mind to the beautiful in art and nature.

The transmission of thought by figures and symbols would, on the whole, therefore, foster those
narrow and material tendencies which the genius of
polysynthetic languages seems calculated to produce.
Its one redeeming trait of strengthening the memory
will serve to explain the strange tenacity with which

certain myths have been preserved through widely dispersed families, as we shall hereafter see.

Besides this of language there are two traits in the history of the red man without parallel in that of any other variety of our species which has achieved any notable progress in civilization.

The one is his *isolation*. Cut off time out of mind from the rest of the world, he never underwent those crossings of blood and culture which so modified and on the whole promoted the growth of the Old World nationalities. In his own way he worked out his own destiny, and what he won was his with a more than ordinary right of ownership. For all those old dreams of the advent of the Ten Lost Tribes, of Buddhist priests, of Northern sea kings, of Welsh princes, or of Phenician merchants on American soil, and there exerting a permanent influence, have been consigned to the dust-bin by every unbiased student, and when we see learned men essaying to resuscitate them, we regretfully look upon it in the light of a literary anachronism. The most competent observers are agreed that American art, whatever similarities may be found in it to that of the Old World, bears an undoubted stamp of indigenous growth. [1]

The second trait is the entire absence of the herdsman's life with its softening associations. Throughout the continent there is not a single authentic instance of a pastoral tribe, not one of an animal raised for its milk, [2] but one for the transportation of per-

[1] See Karl Scherzer, *Die Ruinen von Quiruguá*, p. 11 ; Squier, *The Primeval Monuments of Peru*, p. 16.
[2] Gomara states that De Ayllon found tribes on the Atlantic

sons, and very few for their flesh. It was essentially a hunting race. The most civilized nations looked to the chase for their chief supply of meat, and the courts of Cuzco and Mexico enacted stringent game and forest laws, and at certain periods the whole population turned out for a general crusade against the denizens of the forest. In the most densely settled districts the conquerors found vast stretches of primitive woods.

If we consider the life of a hunter, pitting his skill and strength against the marvellous instincts and quick perceptions of the brute, training his senses to preternatural acuteness, but blunting his more tender feelings, his sole aim to shed blood and take life, dependent on luck for his food, exposed to deprivations, storms, and long wanderings, his chief diet flesh, we may more readily comprehend that conspicuous disregard of human suffering, those sanguinary rites, that vindictive spirit, that inappeasable restlessness, which we so often find in the chronicles of ancient America. The old English law objected to accepting a butcher as a juror on a trial for life; here is a whole race of butchers.

The one softening element was agriculture. On the altar of Mixcoatl, god of hunting, the Aztec priest tore the heart from the human victim and smeared with the spouting blood the snake that coiled its lengths around the idol; flowers and fruits, yellow ears of maize and clusters of rich bananas decked the

shore not far from Cape Hatteras, keeping flocks of deer (*ciervos*) and from their milk making cheese (*Hist. de las Indias*, cap. 43). I give no credence to this statement.

shrine of Centeotl, beneficent patroness of agriculture, and bloodless offerings alone were her appropriate dues. This shows how clear, even to the native mind, was the contrast between these two modes of subsistence. By substituting a sedentary for a wandering life, by supplying a fixed dependence for an uncertain contingency, and by admonishing man that in preservation, not in destruction, lies his most remunerative sphere of activity, we can hardly estimate too highly the wide distribution of the zea mays. This was their only cereal, and it was found in cultivation from the southern extremity of Chili to the fiftieth parallel of north latitude, beyond which limits the low temperature renders it an uncertain crop. In their legends it is represented as the gift of the Great Spirit (Chipeways), brought from the terrestrial Paradise by the sacred animals (Quiches), and symbolically the mother of the race (Nahuas), and the material from which was moulded the first of men (Quiches).

As the races, so the great families of man who speaks dialects of the same tongue are, in a sense, individuals, bearing each its own physiognomy. When the whites first heard the uncouth gutturals of the Indians, they frequently proclaimed that hundreds of radically diverse languages, invented, it was piously suggested, by the Devil for the annoyance of missionaries, prevailed over the continent. Earnest students of such matters—Vater, Duponceau, Gallatin and Buschmann—have, however, demonstrated that nine-tenths of the area of America, at its discovery, was controlled by tribes using dialects traceable to ten or a dozen primitive stems. The names of these, their geographical position in the sixteenth century, and, so far as it is safe to do so, their individual character, I shall briefly mention.

Fringing the shores of the Northern Ocean from Mount St. Elias on the west to the Gulf of St. Lawrence on the east, rarely seen a hundred miles from the coast, were the Eskimos.[1] They are the connecting link between the races of the Old and New Worlds, in physical appearance and mental traits more allied to the former, but in language betraying their nearer kinship to the latter. An amphibious race, born fishermen, in their buoyant skin kayaks they fearlessly meet the tempests, make long voyages, and merit the sobriquet bestowed upon them by Von Baer, "the Phenicians of the north." Contrary to what one might suppose, they are, amid their snows, a contented, light-hearted people, knowing no longing for a sunnier clime, given to song, music, and merry tales. They are cunning handicraftsmen to a degree, but withal, wholly ingulfed in a sensuous existence..

1 The name Eskimo is from the Algonkin word *Eskimantick*, eaters of raw flesh. There is reason to believe that at one time they possessed the Atlantic coast considerably to the south. The Northmen, in the year 1000, found the natives of Vinland, probably near Rhode Island, of the same race as they were familiar with in Labrador. They contemptuously call them *Skralingar*, chips, and describe them as numerous and short of stature (Eric Rothens Saga, in Mueller, *Sagœnbibliothek*, p. 214). It is curious that the traditions of the Tuscaroras, who placed their arrival on the Virginian coast about 1300, spoke of the race they found there (called Tacci or Dogi) as eaters of raw flesh and ignorant of maize (Lederer, *Account of North America*, in Harris, Voyages).

The desperate struggle for life engrosses them, and their mythology is barren.

South of them, extending in a broad band across the continent from Hudson Bay to the Pacific, and almost to the Great Lakes below, is the Athapascan stock. Its affiliated tribes rove far north to the mouth of the Mackenzie River, and wandering still more widely in an opposite direction along both declivities of the Rocky Mountains, people portions of the coast of Oregon south of the mouth of the Columbia, and spreading over the plains of New Mexico, under the names of Apaches, Navajos, and Lipans, almost reach the tropics at the delta of the Rio Grande del Norte, and on the shores of the Gulf of California. No wonder they deserted their fatherland and forgot it altogether, for it is a very *terra damnata*, whose wretched inhabitants are cut off alike from the harvest of the sea and the harvest of the soil. The profitable culture of maize does not extend beyond the fiftieth parallel of latitude, and less than seven degrees farther north the mean annual temperature everywhere east of the mountains sinks below the freezing point.[1] Agriculture is impossible, and the only chance for life lies in the uncertain fortunes of the chase and the penurious gifts of an arctic flora. The denizens of these wilds are abject, slovenly, hopelessly savage, "at the bottom of the scale of humanity in North America," says Dr. Richardson, and their relatives who have wandered to the more genial climes of the south are as savage as they, as perversely hostile to a sedentary life, as gross and

---

[1] Richardson, *Arctic Expedition*, p. 374.

narrow in their moral notions. This wide-spread stock, scattered over forty-five degrees of latitude, covering thousands of square leagues, reaching from the Arctic Ocean to the confines of the ancient empire of the Montezumas, presents in all its subdivisions the same mental physiognomy and linguistic peculiarities. [1]

Best known to us of all the Indians are the Algonkins and Iroquois, peoples of wholly diverse descent and language, who, at the time of the discovery, were the sole possessors of the region now embraced by Canada and the eastern United States north of the thirty-fifth parallel. The latter, under the names of the Five Nations, Hurons, Tuscaroras, Susquehannocks, Nottoways and others, occupied much of the soil from the St. Lawrence and Lake Ontario to the Roanoke, and perhaps the Cherokees, whose homes were in the secluded vales of East Tennessee, were one of their early offshoots. [2] They were a race of warriors,

---

[1] The late Professor W. W. Turner of Washington, and Professor Buschmann of Berlin, are the two scholars who have traced the boundaries of this widely dispersed family. The name is drawn from Lake Athapasca in British America. Mr. Bancroft gives a long list of their sub-tribes. *Native Races of the Pacific States*, III., p. 563.

[2] The Cherokee tongue has a limited number of words in common with the Iroquois, and its structural similarity is close. The name is of unknown origin. It should doubtless be spelled *Tsaiakie*, a plural form, almost the same as that of the river Tellico, properly Tsaliko (Ramsey, *Annals of Tennessee*, p. 87), on the banks of which their principal towns were situated. Adair's derivation from *cheera*, fire, is worthless, as no such word exists in their language.

courageous, cruel, unimaginative, but of rare political sagacity. They are more like ancient Romans than Indians, and are leading figures in the colonial wars.

The Algonkins surrounded them on every side, occupying the rest of the region mentioned, and running westward to the base of the Rocky Mountains, where one of their famous bands, the Blackfeet, still hunts over the valley of the Saskatchewan. They were more genial than the Iroquois, of milder manners and more vivid fancy, and were regarded by these with a curious mixture of respect and contempt. Some writer has connected this difference with their preference for the open prairie country in contrast to the endless and sombre forests where were the homes of the Iroquois. Their history abounds in great men, whose ambitious plans were foiled by the levity of their allies and their want of persistence. They it was who under King Philip fought the Puritan fathers; who at the instigation of Pontiac doomed to death every white trespasser on their soil; who, led by Tecumseh and Black Hawk, gathered the clans of the forest and mountain for the last pitched battle of the races in the Mississippi valley. To them belonged the mild mannered Lenni Lenape, who little foreboded the hand of iron that grasped their own so softly under the elm-tree of Shackamaxon; to them the restless Shawnee, the gypsy of the wilderness; the Chipeways of Lake Superior; and also to them the Indian girl Pocahontas, who in the legend averted from the head of the white man the blow which, rebounding, swept away her father and all his tribe.[1]

---

[1] The term Algonkin may be a corruption of *agomeegwin,*

Between their southernmost outposts and the Gulf of Mexico were a number of clans, mostly speaking dialects of the Chahta-Muskokee tongue, including the Choctaws, Chickasaws, Creeks or Muskokees, the Natchez of Louisiana, and the Apalaches and Seminoles of Florida. Their common legend states that long ago they entered this district from the west, and destroyed or allied themselves with its earlier occupants. The Uchees and Tirmuquas belonged to these. At the discovery, the Chahta-Muskokee dialects stretched from the mountains to the Florida keys, and from the Atlantic to the Mississippi. But no trace of the tongue existed on the Bahamas or Antilles.[1]

North of the Arkansas River on the right bank of

people of the other shore. Algic, often used synonymously, is an adjective manufactured by Mr. Schoolcraft "from the words Alleghany and Atlantic" (*Algic Researches*, ii. p. 12). There is no occasion to accept it, as there is no objection to employing Algonkin both as substantive and adjective. Iroquois is a French compound of the native words *hiro*, I have said, and *kouè*, an interjection of assent or applause, terms constantly heard in their councils.

[1] Since the first edition of this work appeared I have given considerable attention to this interesting family. The results are contained in several papers published by the American Philosophical Society, under the titles : *Contributions to a Grammar of the Muskokee Language*, and *On the Language of the Natchez;* in my edition of Byington's *Grammar of the Choctaw;* and in *The National Legend of the Chahta-Muskokee Tribes*, 1870. The views in regard to the relationship of the Natchez and Mayas, expressed in the former edition, have not been confirmed by the accessions to the vocabularies of that tribe which I have since obtained from one of its last representatives.

the Mississippi, quite to its source, stretching over to Lake Michigan at Green Bay, and up the valley of the Missouri west to the mountains, resided the Dakotas, an erratic folk, averse to agriculture, but daring hunters and bold warriors, tall and strong of body. [1] Their religious notions have been carefully studied, and as they are remarkably primitive and transparent, they will often be referred to. The Sioux and the Winnebagoes are well-known branches of this family, and by some strange chance, one fragment of it, the Tuteloes, was found east of the Alleghanies, in Virginia.

We have seen that Dr. Richardson assigned to a portion of the Athapascas the lowest place among North American tribes, but there are some in New Mexico who might contest the sad distinction, the Root Diggers, Comanches and others, members of the Snake or Shoshonee family, scattered extensively northwest of Mexico. It has been said of a part of these that they are " nearer the brutes than probably any other portion of the human race on the face of the globe." [2] Their habits in some respects are more brutish than those of any brute, for there is no limit to man's moral descent or ascent, and the observer might well be excused for doubting whether such a stock ever had a history in the past, or the possibility of one in the future. Yet these debased creatures speak a dialect with faint traces of a noble kinship, and partake in some measure of the same blood as the famous Aztec race, who founded the empire of Ana-

[1] Dakota, a native word, means friends or allies.
[2] Rep. of the Commissioner of Indian Affairs, 1854, p. 209.

huac, and raised architectural monuments rivalling the most famous structures of the ancient world. This great family, whose language has been traced from Nicaragua to Vancouver's Island, and whose bold intellects colored much of the civilization of the northern continent, was composed in that division of it found in New Spain chiefly of two bands, the Toltecs, whose traditions point to the mountain ranges of Guatemala as their ancient seat, and the Nahuas, who claim to have come at a later period from the north-west coast, and together settled in and near the val ley of Mexico.[1]   Outlying colonies on the shore of

---

[1] According to Professor Buschmann, Aztec is probably from *iztac*, white, and Nahuatlacatl signifies those who speak the language *Nahuatl*, clear sounding, sonorous.   The Abbé Brasseur (de Bourbourg), on the other hand, derives the latter from the Quiche *nawal*, intelligent, and adds the amazing information that this is identical with the English *know all ! !* (*Hist. de Mexique*, etc., i. p. 102).   For in his theory several languages of Central America are derived from the same old Indo-Germanic stock as the English, German, and cognate tongues. Tol-tec, from *Toltecatl*, means inhabitant of Tollan, which latter may be from *tolin*, rush, and signify the place of rushes.   The signification *artificer*, often assigned to Toltecatl, is of later date, and was derived from the famed artistic skill of this early folk (Buschmann, *Aztek. Ortsnamen*, p. 682 : Berlin, 1852). The Toltecs are usually spoken of as anterior to the Nahuas, but the Tlascaltecs and natives of Cholollan or Cholula were in fact Toltecs, unless we assign to this latter name a merely mythical signification.   The early migrations of the two Aztec bands and their relationship, it may be said in passing, are as yet extremely obscure.   The Shoshonees when first known dwelt as far north as the head waters of the Missouri, and in the country now occupied by the Black Feet. Their language, which includes that of the Comanche, Wihinasht, Utah, and kindred

Lake Nicaragua and in the mountains of Vera Paz rose to a civilization that rivalled that of the Montezumas, while others remained in utter barbarism in the far north.

The Aztecs not only conquered a Maya colony, and founded the empire of the Quiches in Central America, a complete body of whose mythology has been brought to light in late years, but seem to have made a marked imprint on the Mayas themselves. These possessed, as has already been said, the peninsula of Yucatan. One of their colonies was the Huastecas, who lived on the river Panuco. Their language is radically distinct from that of the Aztecs, but their calendar and a portion of their mythology are common property. They seem an ancient race, of mild manners and considerable polish. No American nation offers a more promising field for study. Their stone temples still bear testimony to their uncommon skill in the arts. A trustworthy tradition dates the close of the golden age of Yucatan a century anterior to its discovery by Europeans. Previously it had been one kingdom, under one ruler, and prolonged peace had fostered the growth of the fine arts; but when their capital Mayapan fell, internal dissensions ruined most of their cities.

No connection whatever has been shown between the civilization of North and South America. In the latter continent it was confined to two totally foreign

bands, was first shown to have many and marked affinities with that of the Aztecs by Professor Buschmann in his great work, *Ueber die Spuren der Aztekischen Sprache im nördlichen Mexico and höheren Amerikanischen Norden*, p. 648 : Berlin, 1854.

tribes, the Muyscas, whose empire, called that of the Zacs, was in the neighborhood of Bogota, and the Peruvians, who were divided into two primary divisions, the one the Quichuas, including the closely related Incas and Aymaras, possessing the Andean region, and the Yuncas of the coast. The former were the dominant tribe, and their sway extended from the second parallel of north latitude to the twentieth south, embracing a territory about fifteen hundred miles in length by four hundred in width. Lake Titicaca seems to have been the cradle of their civilization, offering another example how inland seas and well-watered plains favor the change from a hunting to an agricultural life.

These four nations, the Aztecs, the Mayas, the Muyscas and the Peruvians, developed spontaneously and independently under the laws of human progress what civilization was found among the red race. They owed nothing to Asiatic or European teachers. The Incas it was long supposed spoke a language of their own, and this has been thought evidence of foreign extraction; but Wilhelm von Humboldt has shown conclusively that it was but a dialect of the common tongue of their country.[1]

[1] His opinion was founded on an analysis of fifteen words of the secret language of the Incas preserved in the Royal Commentaries of Garcilasso de la Vega. On examination, they all proved to be modified forms from the *lengua general* (Meyen, *Ueber die Ureinwohner von Peru,* p. 6). The Quichuas of Peru mnst not be confounded with the Quiches of Guatemala. Quiche is the name of a place, and means "many trees ; " the word Quichua may signify "twisted straw." Muyscas means " men." This nation also called themselves Chibchas. On the ancient geography of Peru, the best article is that of Clement B. Markham, *Jour. of the Royal Geog. Soc.*, 1871.

When Columbus first touched the island of Cuba, he was regaled with horrible stories of one-eyed monsters who dwelt on the other islands, but plundered indiscriminately on every hand. These turned out to be the notorious Caribs, whose other name, *Cannibals*, has descended as a common noun to our language, expressive of one of their inhuman practices. These warlike sea-robbers extended their plundering voyages to Cuba and Haiti, even to Honduras and Yucatan, but pointed for their home to the mainland of South America. This they possessed along the whole northern shore, inland at least as far as the south bank of the Amazon, and west nearly to the Cordilleras. They won renown as bold fighters, daring navigators and skilled craftsmen. Yet the evidence of language is conclusive that they were not remotely related to their victims, the mild and unambitious natives whom Columbus found on the Bahamas, Cuba and Haiti. These in turn were without doubt a branch of the Arawacks who to this day dwell in British and Dutch Guiana ; and they again are an offshoot of the great Tupi-Guaranay stem, which scattered its tribes over the vast region between the Amazon and the Pampas. [1]

Our information of the natives of the Pampas, Patagonia, and the Land of Fire, is too vague to per-

[1] The significance of Carib is probably warrior. It may be the same word as Guarani, which also has this meaning. Tupi or Tupa is the name given the thunder, and should be understood mythically. On the affiliations of the various tribes mentioned in the text I would refer the reader to my essay, *The Arawack Language of Guiana in its Linguistic and Ethnological Relations.* Phila., 1871.

mit their positive identification with the Araucanians of Chili ; but there is much to render the view plausible. Certain physical peculiarities, a common unconquerable love of freedom, and a delight in war, bring them together, and at the same time place them both in strong contrast to their northern neighbors.[1]

There are many tribes whose affinities remain to be decided, especially on the Pacific coast. The lack of inland water communication, the difficult nature of the soil, and perhaps the greater antiquity of the population there, seem to have isolated and split up beyond recognition the indigenous families on that shore of the continent ; while the great river systems and broad plains of the Atlantic slope facilitated migration and intercommunication, and thus preserved national distinctions over thousands of square leagues.

These natural features of the continent, compared with the actual distribution of languages, are our only guides in forming an opinion as to the migrations of these various families in ancient times. Their traditions, take even the most cultivated, are confused, contradictory, and in great part manifestly fabulous. To construct from them by means of daring combinations and forced interpretations a connected account of the race during the centuries preceding Columbus, were with the aid of a vivid fancy an easy matter, but

[1] The Araucanians probably obtained their name from two Quichua words, *ari auccan*, yes ! they fight ; an idiom very expressive of their warlike character. They had had long and terrible wars with the Incas before the arrival of Pizarro.

would be quite unworthy the name of history. The most that can be said with certainty is that the general course of migrations in both Americas was from the high latitudes toward the tropics, and from the great western chain of mountains toward the east. No reasonable doubt exists but that the Athapascas, Algonkins, Iroquois, Chahta-Muskokees and Aztecs all migrated from the north and west to the regions they occupied. In South America, curiously enough, the direction is reversed. The widespread Tupi-Guaranay stem, and the Quichuas seem to have wandered forth from the steppes and valleys at the head waters of the Rio de la Plata toward the Gulf of Mexico, where they came in collision with that other wave of migration surging down from high northern latitudes. For the banks of the river Paraguay and the steppes of the Bolivian Cordilleras are the earliest traditional homes of both Tupis and Quichuas.

These movements took place not in large bodies under the stimulus of a settled purpose, but step by step, family by family, as the older hunting-grounds became too thickly peopled. This fact hints unmistakably at the gray antiquity of the race. It were idle even to guess how great this must be, but it is possible to set limits to it in both directions. On the one hand, not a tittle of evidence is on record to carry the age of man in America beyond the present geological epoch. Dr. Lund examined in Brazil more than eight hundred caverns, out of which number only six contained human bones, and of these six only one had with the human bones those of animals now extinct. Even in that instance the original stratification had been disturbed, and probably the bones had been interred there. [1]   The same is true of the caves of California, Kentucky and Tennessee. This is strong negative evidence. So in every other example where an unbiased and competent geologist has made the examination, the alleged discoveries of human remains in the older strata have proved erroneous.

The cranial forms of the American aborigines have by some been supposed to present anomalies distinguishing their race from all others, and even its chief families from one another. This, too, falls to the ground before a rigid analysis. The last word of craniology, which at one time promised to revolutionize ethnology and even history, is that no one form of the skull is peculiar to the natives of the New World ; that in the same linguistic family one glides into another by imperceptible degrees; and that there is as much diversity among them in this respect as among the races of the Old Continent. [2]   Peculiarities of structure, though they may pass as general truths, offer no firm foundation whereon to construct a scientific ethnology. Anatomy shows nothing unique in the Indian, nothing demanding for its development any special antiquity, still less an original diversity of type.

On the other hand, the remains of primeval art and the impress he made upon nature bespeak for man a residence in the New World coeval with the most distant events of history. By remains of art I do

[1] *Comptes Rendus*, vol. xxi., p. 1368 sqq.

[2] The best authorities on craniology accord in the views expressed in the text, and in the rejection of those advocated by Dr. S. G. Morton in the *Crania Americana.*

not so much refer to those desolate palaces which crumble forgotten in the gloom of tropical woods, nor even the enormous earthworks of the Mississippi valley covered with the mould of generations of forest trees, but rather to the humbler and less deceptive relics of his kitchens and his hunts. On the Atlantic coast one often sees the refuse of Indian villages, where generation after generation have passed their summers in fishing, and left the bones, shells, and charcoal as their only epitaph. How many such summers would it require for one or two hundred people thus gradually to accumulate a mound of offal eight or ten feet high and a hundred yards across, as is common enough? How many generations to heap up that at the mouth of the Altamaha River, examined and pronounced exclusively of this origin by Sir Charles Lyell,[1] which is about this height, and covers ten acres of ground? Those who, like myself, have tramped over many a ploughed field in search of arrow-heads must have sometimes been amazed at the numbers which are sown over the face of our country, betokening a most prolonged possession of the soil by their makers. For a hunting population is always sparse, and the collector finds only those arrow-heads which lie upon the surface. Even a degree of civilization is most ancient; for the evidences are abundant that the mines of California and Lake Superior were worked by tribes using metals at a most remote epoch.

Still more forcibly does nature herself bear witness to this antiquity of possession. Botanists de-

---

[1] *Second Visit to the United States,* i. p. 252.

clare that a very lengthy course of cultivation is required so to alter the form of a plant that it can no longer be identified with the wild species; and still more protracted must be the artificial propagation for it to lose its power of independent life, and to rely wholly on man to preserve it from extinction. Now this is precisely the condition of the maize, tobacco, cotton, quinoa, and mandioca plants, and of that species of palm called by botanists the *Gulielma speciosa;* all have been cultivated from immemorial time by the aborigines of America, and, except cotton, by no other race; all no longer are to be identified with any known wild species; several are sure to perish unless fostered by human care.[1] What numberless ages does this suggest? How many centuries elapsed ere man thought of cultivating Indian corn? How many more ere it had spread over nearly a hundred degrees of latitude, and lost all semblance to its original form? Who has the temerity to answer these questions? The judicious thinker will perceive in them satisfactory reasons for dropping once for all the vexed inquiry, "how America was peopled," and will smile at its imaginary solutions, whether they suggest Jews, Japanese, or, as the latest theory is, Egyptians.

While these and other considerations testify forcibly to that isolation I have already mentioned, they are almost equally positive for an extensive inter-

[1] Martius, *Von dem Rechtzustande unter den Ureinwohnern Brasiliens*, p. 80 : Muenchen, 1832 ; republished in his *Beiträge zur Ethnographie und Sprachenkunde Amerika's :* Leipzig, 1867; see also Lucien de Rosny, *Le Tabac et ses Accessoires parmi les Indigénes de l'Amèrique.* Paris, 1865.

course in very distant ages between the great families of the race, and for a prevalent unity of mental type, or perhaps they hint at a still visible oneness of descent. In their stage of culture, the maize, cotton, and tobacco could hardly have spread so widely by commerce alone. Then there are verbal similarities running through wide families of languages which, in the words of Professor Buschmann, are "calculated to fill us with bewildering amazement,"[1] some of which will hereafter be pointed out; and lastly, passing to the psychological constitution of the race, we may quote the words of a sharp-sighted naturalist, whose monograph on one of its tribes is unsurpassed for profound reflections : "Not only do all the primitive inhabitants of America stand on one scale of related culture, but that mental condition of all in which humanity chiefly mirrors itself, to wit, their religious and moral consciousness, this source of all other inner and outer conditions, is one with all, however diverse the natural influences under which they live."[2]

Penetrated with the truth of these views, all artificial divisions into tropical or temperate, civilized or barbarous, will in the present work, so far as possible, be avoided, and the race will be studied as a unit, its religion as the development of ideas common to all its members, and its myths as the garb thrown

---

[1] *Athapaskische Sprachstamm*, p. 164: Berlin, 1856. Mr. Bancroft (*Native Races*, III., p. 559), who cites two instances in point, is apparently unaware that Prof. Buschmann had already noticed the same ones.

[2] Martius, *Von dem Rechtzustande unter den Ureinwohnern Brasiliens*, p. 77.

around these ideas by imaginations more or less fertile, but seeking everywhere to embody the same notions.

BIBLIOGRAPHICAL NOTE.

As the subject of American mythology is a new one to most readers, and as in its discussion everything depends on a careful selection of authorities, it is well at the outset to review very briefly what has already been written upon it, and to assign the relative amount of weight that in the following pages will be given to the works most frequently quoted. The conclusions I have arrived at are so different from those who have previously touched upon the topic that such a step seems doubly advisable.

The first who undertook a philosophical survey of American religions was Dr. Samuel Farmer Jarvis, in 1819 (A Discourse on the Religion of the Indian Tribes of North America, Collections of the New York Historical Society, vol., iii., New York, 1821). He confined himself to the tribes north of Mexico, a difficult portion of the field, and at that time not very well known. The notion of a state of primitive civilization prevented Dr. Jarvis from forming any correct estimate of the native religions, as it led him to look upon them as deteriorations from purer faiths instead of developments. Thus he speaks of them as having " departed less than among any other nation from the form of primeval truth," and also mentions their " wonderful uniformity " (pp. 219, 221).

The well-known American ethnologist, Mr. E. G. Squier, has also published a work on the subject, of wider scope than its title indicates (The Serpent Symbol in America, New York, 1851). Though written in a much more liberal spirit than the preceding, it is in the interests of a school of mythology now discredited. Thus, with a sweeping generalization, he says : " The religions or superstitions of the American nations, however different they may appear to the superficial glance, are rudimentally the same, and are only modifications of that primitive system which under its physical aspect has been denominated Sun or Fire worship" (p. 111). With this he combines the doctrine, that the chief topic of mythology is the adoration of the generative power ; and to rescue such views from their materializing tendencies, imagines to counterbalance them a clear, universal monotheism. "We claim to have shown," he says (p. 154), "that the grand conception of a Supreme Unity and the doctrine of the reciprocal principles existed in America in a well-defined and clearly recognized form;" and elsewhere that "the monotheistic idea stands out clearly in *all* the religions of America" (p. 151).

The government work on the Indians (*History, Conditions and Prospects of the Indian Tribes of the United States*) published at Washington, 1851-9, was unfortunate in its editor. It is a monument of American extravagance and superficiality. Mr. Schoolcraft was a man of deficient education and narrow prejudices, pompous in style, and inaccurate in statements. The information from original observers it contains is often of real value, but the general views on aboriginal history and religion are shallow.

A German professor, Dr. J. G. Müller, has written quite a voluminous work on American Primitive Religions (*Geschichte der Amerikanischen Ur-religionen*, pp. 707 : Basel, 1855). His theory is that "at the south a worship or nature with the adoration of the sun as its centre, at the north a fear of spirits combined with fetichism, made up the two fundamental divisions of the religion of the red race" (pp. 89, 90). This imaginary antithesis he traces out between the Algonkin and Apalachian tribes, and between the Toltecs of Guatemala and the Aztecs of Mexico. His quotations are nearly all at second-hand, and so little does he criticise his facts as to confuse the Vaudoux worship of the Haitian negroes with that of Votan in Chiapa.

Very much better is the Anthropology of the late Dr. Theodore Waitz (*Anthropologie der Naturvœlker* : Leipzig, 1862-66). No more comprehensive, sound, and critical work on the indigenes of America has ever been written. But on their religions the author is unfortunately defective, being led astray by the hasty and groundless generalizations of others. His great anxiety, moreover, to subject all moral sciences to a realistic philosophy, was peculiarly fatal to any correct appreciation of religious growth, and his views are neither new nor tenable.

For a different reason I must condemn the late enthusiastic and meritorious antiquary, the Abbé E. Charles Brasseur (de Bourbourg), in both his interpretations of American myths, the first that they are history, the second that they record geology !

While heartily regretting the use he made of them, all interested in American antiquity cannot too much thank this indefatigable explorer for the priceless materials he unearthed in the libraries of Spain and Central America, and laid before the public. For the present purpose the most significant of these is the Sacred National Book of the Quiches, a tribe of Guatemala. This contains their legends, written in the original tongue, and transcribed by Father Francisco Ximenes, about 1725. The manuscripts of this missionary were used early in the present century, by Don Felix Cabrera, but were supposed to be entirely lost even by the Abbé Brasseur himself in 1850 (*Lettre à M. le Duc de Valmy,* Mexique, Oct. 15, 1850). Made aware of their importance by the expressions of regret used in the Abbé's letters, Dr. C. Scherzer, in 1854, was fortunate enough to discover them in the library of the University of San Carlos in the city of Guatemala. The legends were in Quiche, with a Spanish translation and scholia. The Spanish was copied by Dr. Scherzer and published in Vienna, in 1856, under the title *Las Historias del Origen de los Indios de Guatemala, por el R. P. F. Francisco Ximenes.* In 1855, the Abbé Brasseur took a copy of the original which he brought out at Paris in 1861, with a translation of his own, under the title *Vuh Popol: Le Livre Sacré des Quichés et les Mythes de l'Antiquité Américaine.* Internal evidence proves that these legends were written down by a converted native some time in the seventeenth century. They carry the national history back about two centuries, beyond which all is professedly mythical. Although both translations are colored by the peculiar views of their makers, this is one of the most valuable bodies of American mythology extant.

Another authority of inestimable value has been placed within the reach of scholars during the last few years. This is the *Relations de la Nouvelle France,* containing the annual reports of the Jesuit missionaries among the Iroquois and Algonkins from and after 1611. My references to this are always to the reprint at Quebec, 1858. Of not less excellence for another tribe, the Creeks, is the brief "Sketch of the Creek Country," by Col. Benjamin Hawkins, written about 1800, and first published in full by the Georgia Historical Society, in 1848. The recent able collation of Mr. H. H. Bancroft, "The Native Races of the Pacific States," contains some previously unpublished myths; but I acknowledge a hesitation in making use of such late material, for fear the old stories of the gods have been leavened by missionary instructions. The same remark applies to the very careful collection of Prof. Carl Knortz, *Sagen der Nord Amerikanischen Indianer.* Most of the other works to which I have referred are too well known to need any special examination here, or will be more particularly mentioned in the foot-notes when quoted.

CHAPTER II.

THE IDEA OF GOD.

A deduction of reason common to the species.—Words expressing it in American languages derived either from ideas of above in space, or of life manifested by breath.—Examples.—No conscious monotheism, and but little idea of immateriality discoverable.—Still less any moral dualism of deities, the Great Good Spirit and the Great Bad Spirit being alike térms and notions of foreign importation.

IF we accept the definition that mythology is the idea of God expressed in symbol, figure, and narrative, and always struggling toward a clearer utterance, it is well not only to trace this idea in its very earliest embodiment in language, but also, for the sake of comparison, to ask what is its latest and most approved expression. The reply to this is given us by Immanuel Kant. He has shown that our reason, dwelling on the facts of experience, constantly seeks the principles which connect them together, and only rests satisfied in the conviction that there is a highest and first principle which reconciles all their discrepancies and binds them into one. This he calls the Ideal of Reason. It must be true, for it is evolved from the laws of reason, our only test of truth. Furthermore, the sense of personality and the voice of conscience, analyzed to their sources, can be explained only by the assumption of an infinite personality and an absolute standard of right. Or, if to some all this appears but wire-drawn, metaphysical subtlety, they are welcome to the definition of the realist, that the idea of God is the sum of those intelligent activities which the individual, reasoning from the analogy of his own actions, imagines to be behind and to bring about natural phenomena. If either of these be correct, it were hard to conceive how any tribe or even any sane man could be without some notion of divinity.

Certainly in America no instance of its absence has been discovered. Obscure, grotesque, unworthy it often was, but everywhere man was oppressed with a *sensus numinis*, a feeling that invisible, powerful agencies were at work around him, who, as they willed, could help or hurt him. In every heart was an altar to the Unknown God. Not that it was customary to attach any idea of unity to these unseen powers. The supposition that in ancient times and in very unenlightened conditions, before mythology had grown, a monotheism prevailed, which afterwards at various times was revived by reformers, is a belief that should have passed away when the delights of savage life and the praises of a state of nature ceased to be the themes of philosophers. We are speaking of a people little capable of abstraction. The exhibitions of force in nature seemed to them the manifestations of that mysterious power felt by their self-consciousness; to combine these various manifestations and recognize them as the operations of one personality, was a step not easily taken. Yet He is not far from every one of us. " Whenever man thinks clearly, or feels deeply, he conceives God as self-conscious unity," says Carriere, with admirable insight ; and elsewhere, " We have monotheism, not in contrast to polytheism, not clear to the thought, but in living intuition in the religious sentiment." [1]

Thus it was among the Indians. Therefore a word is usually found in their languages analogous to none in any European tongue, a word comprehending all manifestations of the unseen world, yet conveying no sense of personal unity. It has been rendered spirit, demon, God, devil, mystery, magic, but commonly and rather absurdly by the English and French, "medicine." In the Algonkin dialects this word is *manito* and *oki*, in Iroquois *oki* and *otkon*, in the Hidatsa *hopa*, the Dakota has *wakan*, the Aztec *teotl*, the Quichua *huaca*, and the Maya *ku*. They all express in its most general form the idea of the supernatural. [2] And as in this word, supernatural, we see a transfer of a conception of place, and that it literally means that which is *above* the natural world, so in such as we can analyze of these vague and primitive terms the same trope appears discoverable. *Wakan* as an adverb means *above*, *oki* is but another orthography for *oghee*, and *otkon* seems allied to *hetken*, both of which have the same signification.

The transfer is no mere figure of speech, but has its origin in the very texture of the human mind. The heavens, the upper regions, are in every religion the supposed abode of the divine. What is higher is

[1] *Die Kunst im Zusammenhang der Culturentwickelung,* i. pp. 50, 252.

[2] On *wakan* see Roehrig, *On the Language of the Dakota,* Smithsonian Report, 1871; on *manito*, Trumbull, in *Old and New*, March, 1870. The criticisms of the latter on the remark in the text are refuted by the consideration that to the savage whatever is præternatural is esteemed divine.

always the stronger and the nobler; a *superior* is one who is better than we are, and therefore a chieftain in Algonkin is called *oghee-ma*, the higher one. Proud, in Latin *superbus*, is in Dakota *wakanicidapi*, etymologically the same. There is, moreover, a naif and spontaneous instinct which leads man in his ecstasies of joy, and in his paroxysms of fear or pain, to lift his hands and eyes to the overhanging firmament. There the sun and bright stars sojourn, emblems of glory and stability. Its azure vault has a mysterious attraction which invites the eye to gaze longer and longer into its infinite depths. [1] Its color brings thoughts of serenity, peace, sunshine, and warmth. Even the rudest hunting tribes felt these sentiments, and as a metaphor in their speeches, and as a paint expressive of friendly design, blue was in wide use among them.[2]

So it came to pass that the idea of God was linked to the heavens long ere man asked himself, are the heavens material and God spiritual, is He one, or is He many ? Numerous languages bear trace of this. The Latin Deus, the Greek Zeus, the Sanscrit Dyaus, the Chinese Tien, all originally referred to the sky above, and our own word heaven is often employed synonymously with God. There is at first no personification in these expressions. They embrace all

---

[1] " As the high heavens, the far-off mountains look to us blue, so a blue superficies seems to recede from us. As we would fain pursue an attractive object that flees from us, so we like to gaze at the blue, not that it urges itself upon us, but that it draws us after it." Goethe, *Farbenlehre*, secs. 780, 781.

[2] Loskiel, *Geschichte der Mission der Evang. Brueder*, p. 63 : Barby, 1789.

unseen agencies, they are void of personality, and yet to the illogical, primitive man, there is nothing contradictory in making them the object of his prayers. The Mayas had legions of gods ; " *ku*," says their historian, [1] " does not signify any particular god ; yet their prayers are sometimes addressed to *kue*," which is the same word in the vocative case.

As the Latins called their united divinities *Superi*, those above, so Captain John Smith found that the Powhatans of Virginia employed the word *oki*, above, in the same sense, and it even had passed into a definite personification among them in the shape of an " idol of wood evil-favoredly carved." In purer dialects of the Algonkin it is always indefinite, as in the terms *nipoon oki*, spirit of summer, *pipoon oki*, spirit of winter. Perhaps the word was introduced into Iroquois by the Hurons, neighbors and associates of the Algonkins. The Hurons applied it to that demoniac power " who rules the seasons of the year, who holds the winds and the waves in leash, who can give fortune to their undertakings, and relieve all their wants." [2] In another and far distant branch of the Iroquois, the Nottoways of southern Virginia, it reappears under the curious form *quaker*, doubtless a corruption of the Powhatan *qui-oki*, lesser gods. [3] The proper Iroquois name of him to whom

[1] Cogolludo, *Historia de Yucathan*, lib. iv. cap. vii.

[2] *Rel. de la Nouv. France.* An. 1636, p. 107.

[3] This word is found in Gallatin's vocabularies (*Transactions of the Am. Antiq. Soc.*, vol. ii.), and may have partially induced that distinguished ethnologist to ascribe, as he does in more than one place, whatever notions the eastern tribes had of a Supreme Being to the teachings of the Quakers.

they prayed was *garonhia*, which again turns out on examination to be their common word for *sky*, and again in all probability from the verbal root *gar*, to be above.[1] The Californian tribes spoke of their chief deity as "The old man above."[2] In the legends of the Aztecs and Quiches such phrases as " Heart of the Sky," " Lord of the Sky," " Prince of the Azure Planisphere," " He above all," are of frequent occurrence, and by a still bolder metaphor, the Araucanians, according to Molina, entitled their greatest god " The Soul of the Sky."

This last expression leads to another train of thought. As the philosopher, pondering on the workings of self-consciousness, recognizes that various pathways lead up to God, so the primitive man, in forming his language, sometimes trod one, sometimes another. Whatever else skeptics have questioned, no one has yet presumed to doubt that if a God and a soul exist at all, they are of like essence. This firm belief has left its impress on language in the names devised to express the supernal, the spiritual world. If we seek hints from languages more familiar to us than the tongues of the Indians, and take for example this word *spiritual*, we find it is from the Latin *spirare*, to blow, to breathe. If in Latin again we look for the derivation of *animus*, the mind, *anima*, the soul, they point to the Greek *anemos*, wind, and *aémi*, to blow. In Greek the

---

[1] Bruyas, *Radices Verborum Iroquœorum*, p. 84. This work is in Shea's Library of American Linguistics, and is a most valuable contribution to philology. The same etymology is given by Lafitau, *Mœurs des Sauvages*, etc., Germ. trans., p. 65.

[2] Bancroft, *Native Races*, iii. 158.

words for soul or spirit, *psuche*, *pneuma*, *thumos*, all are directly from verbal roots expressing the motion of the wind or the breath. The Hebrew word *ruah* is translated in the Old Testament sometimes by wind, sometimes by spirit, sometimes by breath. The Egyptian *Kneph* is another instance in point. Etymologically, in fact, ghosts and gusts, breaths and breezes, the Great Spirit and the Great Wind, are one and the same. It is easy to guess the reason of this. The soul is the life, the life is the breath. Invisible, imponderable, quickening with vigorous motion, slackening in rest and sleep, passing quite away in death, it is the most obvious sign of life. All nations grasped the analogy and identified the one with the other. But the breath is nothing but wind. How easy, therefore, to look upon the wind that moves up and down and to and fro upon the earth, that carries the clouds, itself unseen, that calls forth the terrible tempests and the various seasons, as the breath, the spirit of God, as God himself ? So in the Mosaic record of creation, it is said " a mighty wind " passed over the formless sea and brought forth the world, and when the Almighty gave to the clay a living soul, he is said to have breathed into it " the wind of lives."

Armed with these analogies, we turn to the primitive tongues of America, and find them there as distinct as in the Old World. In Dakota *niya* is literally breath, figuratively life ; Elliott in his Bible translates soul by *nashanonk*, a breathing ; in Netela *piuts* is life, breath, and soul ; *silla*, in Eskimo, means air, it means wind, but it is also the word that conveys the highest idea of the world as a whole, and

the reasoning faculty. The supreme existence they
call *Sillam· Innua*, Owner of the Air, or of the All ;
or *Sillam Nelega*, Lord of the Air or Wind. In the
Yakama tongue of Oregon *wkrisha* signifies there is
wind, *wkrishwit*, life ; with the Aztecs, *ehecatl* expressed both air, life, and the soul, and personified in
their myths it was said to have been born of the
breath of Tezcatlipoca, their highest divinity, who
himself is often called Yoalliehecatl, the Wind of
Night. [1]

The descent is, indeed, almost imperceptible which
leads to the personification of the wind as God, which
merges this manifestation of life and power in one
with its unseen, unknown cause. Thus it is a worthy
epithet which the later Creeks apply to the supreme
ruler, when they address him as HESAKETŬMESE, Source
of Breath ; and doubtless it was at first but a title
of equivalent purport which the Cherokees, their
neighbors, were wont to employ, OONAWLEH UNGGI,
Eldest of Winds, but rapidly leading to a complete
identification of the divine with the natural phenomena of meteorology. This seems to have taken
place in the same group of nations, for the original
Choctaw word for Deity is given as HUSHTOLI, the
Storm Wind. [2] The idea, indeed, was constantly

[1] My authorities are Riggs, *Dict. of the Dakota*, Boscana, *Ac-
count of New California*, Richardson's and Egede's Eskimo
Vocabularies, Pandosy, *Gram. and Dict. of the Yakama* (Shea's
Lib. of Am. Linguistics), and the Abbé Brasseur for the Aztec.

[2] These terms are found in Gallatin's vocabularies. The last
mentioned is not, as Adair thought, derived from *issto ulla* or
ishto hoollo, strong man (properly *hatak kollo*), for in Choctaw
the adjective cannot precede the noun it qualifies. Its true
sense seems visible in the analogous Creek word *hotvle*, the wind.

being lost in the symbol. In the legends of the Quiches, the mysterious creative power is HURAKAN, a name of no signification in their language, one which some have thought they brought from the Antilles, which finds its meaning in the ancient tongue of Haiti, and which, under the forms of *hurricane, ouragan, orkan,* was adopted into European marine languages as the native name of the terrible tornado of the Caribbean Sea. [1] Mixcohuatl, the Cloud Serpent, chief divinity of several tribes in ancient Mexico, is to this day the correct term in their language for the tropical whirlwind, and the natives of Panama worshipped the same phenomenon under the name Tuyra. [2] To kiss the air was in Peru the commonest and simplest sign of adoration to the collective divinities. [3]

---

[1] Webster derives hurricane from the Latin *furio.* But Oviedo tells us in his description of Hispaniola that " Hurakan, in lingua di questa isola vuole dire propriamente fortuna tempestuosa molto eccessiva, perche en effetto non è altro que un grandissimo vento è pioggia insieme." *Historia dell' Indie,* lib. vi. cap. iii. The word Hurakan is puzzling in its presence in Yucatan. I cannot doubt it is from a Tupi root. Denis in his notes to the *Histoire de Maragnan* of the Père Yves d'Evreux gives the form *Hyorocan* as known in or near that province. In the Macusi and Arekuna dialects of Guiana *Hori* now means devil, bad spirit (*Schombergk, Reisen in Britisch Guiana*). *An* in Tupi is soul, *Anan* the name of one of the Arawack gods. The *Dictionarium Galibi,* Paris, 1763, gives the forms *iroucan, youroucan, jeroucan* and *hyorocan.* On the whole, I am inclined to believe the Mayas adopted the name from the Spaniards.

[2] Oviedo, *Rel. de la Prov. de Cueba,* p. 141, ed. Ternaux-Compans.

[3] Garcia, *Origen de los Indios,* lib. iv. cap. xxii.

Many writers on mythology have commented on
the prominence so frequently given to the winds.
None have traced it to its true source. The facts of
meteorology have been thought all sufficient for a
solution. As if man ever did or ever could draw the
idea of God from nature! In the identity of wind
with breath, of breath with life, of life with soul, of
soul with God, lies the far deeper and far truer reason, whose insensible development I have here traced,
in outline indeed, but confirmed by the evidence of
language itself.

Let none of these expressions, however, be construed to prove the distinct recognition of One Supreme Being. Of monotheism either as displayed in
the one personal definite God of the Semitic races, or
in the dim pantheistic sense of the Brahmins, there
was not a single instance on the American continent.
The missionaries found no word in any of their languages fit to interpret *Deus*, God. How could they
expect it? The associations we attach to that name
are the accumulated fruits of nigh two thousand
years of Christianity. The phrases Good Spirit,
Great Spirit, and similar ones, have occasioned endless
discrepancies in the minds of travellers. In most
instances they are entirely of modern origin, coined
at the suggestion of missionaries, applied to the white
man's God. Very rarely do they bring any conception of personality to the native mind, very rarely do
they signify any object of worship, perhaps never did
in the olden times. The Jesuit Relations state
positively that there was no one immaterial god recognized by the Algonkin tribes, and that the title,
the Great Manito, was introduced first by themselves

in its personal sense. [1] The supreme Iroquois Deity Neo or Hawaneu, triumphantly adduced by many writers to show the monotheism underlying the native creeds, and upon whose name Mr. Schoolcraft has built some philological reveries, turns out on closer scrutiny to be the result of Christian instruction, and the words themselves to be but corruptions of the French *Dieu* and *le bon Dieu!* [2]

Innumerable mysterious forces are in activity around the child of nature; he feels within him something that tells him they are not of his kind, and yet not altogether different from him; he sums them up in one word drawn from sensuous experience. Does he wish to express still more forcibly this sentiment, he doubles the word, or prefixes an adjective, or adds an affix, as the genius of his language may dictate. But it still remains to him but an unapplied abstraction, a mere category of thought, a frame for the All. It is never the object of veneration or sacrifice, no myth brings it down to his comprehension, it is not installed in his temples. Man cannot escape the belief that behind all form is one essence; but the moment he would seize and define it, it eludes his grasp, and by a sorcery more sadly ludicrous than that which blinded Titania, he worships not the Infinite he thinks, but a base idol of his own making.

---

[1] See the *Rel. de la Nouv. France pour l'An* 1637, p. 49.

[2] Mr. Morgan, in his excellent work, *The League of the Iroquois*, has been led astray by an ignorance of the etymology of these terms. For Schoolcraft's views see his *Oneota*, p. 147. The matter is ably discussed in the *Etudes Philologiques sur Quelques Langues Sauvages de l'Amérique*, p. 14: Montreal, 1866; but comp. Shea, *Dict Français-Onontagué*, preface.

As in the Zend Avesta behind the eternal struggle
of Ormuzd and Ahriman looms up the undisturbed
and infinite Zeruana Akerana, as in the pages of the
Greek poets we here and there catch glimpses of a
Zeus who is not he throned on Olympus, nor he who
takes part in the wrangles of the gods, but stands
far off and alone, one yet all, " who was, who is, who
will be," so the belief in an Unseen Spirit, who asks
neither supplication nor sacrifice, who, as the natives
of Texas told Joutel in 1684, " does not concern himself about things here below," [1] who has no name to
call him by, and is never a figure in mythology, was
doubtless occasionally present to their minds. Said
a sagamore of Newfoundland to a missionary : " There
is one only God, one Son, one Mother and the Sun,
which are four, but God is above all." [2] It was
present not more but far less distinctly and often not
at all in the more savage tribes, and no assertion can
be more contrary to the laws of religious progress
than that which pretends that a purer and more
monotheistic religion exists among nations devoid of
mythology.   There are only two instances on the
American continent where the worship of an immaterial God is asserted to have been instituted, and
these as the highest conquests of American natural
religions deserve especial mention.

They occurred, as we might expect, in the two
most civilized nations, the Quichuas of Peru, and the

[1] " Qui ne prend aucun soin des choses icy bas." *Jour.
Hist. d'un Voyage de l'Amérique*, p. 225 : Paris, 1713.

[2] Blomes, *State of his Majestie's Territories in America*, p.
241, Lond. 1687.

Nahuas of Tezcuco.   It is related that about the year
1440, at a grand religious council held at the conse-
cration of the newly-built temple of the Sun at Cuzco,
the Inca Yupanqui rose before the assembled multitude and spoke somewhat as follows:—

" Many say that the Sun is the Maker of all things.
But he who makes should abide by what he has made.
Now many things happen when the Sun is absent;
therefore he cannot be the universal creator.   And
that he is alive at all is doubtful, for his trips do not
tire him.   Were he a living thing, he would grow
weary like ourselves ; were he free, he would visit
other parts of the heavens.   He is like a tethered
beast who makes a daily round under the eye of a
master ; he is like an arrow, which must go whither
it is sent, not whither it wishes.   I tell you that he,
our Father and Master the Sun, must have a lord and
master more powerful than himself, who constrains
him to his daily circuit without pause or rest." [1]

To express this greatest of all existences, a name
was proclaimed, based upon that of the highest divinities known to the ancient Aymara clans, Illatici
Viracocha Pachacamac, literally, the thunder vase,
the foam of the sea, animating the world, mysterious
and symbolic names drawn from the deepest religious
instincts of the soul, whose hidden meanings will be

---

[1] In attributing this speech to the Inca Yupanqui, I have followed Balboa, who expressly says this was the general opinion
of the Indians (*Hist. du Pérou*, p. 62, ed. Ternaux-Compans).
Others assign it to other Incas.   See Garcilasso de la Vega, *Hist.
des Incas*, lib. viii. chap. 8, and Acosta, *Nat. and Morall Hist.
of the New World*, chap. 5.   The fact and the approximate time
are beyond question.

unravelled hereafter. A temple was constructed in a vale by the sea near Callao, wherein his worship was to be conducted without images or human sacrifices. The Inca was ahead of his age, however, and when the Spaniards visited the temple of Pachacamac in 1525, they found not only the walls adorned with hideous paintings, but an ugly idol of wood representing a man of colossal proportions set up therein, and receiving the prayers of the votaries.[1]

No better success attended the attempt of Nezahuatl, lord of Tezcuco, said to have taken place about the same time. He had long prayed to the gods of his forefathers for a son to inherit his kingdom, and the altars had smoked vainly with the blood of slaughtered victims. At length, in indignation and despair, the prince exclaimed, " Verily, these gods that I am adoring, what are they but idols of stone without speech or feeling? They could not have made the beauty of the heaven, the sun, the moon, and the stars which adorn it, and which light the earth, with its countless streams, its fountains and waters, its trees and plants, and its various inhabitants. There must be some god, invisible and unknown, who is the universal creator. He alone can console me in my affliction and take away my sorrow." Strengthened in this conviction by a timely fulfilment of his heart's desire, he erected a temple nine stories high to represent the nine heavens, which he dedicated " to the Unknown God, the Cause of Causes." This temple, he ordained, should never be polluted by blood, nor

---

[1] Xeres, *Rel. de la Conq. du Pérou*, p. 151, ed. Ternaux-Compans.

should any graven image ever be set up within its precincts.[1]

In neither case, be it observed, was any attempt made to substitute another and purer religion for the popular one. The Inca continued to receive the homage of his subjects as a brother of the sun, and the regular services to that luminary were never interrupted. Nor did the prince of Tezcuco afterwards neglect the honors due his national gods, nor even refrain himself from plunging the knife into the breasts of captives on the altar of the god of war.[2] They were but expressions of that monotheism which is ever present, "not in contrast to polytheism, but in living intuition in the religious sentiments." If this subtle but true distinction be rightly understood, it will excite no surprise to find such epithets as "endless," "omnipotent," "invisible," "adorable," such appellations as "the Maker and Moulder of All," "the Mother and Father of Life," "the One God complete in perfection and unity," "the Creator of all that is," "the Soul of the World," in use and of undoubted indigenous origin not only among the civilized Aztecs, but even among the Haitians, the Araucanians, the Lenni Lenape, and others.[3] It will

[1] Prescott, *Conq. of Mexico*, i. pp. 192, 193, on the authority of Ixtlilxochitl.

[2] Brasseur, *Hist. du Mexique*, iii. p. 297, note.

[3] Of very many authorities that I have at hand, I shall only mention Heckewelder, *Acc. of the Inds.* p. 422; Duponceau, *Mem. sur les Langues de l'Amér. du Nord*, p. 310; Peter Martyr, *De Rebus Oceanicis*, Dec. i., cap. 9; Molina, *Hist of Chili*, ii. p. 75; Ximenes, *Origen de los Indios de Guatemala*, pp. 4,5; Ixtlilxochitl, *Rel. des Conq. du Mexique*, p. 2. These terms bear the

not seem contradictory to hear of them in a purely
polytheistic worship ; we shall be far from regarding them as familiar to the popular mind, and we
shall never be led so far astray as to adduce them in
evidence of a monotheism in either technical sense of
that word. In point of fact they were not applied to
any particular god even in the most enlightened nations, but were terms of laudation and magniloquence
used by the priests and devotees of every several god
to do him honor. They prove something in regard
to a consciousness of divinity hedging us about, but
nothing at all in favor of a recognition of one God ;
they exemplify how profound is the conviction of a
highest and first principle, but they do not offer the
least reason to surmise that this was a living reality
in doctrine or practice.

The confusion of these distinct ideas has led to
much misconception of the native creeds. But another
and more fatal error was that which distorted them

severest scrutiny. The Aztec appellation of the Supreme Being
Tloque nahuaque is compounded of *tloc*, together, with, and *na-*
huac, at, by, with, with possessive forms added, giving the signification, Lord of all existence and coexistence (alles Mitseyns
und alles Beiseyns, bei welchem das Seyn aller Dinge ist. Buschmann, *Ueber die Aztekischen Ortsnamen*, p. 642). In the Quiche
legends the Supreme Being is called *Bitol*, the substantive form
of *bit*, to make pottery, to form, and *Tzakol*, substantive form of
tzak, to build, the Creator, the Constructor. The Arowacks of
Guyana applied the term *Aluberi* to their highest conception of
a first cause, from the verbal form *alin*, he who makes (Martius,
Ethnographie und Sprachenkunde Amerika's, i. p. 696). So some
of the Minnetarees interpret the name of their deity *Itsikamahi-*
dis as " he who first made " (Matthews, *Grammar of the Hidatsa*,
p. xxi. New York, 1873).

into a dualistic form, ranging on one hand the good spirit with his legions of angels, on the other the evil one with his swarms of fiends, representing the world as the scene of their unending conflict, man as the unlucky football who gets all the blows. This notion, which has its historical origin among the Parsees of ancient Iran, is unknown to savage nations. "The Hidatsa," says Dr. Matthews, "believe neither in a hell nor in a devil." [1] "The idea of the Devil," justly observes Jacob Grimm, "is foreign to all primitive religions." Yet Professor Mueller, in his voluminous work on those of America, after approvingly quoting this saying, complacently proceeds to classify the deities as good or bad spirits! [2]

This view, which has obtained without question in every work on the native religions of America, has arisen partly from habits of thought difficult to break, partly from mistranslations of native words, partly from the foolish axiom of the early missionaries, "The gods of the gentiles are devils." Yet their own writings furnish conclusive proof that no such distinction existed out of their own fancies. The same word (*otkon*) which Father Bruyas employs to translate into Iroquois the term "devil," in the passage "the Devil took upon himself the figure of a serpent," he is obliged to use for "spirit" in the phrase, "at the resurrection we shall be spirits," [3] which is a rather amusing illustration how impossible it was by any native word to convey the idea of the spirit of evil.

---

[1] *Grammar of the Hidatsa*, p. xxii.
[2] *Geschichte der Amerikanischen Urreligionen*, p. 403.
[3] Bruyas, *Rad. Verb. Iroquæorum*, p. 38.

When in 1570, Father Rogel commenced his labors among the tribes near the Savannah River, he told them that the deity they adored was a demon who loved all evil things, and they must hate him ; whereupon his auditors replied, that so far from this being the case, whom he called a wicked being was the power that sent them all good things, and indignantly left the missionary to preach to the winds.[1]

A passage often quoted in support of this mistaken view is one in Winslow's " Good News from New England," written in 1622. The author says that the Indians worship a good power called Kiehtan, and another " who, as farre as wee can conceive, is the Devill," named, Hobbamock, or Hobbamoqui. The former of these names is merely the word "great," in their dialect of Algonkin, with a final *n*, and is probably an abbreviation of Kittanitowit, the great manito, a vague term mentioned by Roger Williams and other early writers, introduced, Mr. Trumbull thinks, to express a conception received from the missionaries. The latter, so far from corresponding to the power of evil, was, according to Winslow's own statement, the kindly god who cured diseases, aided them in the chase, and appeared to them in dreams as their protector. Therefore, with great justice, Dr. Jarvis has explained it to mean " the *oke* or tutelary deity which each Indian worships," as the word itself signifies.[2]

---

[1] Alcazar, *Chrono-historia de la Prov. de Toledo*, Dec. iii., Año viii., cap. iv. : Madrid, 1710. This rare work contains the only faithful copies of Father Rogel's letters extant. Mr. Shea, in his History of Catholic Missions, erroneously calls him Roger.

[2] *Discourse on the Religion of the Ind. Tribes of N. Am.*, p. 252 in the Trans. N. Y. Hist. Soc.

So in many instances it turns out that what has been reported to be the evil divinity of a nation, to whom they pray to the neglect of a better one, is in reality the highest power they recognize.   Thus Juripari, worshipped by certain tribes of the Tupi-Guaranay stock, and said to be their wicked spirit, is in fact the name in their language for spiritual existence in general ; [1] and Aka-kanet, sometimes mentioned as the father of evil in the mythology of the Araucanians, is the benign power appealed to by their priests, who is throned in the Pleiades, who sends fruits and flowers to the earth, and is addressed as "grandfather." [2]   The Cupay of the Peruvians never was, as Prescott would have us believe, "the shadowy embodiment of evil," but simply and solely their god of the dead, the Pluto of their pantheon, corresponding to the Mictla of the Mexicans.

The evidence on the point is indeed conclusive. The Jesuit missionaries very rarely distinguish between good and evil deities when speaking of the

---

[1] " Giropari semble apartenir plus specialement au nord du Bresil," says Denis in his notes to Father d'Evreux's *Histoire de Marignan*, p. 405. He sent both pleasant and unpleasant events ; on the Pampas it seems to have been a common, not a proper name.   The derivation given is *jerupiar pari*, the lame proud one (Martius, *Die Indianischen Völkerschaften in Brasilien*, p. 468).

[2] Mueller, *Amer. Urreligionen*, pp. 265, 272, 274. Well may he remark : " The dualism is not very striking among these tribes ; " as a few pages previous he says of the Caribs, " The dualism of gods is anything but rigidly observed.   The good gods do more evil than good.   Fear is the ruling religious sentiment."   To such a lame conclusion do these venerable prepossessions lead. *Grau ist alle Theorie.*

religion of the northern tribes; and the Moravian Brethren among the Algonkins and Iroquois place on record their unanimous testimony that " the idea of a devil, a prince of darkness, they first received in later times through the Europeans." [1] So the Cherokees, remarks an intelligent observer, " know nothing of the Evil One and his domains, except what they have learned from white men." [2] The term Great Spirit conveys, for instance, to the Chipeway just as much the idea of a bad as of a good spirit; he is unaware of any distinction until it is explained to him. [3] " I have never been able to discover from the Dakotas themselves," remarks the Rev. G. H. Pond, who had lived among them as a missionary for eighteen years, [4] " the least degree of evidence that they divide the gods into classes of good and evil, and am persuaded that those persons who represent them as doing so, do it inconsiderately, and because it is so natural to subscribe to a long cherished popular opinion."

Very soon after coming in contact with the whites, the Indians caught the notion of a bad and good spirit, pitted one against the other in eternal warfare, and engrafted it on their ancient traditions. Writers anxious to discover Jewish or Christian analogies, forcibly construed myths to suit their pet theories, and for indolent observers it was convenient to cata-

---

[1] Loskiel, *Ges. der Miss. der evang. Brueder,* p. 46.

[2] Whipple, *Report on the Ind. Tribes,* p. 35: Washington, 1855. Pacific Railroad Docs.

[3] Schoolcraft, *Indian Tribes,* i. p. 359.

[4] In Schoolcraft, *Ibid.,* iv. p. 642.

logue their gods in antithetical classes. In Mexican
and Peruvian mythology this is so plainly false that
historians no longer insist upon it, but as a popular
error it still holds its ground with reference to the
more barbarous and less known tribes.

Perhaps no myth has been so often quoted in its
confirmation as that of the ancient Iroquois, which
narrates the conflict between the first two brothers
of our race. It is of undoubted native origin, and
venerable antiquity. The version given by the Tuscarora chief Cusic, in 1825, relates that in the beginning of things there were two brothers, Enigorio and
Enigohahetgea, names literally meaning the Good
Mind and the Bad Mind. [1] The former went about
the world furnishing it with gentle streams, fertile
plains, and plenteous fruits, while the latter ma-
liciously followed him creating rapids, thorns, and
deserts. At length the Good Mind turned upon his
brother in anger, and crushed him into the earth.
He sank out of sight in its depths, but not to perish,
for in the dark realms of the underworld he still
lives, receiving the souls of the dead and being
the author of all evil. Now when we compare this
with the version of the same legend given by Father
Brebeuf, missionary to the Hurons in 1636, we find
its whole complexion altered; the moral dualism
vanishes; the names Good Mind and Bad Mind do not
appear; it is the struggle of Ioskeha, the White one,

---

[1] Or more exactly, the Beautiful Spirit, the Ugly Spirit. In
Onondaga the radicals are *onigonra*, spirit, *hio* beautiful, *ahetken*
ugly. *Dictionnaire Français-Onontagué, édité par Jean-Marie
Shea:* New York, 1859.

with his brother Tawiscara, the Dark one, and we at once perceive that Christian influence in the course of two centuries had given the tale a meaning foreign to its original intent.

So it is with the story the Algonkins tell of their hero Manibozho, who, in the opinion of a well-known writer, " is always placed in antagonism to a great serpent, a spirit of evil." [1] It is to the effect that after conquering many animals, this famous magician tried his arts on the prince of serpents. After a prolonged struggle, which brought on the general deluge and the destruction of the world, he won the victory. The first authority we have for this narrative is even later than Cusic; it is Mr. Schoolcraft in our own day; the legendary cause of the deluge as related by Father Le Jeune, in 1634, is quite dissimilar, and makes no mention of a serpent; and as we shall hereafter see, neither among the Algonkins nor any other Indians, was the serpent usually a type of evil, but quite the reverse.[2]

The comparatively late introduction of such views into the native legends finds a remarkable proof in the myths of the Quiches, which were committed to writing in the seventeenth century. They narrate the struggles between the rulers of the upper and the nether world, the descent of the former into Xibalba, the Realm of Phantoms, and their victory over its lords, One Death and Seven Deaths. The writer adds

[1] Squier, *The Serpent Symbol in America.*

[2] Both these legends will be analyzed in a subsequent chapter, and an attempt made not only to restore them their primitive form, but to explain their meaning.

5

of the latter, who clearly represent to his mind the
Evil One and his adjutants, " in the old times they
did not have much power ; they were but annoyers
and opposers of men, and in truth they were not regarded as gods. But when they appeared it was terrible. They were of evil, they were owls, fomenting
trouble and discord." In this passage, which, be it
said, seems to have impressed the translators very
differently, the writer appears to compare the great
power assigned by the Christian religion to Satan and
his allies, with the very much less potency attributed
to their analogues in heathendom, the rulers of the
world of the dead.[1]

A little reflection will convince the most incredulous that any such dualism as has been fancied to
exist in the native religions, could not have been of
indigenous growth. The gods of the primitive man
are beings of thoroughly human physiognomy,
painted with colors furnished by intercourse with his
fellows. These are his enemies or his friends, as he
conciliates or insults them. No mere man, least of
all a savage, is kind and benevolent in spite of neglect and injury, nor is any man causelessly and cease-
lessly malicious. Personal, family, or national feuds
render some more inimical than others, but always
from a desire to guard their own interests, never out
of a delight in evil for its own sake. Thus the
cruel gods of death, disease, and danger, were never
of Satanic nature, while the kindliest divinities were

---

[1] Compare the translation and remarks of Ximenes, *Or, de
los Indios de Guat.*, p. 76, with those of Brasseur, *Le Livre
Sacré des Quichés*, p. 189.

disposed to punish, and that severely, any neglect of their ceremonies.

I must not be understood to mean that there was no dichotomic classification of deities. This there was, and very generally. Some gods favored man, and others hurt him; some were his friends, others his foes. But what I would warn against is the common error of confounding this with a *moral* dualism. This can only arise in minds where the ideas of good and evil are not synonymous with those of pleasure and pain, for the conception of a wholly good or a wholly evil nature requires the use of these terms in their higher, ethical sense. The various deities of the Indians, it may safely be said in conclusion, present no stronger antithesis in this respect than those of ancient Greece and Rome.

CHAPTER III.

THE SACRED NUMBER, ITS ORIGIN AND APPLICATIONS.

The number FOUR sacred in all American religions, and the key to their symbolism.—Derived from the CARDINAL POINTS.—Appears constantly in government, arts, rights, and myths.—The Cardinal Points identified with the Four Winds, who in myths are the four ancestors of the human race, and the four celestial rivers watering the terrestrial Paradise.—Associations grouped around each Cardinal Point.—From the number four was derived the symbolic value of the number *Forty*, and the *Sign of the Cross*.

EVERY one familiar with the ancient religions of the world must have noticed the mystic power they attached to certain numbers, and how these numbers became the measures and formative quantities, as it were, of traditions and ceremonies, and had a symbolical meaning nowise connected with their arithmetical value. For instance, in many eastern religions, that of the Jews among the rest, *seven* was the most sacred number, and after it, *four* and *three*. The most cursory reader must have observed in how many connections the seven is used in the Hebrew Scriptures, occurring, in all, something over three hundred and sixty times, it is said. Why these numbers were chosen rather than others has not been clearly explained. Their sacred character dates beyond the earliest history, and must have been coeval with the first expressions of the religious sentiment. Only one of them, the FOUR, has any prominence in the religions of the red race, but this is so marked and so universal, that at a very early period in my studies I felt convinced that if the reason for its adoption could be discovered, much of the apparent confusion which reigns among them would be dispelled.

Such a reason must take its rise from some essential relation of man to nature, everywhere prominent, everywhere the same. It is found in the *adoration of the cardinal points.*

The red man, as I have said, was a hunter; he was ever wandering through pathless forests, coursing over boundless prairies. It seems to the white race not a faculty, but an instinct that guides him so unerringly. He is never at a loss. Says a writer who has deeply studied his character: "The Indian ever has the points of the compass present to his mind, and expresses himself accordingly in words, although it shall be of matters in his own house."[1]

The assumption of precisely four cardinal points is not of chance; it is recognized in every language; it is rendered essential by the anatomical structure of the body; it is derived from the immutable laws of the universe. Whether we gaze at the sunset or the sunrise, or whether at night we look for guidance to the only star of the twinkling thousands that is constant to its place, the anterior and posterior planes of our bodies, our right hands and our left coincide with the parallels and meridians. Very early in his history did man take note of these four points, and recognizing in them his guides through the night and the wilderness, call them his gods. Long after-

[1] Buckingham Smith, *Gram. Notices of the Heve Language*, p. 26 (Shea's Lib. Am. Linguistics).

wards, when centuries of slow progress had taught
him other secrets of nature—when he had discerned
in the motions of the sun, the elements of matter, and
the radicals of arithmetic a repetition of this number
—they were to him further warrants of its sacredness. He adopted it as a regulating· quantity in his
institutions and his arts; he repeated it in its multiples and compounds ; he imagined for it novel applications; he constantly magnified its mystic meaning ;
and finally, in his philosophical reveries, he called it
the key to the secrets of the universe, " the source of
everflowing nature." [1]

In primitive geography the figure of the earth is a
square plain; in the legend of the Quichés it is
" shaped as a square, divided into four parts, marked
with lines, measured with cords, and suspended from
the heavens by a cord to its four corners and its four
sides." [2] The earliest divisions of territory were in
conformity to this view. Thus it was with ancient
Egypt, Syria, Mesopotamia, India and China;[3] and

---

[1] I refer to the four " ultimate elementary particles " of Em-
pedocles. The number was sacred to Hermes, and lay at the root
of the physical philosophy of Pythagoras. The quotation in the
text is from the "·Golden Verses," given in Passow's lexicon
under the word τετρακτὺς : ναι μα τον ἁμετερᾳ ψυχᾳ παραδοντα τε-
τρακτυν παγαν αεναου φυσεως. " The most sacred of all things," said
this famous teacher, " is Number ; and next to it, that which
gives Names ; " a truth that the lapse of three thousand years
is just enabling us to appreciate.

[2] Ximenes, *Or. de los Indios*, etc., p. 5.

[3] See Sepp, *Heidenthum und dessen Bedeutung für das Christenthum*, i. p. 464 sqq., a work full of learning, but written in
the wildest vein of Joseph de Maistre's school of Romanizing
mythology.

in the new world, the states of Peru, Araucania, the
Muyscas, the Quichés, and Tlascala were tetrarchies
divided in accordance with, and in the first two instances named after, the cardinal points. So their
chief cities—Cuzco, Quito, Tezcuco, Mexico, Cholula—were quartered by streets running north, south,
east, and west. It was a necessary result of such a
division that the chief officers of the government
were four in number, that the inhabitants of town
and country, that the whole social organization acquired a quadruplicate form. The official title of the
Incas was " Lord of the four quarters of the earth,"
and the venerable formality in taking possession of
land, both in their domain and that of the Aztecs,
was to throw a stone, to shoot an arrow, or to hurl a
firebrand to each of the cardinal points.[1] They carried out the idea in their architecture, building their
palaces in squares with doors opening, their tombs
with their angles pointing, their great causeways
running in these directions. These architectural
principles repeat themselves all over the continent ;
they recur in the sacred structures of Yucatan, in the
ancient cemetery of Teo-tihuacan, near Mexico, where
the tombs are arranged along avenues corresponding
exactly to the parallels and meridians of the central
tumuli of the sun and moon ;[2] and however ignorant

[1] Brasseur, *Hist. du Mexique*, ii. p. 227, *Le Livre Sacré des
Quichés*, introd. p. ccxlii. The four provinces of Peru were
Anti, Cunti, Chincha, and Colla The meaning of these names has
been lost, but to repeat them, says La Vega, was the same as to
use our words, east, west, north, and south (*Hist. des Incas*, lib.
ii. cap.11).

[2] Humboldt, *Polit. Essay on New Spain*, ii. p. 44.

we **are** about the mound builders of the Mississippi valley, we know that they constructed their earthworks with a constant regard to the quarters of the compass.

Nothing can be more natural than to take into consideration the regions of the heavens in the construction of buildings; I presume that at any time no one plans an edifice of pretensions without doing so. Yet this is one of those apparently trifling transactions which in their origin and applications have exerted a controlling influence on the history of the human race.

When we reflect how indissolubly the mind of the primitive man is welded to his superstitions, it were incredible that his social life and his architecture could thus be as it were in subjection to one idea, and his rites and myths escape its sway. As one might expect, it reappears in these latter more vividly than anywhere else. If there is one formula more frequently mentioned by travellers than another as an indispensable preliminary to all serious business, it is that of smoking, and the prescribed and traditional rule was that the first puff should be to the sky, and then one to each of the corners of the earth, or the cardinal points.[1] These were the spirits who made and governed the earth, and under whatever difference of guise the uncultivated fancy portrayed them, they were the leading figures in the

[1] This custom has been often mentioned among the Iroquois, Algonkins, Dakotas, Creeks, Natchez, Araucanians, and other tribes. Nuttall points out its recurrence among the Tartars of Siberia also. (*Travels*, p. 175.)

tales and ceremonies of nearly every tribe of the red race. These were the divine powers summoned by the Chipeway magicians when initiating neophytes into the mysteries of the meda craft. They were asked to a lodge of four poles, to four stones that lay before its fire, there to remain four days, and attend four feasts. At every step of the proceeding this number or its multiples were repeated.[1] With their neighbors the Dakotas the number was also distinctly sacred; it was intimately inwoven in all their tales concerning the wakan power and the spirits of the air, and their religious rites. The artist Catlin has given a vivid description of the great annual festival of the Mandans, a Dakota tribe, and brings forward with emphasis the ceaseless reiteration of this number from first to last.[2] He did not detect its origin in the veneration of the cardinal points, but the information that has since been furnished of the myths of this stock leaves no doubt that such was the case.[3]

Proximity of place had no part in this similarity of rite. In the grand commemorative festival of the Creeks called the Busk, which wiped out the memory of all crimes but murder, which reconciled the proscribed criminal to his nation and atoned for his guilt, when the new fire was kindled and the green corn

---

[1] Schoolcraft, *Indian Tribes*, v. pp. 424 et seq.

[2] *Letters on the North American Indians*, vol. i., Letter 22.

[3] Schoolcraft, *Indian Tribes*, iv. p. 643 sq. " Four is their sacred number," says Mr. Pond (p. 646). Their neighbors, the Pawnees, though not the most remote affinity can be detected between their languages, coincide with them in this sacred number, and distinctly identified it with the cardinal points. See De Smet, *Oregon Missions*, pp. 360, 361.

served up, every dance, every invocation, every ceremony, was shaped and ruled by the application of the
number four and its multiples in every imaginable
relation. So it was at that solemn probation which
the youth must undergo to prove himself worthy of
the dignities of manhood and to ascertain his guardian
spirit; here again his fasts, his seclusions, his trials,
were all laid down in fourfold arrangement.[1]

Not alone among these barbarous tribes were the
cardinal points thus the foundation of the most
solemn mysteries of religion. An excellent authority
relates that the Aztecs of Micla, in Guatemala, celebrated their chief festival four times a year, and that
four priests solemnized its rites. They commenced
by invoking and offering incense to the sky and the
four cardinal points; they conducted the human
victim four times around the temple, then tore out
his heart, and catching the blood in four vases scattered it in the same directions.[2] So also the Peruvians had four principal festivals annually, and at
every new moon one of four days' duration. In fact
the repetition of the number in all their religious
ceremonies is so prominent that it has been a subject
of comment by historians. They have attributed it to
the knowledge of the solstices and equinoxes, but

[1] Benj. Hawkins, *Sketch of the Creek Country*, pp. 75, 78:
Savannah, 1848. The description he gives of the ceremonies of
the Creeks was transcribed word for word and published in the
first volume of the American Antiquarian Society's Transactions
as of the Shawnees of Ohio. This literary theft has not before
been noticed.

[2] Palacios, *Des. de la Prov. de Guatemala*, pp. 31, 32, ed.
Ternaux-Compans.

assuredly it is of more ancient date than this. The same explanation has been offered for its recurrence among the Nahuas of Mexico, whose whole lives were subjected to its operation. At birth the mother was held unclean for four days, a fire was kindled and kept burning for a like length of time, at the baptism of the child an arrow was shot to each of the cardinal points. Their prayers were offered four times a day, the greatest festivals were every fourth year, and their offerings of blood were to the four points of the compass. At death food was placed on the grave, as among the Eskimos, Creeks, Dakotas and Algonkins, for four days (for all these nations and many others supposed that the journey to the land of souls was accomplished in that time), and mourning for the dead was for four months or four years.[1]

It were fatiguing and unnecessary to extend the catalogue much further. Yet it is not nearly exhausted. From tribes of both continents and all stages of culture, the Muyscas of Columbia and the Natchez of Louisiana, the Quichés of Guatemala and the Caribs of the Orinoko, instance after instance might be marshalled to illustrate how universally a sacred character was attached to this number, and how uniformly it is traceable to a veneration of the cardinal points

---

[1] All familiar with Mexican antiquity will recall many such examples. I may particularly refer to Kingsborough, *Antiqs. of Mexico*, v. p. 480, Ternaux-Compans' *Recueil de pièces rel. à la Conq. du Mexique*, pp. 307, 310, and Gama, *Des. de las dos Piedras que se hallaron en la plaza principal de Mexico*, ii. sec. 126 (Mexico, 1832), who gives numerous instances beyond those I have cited, and directs with emphasis the attention of the reader to this constant repetition.

It is sufficient that it be displayed in some of its more unusual applications.

It is well known that the calendar common to the Aztecs and Mayas divides the month into four weeks, each containing a like number of secular days; that their indiction is divided into four periods; and that they believed the world had passed through four cycles. It has not been sufficiently emphasized that in many of the picture writings these days of the week are placed respectively north, south, east, and west, and that in the Maya language the quarters of the indiction still bear the names of the cardinal points, hinting the reason of their adoption.[1] This cannot be fortuitous. Again, the division of the year into four seasons—a division as devoid of foundation in nature as that of the ancient Aryans into three, and unknown among many tribes, yet obtained in very early times among Algonkins, Cherokees, Choctaws, Creeks, Aztecs, Muyscas, Peruvians, and Araucanians. They were supposed to be produced by the unending struggles and varying fortunes of the four aerial giants who rule the winds.

We must seek in mythology the key to the monotonous repetition and the sanctity of this number; and furthermore, we must seek it in those natural modes of expression of the religious sentiment which are above the power of blood or circumstance to control. One of these modes, we have seen, was that which led to the identification of the divinity with the wind, and this it is that solves the enigma in the

---

[1] Albert Gallatin, *Trans. Am. Ethnol. Soc.*, ii. p. 316, from the Codex Vaticanus, No. 3738.

present instance. Universally the spirits of the cardinal points were imagined to be in the winds that blew from them. The names of these directions and of the corresponding winds are often the same, and when not, there exists an intimate connection between them. For example, take the languages of the Mayas, Huastecas, and Moscos of Central America ; in all of them the word for *north* is synonymous with *north wind*, and so on for the other three points of the compass. Or again, that of the Dakotas, and the word *tate-ouye-toba*, translated " the four quarters of the heavens," means literally, " whence the four winds come." [1] It were not difficult to extend the list ; but illustrations are all that is required. Let it be remembered how closely the motions of the air are associated in thought and language with the operations of the soul and the idea of God ; let it further be considered what support this association receives from the power of the winds on the weather, bringing as they do the lightning and the storm, the zephyr that cools the brow, and the tornado that levels the forest ; how they summon the rain to fertilize the seed and refresh the shrivelled leaves ; how they aid the hunter to stalk the game, and usher in the varying seasons ; how, indeed, in a hundred ways, they intimately concern his comfort and his life ; and it will not seem strange that they almost occupied the place of all other gods in the mind of the child of nature. Especially as those who gave or withheld the rains were the objects of his anxious solicitation. " Ye who dwell at the four corners of the earth—at the north, at the south, at

---

[1] Riggs, *Gram. and Dict. of the Dakota Lang.*, s. v.

the east, and at the west," commenced the Aztec prayer to the Tlalocs, gods of the showers.[1] For they, as it were, hold the food, the life of man in their power, garnered up on high, to grant or deny, as they see fit. It was from them that the prophet of old was directed to call back the spirits of the dead to the dry bones of the valley. "Prophesy unto the wind, prophesy, son of man, and say to the wind, thus saith the Lord God, come forth from the four winds, O breath, and breathe upon these slain, that they may live." (Ezek. xxxvii. 9.)

In the same spirit the priests of the Eskimos prayed to *Sillam Innua*, the Owner of the Winds, as the highest existence; the abode of the dead they called *Sillam Aipane*, the House of the Winds; and in their incantations, when they would summon a new soul to the sick, or order back to its home some troublesome spirit, their invocations were ever addressed to the winds from the cardinal points—to Pauna the East, and Sauna the West, to Kauna the South and Auna the North.[2]

As the rain-bringers, as the life-givers, it were no far-fetched metaphor to call them the fathers of our race. Hardly a nation on the continent but seems to have had some vague tradition of an origin from four brothers, to have at some time been led by four leaders or princes, or in some manner to have connected the appearance and action of four important person-

[1] Sahagun, *Hist. de la Nueva España*, in Kingsborough, v. p. 375.

[2] Egede, *Nachrichten von Grönland*, pp. 137, 173, 285. (Kopenhagen, 1790.)

ages with its earliest traditional history. Sometimes the myth defines clearly these fabled characters as the spirits of the winds, sometimes it clothes them in uncouth, grotesque metaphors, sometimes again it so weaves them into actual history that we are at a loss where to draw the line that divides fiction from truth.

I shall attempt to follow step by step the growth of this myth from its simplest expression, where the transparent drapery makes no pretence to conceal its true meaning, through the ever more elaborate narratives, the more strongly marked personifications of more cultivated nations, until it assumes the outlines of, and has palmed itself upon the world as actual history.

This simplest form is that which alone appears among the Algonkins and Dakotas. They both traced their lives back to four ancestors, personages concerned in various ways with the first things of time, not rightly distinguished as men or gods, but very positively identified with the four winds. Whether from one or all of these the world was peopled, whether by process of generation or some other more obscure way, the old people had not said, or saying, had not agreed.[1]

It is a shade more complex when we come to the Creeks. They told of four men who came from the four corners of the earth, who brought them the sacred fire, and pointed out the seven sacred plants. They were called the Hi-you-yul-gee, a sort of cabal-

[1] Schoolcraft, *Algic Researches,* i. p. 139, and *Indian Tribes,* iv. p. 229.

istic word, the plural form of their common invocation, *hi-yo-yu.* Having rendered them this service,
the kindly visitors disappeared in a cloud, returning
whence they came. When another and more ancient
legend informs us that the Creeks were at first divided into four clans, and alleged a descent from four
female ancestors, it will hardly be venturing too far
to recognize in these four ancestors the four friendly
patrons from the cardinal points.[1]

The ancient inhabitants of Haiti, when first discovered by the Spaniards, had a similar genealogical
story, which Peter Martyr relates with various ex-
cuses for its silliness and exclamations at its absurdi-
ty. Perhaps the fault lay less in its lack of meaning
than in his want of insight. It was to the effect
that men lived in caves, and were destroyed by the
parching rays of the sun, and were destitute of means
to prolong their race, until they caught and subjected to their use four women who were swift of foot
and slippery as eels. These were the mothers of the
race of men. Or again, it was said that a certain
king had a huge gourd which contained all the waters of the earth; four brothers, who coming into
the world at one birth had cost their mother her life,
ventured to the gourd to fish, picked it up, but frightened by the old king's approach, dropped it on the
ground, broke it into fragments, and scattered the
waters over the earth, forming the seas, lakes, and
rivers, as they now are. These brothers in time became the fathers of a nation, and to them they traced

---

[1] Hawkins, *Sketch of the Creek Country,* pp. 81, 82, and my
essay, *The National Legend of the Chahta Muskokee Tribe,* p. 11.

their lineage.[1] With the previous examples before our eyes, it asks no vivid fancy to see in these quaternions once more the four winds, the bringers of rain, so swift and so slippery.

The Navajos are a rude tribe north of Mexico. Yet even they have an allegory to the effect that when the first man came up from the ground under the figure of the moth-worm, the four spirits of the cardinal points were already there, and hailed him with the exclamation, " Lo, he is of our race." [2] It is a poor and feeble effort to tell the same old story.

The Mayas of Yucatan shared this ancestral legend, for in an ancient manuscript found by Mr. Stephens during his travels, it appears they looked back to four parents or leaders called the Tutul Xiu. But, indeed, this was a trait of all the civilized nations of Central America and Mexico. An author who was very unwilling to admit any mythical interpretation of the coincidence, has adverted to it in tones of astonishment: " In all the Aztec and Toltec histories there are four characters who constantly reappear; either as priests or envoys of the gods, or of hidden and disguised majesty ; or as guides and chieftains of tribes during their migrations; or as kings and rulers of monarchies after their foundation; and even to the time of the conquest, there are always four princes

---

[1] Peter Martyr, *De Reb. Ocean.*, Dec. i. lib. ix. The story is told more at length by the Brother Ramon Pane, in the abstract of native traditions he drew up by the order of Columbus. I have given them from several sources, among others the unpublished works of Las Casas, in *The Arawack Language in its Linguistic and Ethnological Relations*, Phila., 1871.

[2] Schoolcraft, *Ind. Tribes*, iv. p. 89.

who compose the supreme government, whether in Guatemala, or in Mexico."[1] This fourfold division points not to a common history but to a common nature. The ancient heroes and demigods, who, four in number, figure in all these antique traditions, were not men of flesh and blood, but the invisible currents of air who brought the fertilizing showers.

They corresponded to the four gods Bacab, who in the Yucatecan mythology were supposed to stand one at each corner of the world, supporting, like gigantic caryatides, the overhanging firmament. When at the general deluge all other gods and men were swallowed by the waters they alone escaped to people it anew. These four, known by the names of Kan, Muluc, Ix, and Cauac, represented respectively the east, north, west, and south, and as in Oriental symbolism, so here each quarter of the compass was distinguished by a color, the east by yellow, the south by red, the west by black, and the north by white. The names of these mysterious personages, employed somewhat as we do the Dominical letters, adjusted the calendar of the Mayas, and by their propitious or portentous combinations was arranged their system of judicial astrology. They were the gods of rain, and under the title Chac, the Red Ones, were the chief ministers of the highest power. As such they were represented in the religious ceremonies by four old men, constant attendants on the high priest in his official functions.[2] In this most civilized branch of the

---

[1] Brasseur, *Le Liv. Sac.*, Introd., p. cxvii.

[2] Diego de Landa, *Rel. de las Cosas de Yucatan*, pp. 160, 206, 208, ed. Brasseur. The learned editor, in a note to p. 208, states erroneously the disposition of the colors, as may be seen

red race, as everywhere else, we thus find four mythological characters prominent beyond all others,
giving a peculiar physiognomy to the national legends, arts, and sciences, and in them once more
we recognize by signs infallible, personifications of
the four cardinal points and the four winds.

They rarely lose altogether their true character.
The Quiché legends tell us that the four men who
were first created by the Heart of Heaven, Hurakan,
the Air in Motion, were infinitely keen of eye and
swift of foot, that " they measured and saw all that
exists at the four corners and the four angles of the
sky and the earth ;" that they did not fulfil the design
of their maker " to bring forth and produce when
the season of harvest was near," until he blew into
their eyes a cloud, " until their faces were obscured
as when one breathes on a mirror." Then he
gave them of wives the four mothers of our species,
names were Falling Water, Beautiful Water, Water
of Serpents, and Water of Birds.[1] Truly he who
can see aught but a transparent myth in this

by comparing the document on p. 395. This dedication of
colors to the cardinal points is universal in Central Asia. The
geographical names of the Red Sea, the Black Sea, the Yellow
Sea, or Persian Gulf, and the White Sea or the Mediterranean,
are derived from this association. The cities of China, many
of them at least, have their gates which open toward the cardinal points painted of certain colors, and precisely these four,
the white, the black, the red, and the yellow, are those which
in Oriental myth the mountain in the centre of Paradise shows
to the different cardinal points. (Sepp, *Heidenthum und Christenthum* i. p. 177.) The coincidence furnishes food for reflection.

[1] *Le Livre Sacré des Quichés*, pp. 203–5, note.

recital, is a realist that would astonish Euhemerus himself.

There is in these Aztec legends a quaternion besides this of the first men, one that bears marks of a profound contemplation on the course of nature, one that answers to the former as the heavenly phase of the earthly conception. It is seen in the four personages, or perhaps we should say modes of action, that make up the one Supreme Cause of All, Hurakan, the breath, the wind, the Divine Spirit. They are He who creates, He who gives Form, He who gives Life, and He who reproduces.[1] This acute and extraordinary analysis of the origin and laws of organic life, clothed under the ancient belief in the action of the winds, reveals a depth of thought for which we were hardly prepared, and is perhaps the single instance of anything like metaphysics among the red race. It is clearly visible in the earlier portions of the legends of the Quichés, and is the more surely of native origin as it has been quite lost on both their translators.

Go where we will, the same story meets us. The empire of the Incas was attributed in the sacred

---

[1] The analogy is remarkable between these and the " quatre actes de la puissance generatrice jusqu'à l'entier développément des corps organisés,'' portrayed by four globes in the Mycenean bas-reliefs. See Guigniaut, *Religions de l'Antiquité,* i. p. 374. It were easy to multiply the instances of such parallelism in the growth of religious thought in the Old and New World, but I designedly refrain from doing so. They have already given rise to false theories enough, and a discussion of their significance is not embraced in the design of the present work. For this I must refer the reader to the general principles of mythology laid down in my work entitled: *The Religious Sentiment, its Source and Aim.*

chants of the Amautas, the priests assigned to take
charge of the records, to four brothers and their
wives. These mythical civilizers are said " to have
emerged from a cave called *Pacari tampu*, a birthplace,"
which may also mean " the House of Subsistence,"
reminding us of the four heroes who in Aztec legend
set forth to people the world from Tonacatepec, " the
mountain of our subsistence ; " or again it may mean
—for like many of these mythical names it seems to
have been designedly chosen to bear a double construction—the Lodgings of the Dawn, recalling another Aztec legend which points for the birthplace of
the race to Tula in the distant orient. The cave itself suggests to the classical reader that of Eolus, or
may be paralleled with that in which the Iroquois
fabled the winds were imprisoned by their lord,[1] or
with that in which, according to early Christian legend, Jesus was born. These brothers were of no
common kin. Their voices could shake the earth
and their hands heap up mountains. Like the thunder god, they stood on the hills and hurled their
sling-stones to the four corners of the earth. When
one was overpowered he fled upward to the heaven
or was turned into stone, and it was by their aid and
counsel that the savages who possessed the land re-
nounced their barbarous habits and commenced to
till the soil. There can be no doubt but that this
in turn is but another transformation of the Protean
myth we have so long pursued.[2]

[1] Müller, *Amer. Urreligionen*, p. 105, after Strahlheim, who is,
however, no authority.

[2] Müller, *ubi supra*, pp. 308 sqq., gives a good résumé of the
different versions of the myth of the four brothers in Peru.

There are traces of the same legend among many other tribes of the continent, but the trustworthy reports we have of them are too scanty to permit analysis. Enough that they are mentioned in a note, for it is every way likely that could we resolve their meaning they too would carry us back to the four winds.[1]

[1] The Tupis of Brazil claim a descent from four brothers, three of whose names are given by Hans Staden, a prisoner among them about 1550, as Krimen, Hermittan, and Coem; the latter he explains to mean the morning, the east (*le matin*, printed by mistake *le mutin*, *Relation de Hans Staden de Homberg*, p. 274, ed. Ternaux Compans; compare Dias, *Dicc. da Lingua Tupy*, p. 47). Their southern relatives, the Guaranis of Paraguay, also spoke of the four brothers and gave two of their names as Tupi and Guarani, respectively parents of the tribes called after them (Guevara, *Hist. del Paraguay*, lib. i. cap. ii., in Waitz). The fourfold division of the Muyscas of Bogota was traced back to four chieftains created by their hero god Nemqueteba (A. von Humboldt, *Vues des Cordillères*, p. 246). The Nahuas of Mexico much more frequently spoke of themselves as descendants of four or eight original families than of seven (Humboldt, *ibid.*, p. 317, and others in Waitz, *Anthropologie*, iv. pp. 36, 37). The Sacs or Sauks of the Upper Mississippi supposed that two men and two women were first created, and from these four sprang all men (Morse, *Rep. on Ind. Affairs*, App. p. 138). The Ottoes, Pawnees, "and other Indians," had a tradition that from eight ancestors all nations and races were descended (Id., p. 249). This duplication of the number probably arose from assigning the first four men four women as wives. The division into clans or totems which prevails in most northern tribes rests theoretically on descent from different ancestors. The Shawnees and Natchez were divided into four such clans, the Choctaws, Navajos, and Iroquois into eight, thus proving that in those tribes also the myth I have been discussing was recognized. The tribe visited by Lederer in southern Virginia was composed of four clans, who did not in-

Let no one suppose, however, that this was the only myth of the origin of man. Far from it. It was but one of many, for, as I shall hereafter attempt to show, the laws that governed the formations of such myths not only allowed but enjoined great divergence of form. Equally far was it from being the only image which the inventive fancy hit upon to express the action of the winds as the rain bringers. They too were many, but may all be included in a twofold division, either as the winds were supposed to flow in from the corners of the earth or outward from its central point. Thus they are spoken of under such figures as four tortoises at the angles of the earthly plane who vomit forth the rains,[1] or four gigantic caryatides who sustain the heavens and blow the winds from their capacious lungs,[2] or more frequently as four rivers flowing from the broken calabash on high, as the Haitians, draining the waters of the primitive world,[3] as four animals who bring from heaven the maize,[4] as four messengers whom the god of air sends forth, or under a coarser trope as the spittle he ejects toward the cardinal points which is straightway transformed into wild rice, tobacco, and maize.[5]

Constantly from the palace of the lord of the world, seated on the high hill of heaven, blow four

termarry and had separate burial places (*Discoveries*, p. 5. London, 1672).

[1] Mandans in Catlin, *Letts. and Notes*, i. p. 181.
[2] The Mayas, Cogolludo, *Hist. de Yucathan*, lib. iv. cap. 8.
[3] The Navajos, Schoolcraft, *Ind. Tribes*, iv. p. 89.
[4] The Quichés, Ximenes, *Or. de los Indios*, p. 79.
[5] The Iroquois, Müller, *Amer. Urreligionen*, p. 109.

winds, pour four streams, refreshing and fecundating
the earth.   Therefore, in the myths of ancient Iran
there is mention of a celestial fountain, Arduisur, the
virgin daughter of Ormuzd, whence four all nourish-
ing rivers roll their waves toward the cardinal
points; therefore the Thibetans believe that on the
sacred mountain Himavata grows the tree of life
Zampu, from whose foot once more flow the waters
of life in four streams to the four quarters of the
world; and therefore it is that the same tale is told
by the Chinese of the mountain Kouantun, by the
Brahmins of Mount Meru, by the Edda of the mountain in Asaheim whence flows the spring Hvergelmir,
and by the Parsees of Mount Albors in the Cau-
casus.[1]   Each nation called their sacred mountain
"the navel of the earth;" for not only was it the
supposed centre of the habitable world, but through
it, as the fœtus through the umbilical cord, the earth
drew her increase.   Beyond all other spots were they
accounted fertile, scenes of joyous plaisance, of repose, and eternal youth; there rippled the waters
of health, there blossomed the tree of life; they were
fit trysting spots of gods and men.   Hence came the
tales of the terrestrial paradise, the rose garden of
Feridun, the Eden gardens of the world.   The name
shows the origin, for paradise (in Sanscrit, *para desa*)
means literally *high land*.   There, in the unanimous
opinion of the Orient, dwelt once in unalloyed delight the first of men; thence driven by untoward
fate, no more anywhere could they find the path

---

[1] For these myths see Sepp, *Das Heidenthum und dessen Bedeutung für das Christenthum,* i. p. 111 sqq.   The interpretation
is of course my own.

thither. Some thought that in the north, among the fortunate Hyperboreans, others that in the mountains of the moon where dwelt the long-lived Ethiopians, and others again that in the furthest east, underneath the dawn, was situate the seat of pristine happiness; but many were of opinion that somewhere in the western sea, beyond the pillars of Hercules and the waters of the Outer Ocean, lay the garden of the Hesperides, the Islands of the Blessed, the earthly Elysion.

It is not without design that I recall this early dream of the religious fancy. When Christopher Columbus, fired by the hope of discovering this terrestrial paradise,[1] broke the enchantment of the cloudy sea and found a new world, it was but to light upon the same race of men, deluding themselves with the same hope of earthly joys, the same fiction of a long lost garden of their youth. They told him that still to the west, amid the mountains of Paria, was a spot whence flowed mighty streams over all lands, and which in sooth was the spot he sought;[2] and when that baseless fabric had vanished, there still remained the fabled island of Boiuca, or Bimini, hundreds of leagues north of Hispaniola, whose glebe was watered by a fountain of such noble virtue as to restore youth and vigor to the worn out and the aged.[3] This was no fiction of the natives to rid themselves of burdensome guests. Long before the white man approached their shores, families had started

---

[1] See Navarrete, *Viages*, i. p. 259.

[2] Peter Martyr, *De Reb. Ocean.*, Dec. iii., l.b. ix. p. 195 : Colon, 1574.

[3] Ibid., Dec. iii., lib. x. p. 202.

from Cuba, Yucatan, and Honduras in search of these renovating waters, and not returning, were supposed by their kindred to have been detained by the delights of that enchanted land, and to be revelling in its seductive joys, forgetful of former ties.[1]

Perhaps it was but another rendering of the same belief that pointed to the impenetrable forests of the Orinoko, the ancient homes of the Caribs and Arawacks, and there located the famous realm of El Dorado with its imperial capital Manoa, abounding in precious metals and all manner of gems, peopled by a happy race, and governed by an equitable ruler.

The Aztec priests never chanted more regretful dirges than when they sang of Tulan, the cradle of their race, where once it dwelt in peaceful, indolent happiness, whose groves were filled with birds of sweet voices and gay plumage, whose generous soil brought forth spontaneously maize, cocoa, aromatic gums, and fragrant flowers. "Land of riches and plenty, where the gourds grow an arm's length across, where an ear of corn is a load for a stout man, and its stalks are as high as trees ; land where the cotton ripens of its own accord of all rich tints ; land abounding with limpid emeralds, turquoises, gold and silver." [2] This land was also called Tlalocan,

---

[1] Florida was also long supposed to be the site of this wondrous spring, and it is notorious that both Juan Ponce de Leon and De Soto had some lurking hope of discovering it in their expeditions thither. I have examined the myth somewhat at length in *Notes on the Floridian Peninsula, its Literary History, Indian Tribes, and Antiquities*, pp. 99, 100 : Philadelphia, 1859.

[2] Sahagun, *Hist. de la Nueva España*, lib. iii. cap. iii.

from Tlaloc, the god of rain, who there had his dwelling-place, and Tlapallan, the land of colors, or the red land, for the hues of the sky at sunrise floated over it. Its inhabitants were surnamed children of the air, or of Quetzalcoatl, and from its centre rose the holy mountain Tonacatepec, the mountain of our life or subsistence. Its supposed location was in the east, whence in that country blow the winds that bring mild rains, says Sahagun, and that missionary was himself asked, as coming from the east, whether his home was in Tlapallan ; more definitely by some it was situated among the lofty peaks on the frontiers of Guatemala, and all the great rivers that water the earth were supposed to have their sources there.[1] But here, as elsewhere, its site was not determined. " There is a Tulan," says an ancient authority, " where the sun rises, and there is another in the land of shades, and another where the sun reposes, and thence came we ; and still another where the sun reposes, and there dwells God." [2]

---

[1] *Le Livre Sacré des Quichés*, Introd., p. clviii.

[2] *Memorial de Tecpan Atitlan*, in Brasseur, *Hist. de Mexique*, i. p. 167. The derivation of Tulan, or Tula, is extremely uncertain. The Abbé Brasseur saw in it the *ultima Thule* of the ancient geographers, which suited his idea of early American history. Hernando De Soto found a village of this name on the Mississippi, or near it. But on looking into Gallatin's vocabularies, *tulla* turns out to be the Choctaw word for *stone,* and as De Soto was then in the Choctaw country, the coincidence is explained at once. Buschmann, who spells it *Tollan,* takes it from *tolin,* a rush, and translates *juncetum, Ort der Binsen. (Ueber die Aztekischen Orstnamen,* p. 682.) Those who have attempted to make history from these mythological fables have been much puzzled about the location of this mystic land. Humboldt has

The myth of the Quichés but changes the name of this pleasant land. With them it was *Pan-paxil-pa-cayala*, where the waters divide in falling, or, between the waters parcelled out and mucky. This was "an excellent land, full of pleasant things, where was store of white corn and yellow corn, where one could not count the fruits, nor estimate the quantity of honey and food." Over it ruled the lord of the air, and from it the four sacred animals carried the corn to make the flesh of men. [1]

Once again, in the legends of the Mixtecas, we hear the old story repeated of the garden where the first two brothers dwelt. It lay between a meadow and that lofty peak which supports the heavens and the palaces of the gods. "Many trees were there, such as yield flowers and roses, very luscious fruits, divers herbs, and aromatic spices." The names of the brothers were the Wind of Nine Serpents, and the Wind of Nine Caverns. The first was as an eagle, and flew aloft over the waters that poured

placed it on the northwest coast, Cabrera at Palenque, Clavigero north of Anahuac, etc., etc. M. de Charencey remarks that more than twenty cities in Mexico and Central America bore this name (*Le Mythe de Votan*, p. 29. Alençon, 1871). In view of this it is amusing to find Mr. Bancroft locate it so definitely (*Native Races*, ii. p. 99.) Aztlan, literally, the White Land, is another name of originally mythical purport, which it would be equally vain to seek on the terrestrial globe. In the extract in the text, the word translated God is *Qabavil*, an old word for the highest god, either from a root meaning to open, to disclose, or from one of similar form signifying to wonder, to marvel ; literally, therefore, the Revealer, or the Wondrous One (*Vocab. de la Lengua Quiché*, p. 209 : Paris, 1862).

[1] Ximenes, *Or. de los Indios*, p. 80, *Le Livre Sacré*, p, 195.

around their enchanted garden; the second was as a serpent with wings, who proceeded with such velocity that he pierced rocks and walls. They were too swift to be seen by the sharpest eye, and were one near as they passed, he was only aware of a whisper and a rustling like that of the wind in the leaves.[1]

Wherever, in short, the lust of gold lured the early adventurers, they were told of some nation a little further on, some wealthy and prosperous land, abundant and fertile, satisfying the desire of the heart. It was sometimes deceit, and it was sometimes the credited fiction of the earthly paradise, that in all ages has with a promise of perfect joy consoled the aching heart of man.

It is instructive to study the associations that naturally group themselves around each of the cardinal points, and watch how these are mirrored on the surface of language, and have directed the current of thought. Jacob Grimm has performed this task with fidelity and beauty as regards the Aryan race, but the means are wanting to apply his searching method to the indigenous tongues of America. Enough if in general terms their mythological value be determined.

When the day begins, man wakes from his slumbers, faces the rising sun and prays. The east is before him; by it he learns all other directions; it is to him what the north is to the needle; with reference to it he assigns in his mind the position of the three other cardinal points.[2] There is the starting-

---

[1] Garcia, *Origen de los Indios*, lib. iv. cap. 4.

[2] Compare the German expression *sich orientiren*, to right one's self by the east, to understand one's surroundings.

place of the celestial fires, the home of the sun, the womb of the morning. It represents in space the beginning of things in time, and as the bright and glorious creatures of the sky come forth thence, man conceits that his ancestors also in remote ages wandered from the orient; there in the opinion of many in both the old and new worlds was the cradle of the race; there in Aztec legend was the fabled land of Tlapallan, and the wind from the east was called the wind of Paradise, Tlalocavitl.

From this direction came, according to the almost unanimous opinion of the Indian tribes, those hero gods who taught them arts and religion; thither they returned, and from thence they would again appear to resume their ancient sway. As the dawn brings light, and with light is associated in every human mind the ideas of knowledge, safety, protection, majesty, divinity, as it dispels the spectres of night, as it defines the cardinal points, and brings forth the sun and the day, it occupied the primitive mind to an extent that can hardly be magnified beyond the truth. It is in fact the central figure in most natural religions.

The west, as the grave of the heavenly luminaries, or rather as their goal and place of repose, brings with it thoughts of sleep, of death, of tranquillity, of rest from labor. When the evening of his days was come, when his course was run, and man had sunk from sight, he was supposed to follow the sun and find some spot of repose for his tired soul in the distant west. There, with general consent, the tribes north of the Gulf of Mexico supposed the happy hunting-grounds; there, taught by the same analogy, the ancient Aryans placed the Nerriti, the exodus, the land of the dead. " The old notion among us," said on one occasion a distinguished chief of the Creek nation, " is that when we die, the spirit goes the way the sun goes, to the west, and there joins its family and friends who went before it.' [1]

In the northern hemisphere the shadows fall to the north, thence blow cold and furious winds, thence come the snow and early thunder. Perhaps all its primitive inhabitants, of whatever race, thought it the seat of the mighty gods.[2]   A floe of ice in the Arctic Sea was the home of the guardian spirit of the Algonkins ;[3] on a mountain near the north star the Dakotas thought Heyoka dwelt who rules the seasons; and the realm of Mictla, the Aztec god of death, lay where the shadows pointed.   From that cheerless abode his sceptre reached over all creatures, even the gods themselves, for sooner or later all must fall before him.   The great spirit of the dead, said the Ottawas, lives in the dark north,[4] and there, in the opinion of the Monquis of California, resided their chief god, Gumongo.[5]

Unfortunately the makers of vocabularies have rarely included the words north, south, east, and west in their lists, and the methods of expressing these ideas adopted by the Indians can only be partially discovered.   The east and west were usually called from the rising and setting of the sun as in our words

---

[1] Hawkins, *Sketch of the Creek Country*, p. 80.
[2] See Jacob Grimm, *Geschichte der Deutschen Sprache*, p. 681.
[3] De Smet, Oregon Missions, p. 352.
[4] Bressani, *Relation Abrégé*, p. 93.
[5] Venegas, *Hist. of California*, i. p. 91 : London, 1759.

orient and occident, but occasionally from traditional notions. The Mayas named the west the greater, the east the lesser debarkation; believing that while their culture hero Zamna came from the east with a few attendants, the mass of the population arrived from the opposite direction.[1] The Aztecs spoke of the east as "the direction of Tlalocan," the terrestrial paradise. But for north and south there were no such natural appellations, and consequently the greatest diversity is exhibited in the plans adopted to express them. The north in the Caddo tongue is "the place of cold," in Dakota "the situation of the pines," in Creek "the abode of the (north) star," in Algonkin "the home of the soul," in Aztec "the direction of Mictla" the realm of death, in Quiché and Quichua, "to the right hand;"[2] while for the south we find such terms as in Dakota "the downward direction," in Algonkin "the place of warmth," in Quiché "to the left hand," while among the Eskimos who look in this direction for the sun, its name implies "before one," just as does the Hebrew word

---

[1] Cogolludo, *Hist. de Yucathan*, lib. iv. cap. iii.

[2] Alexander von Humboldt has asserted that the Quichuas had other and very circumstantial terms to express the cardinal points drawn from the positions of the sun (*Ansichten der Natur*, ii. p. 368). But the distinguished naturalist overlooked the literal meaning of the phrases he quotes for north and south, *intip chaututa chayananpata* and *intip chaupunchau chayananpata*, literally, the sun arriving toward the midnight, the sun arriving toward the midday. These are evidently translations of the Spanish *hacia la media noche, hacia el medio dia*, for they could not have originated among a people under or south of the equatorial line.

kedem, which, however, this more southern tribe applied to the east.

We can trace the sacredness of the number four in other curious and unlooked-for developments. Multiplied into the number of the fingers—the arithmetic of every child and ignorant man—or by adding together the first four members of its arithmetical series (4+8+12+16), it gives the number forty. This was taken as a limit to the sacred dances of some Indian tribes, and by others as the highest number of chants to be employed in exorcising diseases. Consequently it came to be fixed as a limit in exercises of preparation or purification. The females of the Orinoco tribes fasted forty days before marriage, and those of the upper Mississippi were held unclean the same length of time after childbirth; such was the term of the Prince of Tezcuco's fast when he wished an heir to his throne, and such the number of days the Mandans supposed it required to wash clean the world at the deluge.[1]

No one is ignorant how widely this belief was prevalent in the old world, nor how the quadrigesimal is still a sacred term with some denominations of Christianity. But a more striking parallelism awaits us. The symbol that beyond all others has fascinated the human mind, THE CROSS, finds here its source and meaning. Scholars have pointed out its sacredness in many natural religions, and have reverently accepted it as a mystery, or offered scores of conflicting and often debasing interpretations. It is but

---

[1] Catlin, *Letters and Notes,* i., Letter 22; La Hontan, *Mémoires,* ii. p. 151; Gumilla, *Hist. del Orinoco,* p. 159.

another symbol of the four cardinal points, the four winds of heaven. This will luminously appear by a study of its use and meaning in America.

The Catholic missionaries found it was no new object of adoration to the red race, and were in doubt whether to ascribe the fact to the pious labors of Saint Thomas or the sacrilegious subtlety of Satan. It was the central object in the great temple of Cozumel, and is still preserved on the bas-reliefs of the ruined city of Palenque. From time immemorial it had received the prayers and sacrifices of the Aztecs and Toltecs, and was suspended as an august emblem from the walls of temples in Popoyan and Cundinamarca. In the Mexican tongue it bore the significant and worthy name " Tree of Our Life," or " Tree of our Flesh" (Tonacaquahuitl). It represented the god of rains and of health, and this was everywhere its simple meaning. " Those of Yucatan," say the chroniclers, " prayed to the cross as the god of rains when they needed water." The Aztec goddess of rains bore one in her hand, and at the feast celebrated to her honor in the early spring victims were nailed to a cross and shot with arrows. Quetzalcoatl, god of the winds, bore as his sign of office " a mace like the cross of a bishop ; " his robe was covered with them strown like flowers, and its adoration was throughout connected with his worship.[1] When the

---

[1] On the worship of the cross in Mexico and Yucatan and its invariable meaning as representing the gods of rain, consult Ixtlilxochitl, *Hist. des Chichimeques*, p. 5 ; Sahagun, *Hist. de la Nueva España*, lib. i. cap. ii.; Garcia. *Or. de los Indios*, lib. iii. cap. vi. p. 109 ; Palacios, *Des. de la Prov. de Guatemala*, p. 29 ; Cogolludo, *Hist. de Yucathan*, lib. iv. cap. ix ; Villagutierre

Muyscas would sacrifice to the goddess of waters they extended cords across the tranquil depths of some lake, thus forming a gigantic cross, and at their point of intersection threw in their offerings of gold, emeralds, and precious oils.[1] The arms of the cross were designed to point to the cardinal points and represent the four winds, the rain bringers. To confirm this explanation, let us have recourse to the simpler ceremonies of the less cultivated tribes, and see the transparent meaning of the symbol as they employed it.

When the rain maker of the Lenni Lenape would exert his power, he retired to some secluded spot and drew upon the earth the figure of a cross (its arms toward the cardinal points?), placed upon it a piece of tobacco, a gourd, a bit of some red stuff, and commenced to cry aloud to the spirits of the rains.[2] In the Blackfoot country are occasionally found ruins of large boulders, arranged in the form of a cross. These, Gen. J. M. Brown informs me are attributed to "the old man in the sun," Natose, who sends the winds. They mark his resting-places, the limbs of the cross representing his body and arms. Gen. Brown thinks they indicate the cardinal points. The Creeks at the festival of the Busk, celebrated, as we have seen, to the four winds, and according to their legends instituted by them, commenced with making the new

Sotomayor, *Hist. de el Itza y de el Lacandon*, lib. iii. cap. 8; and many others might be mentioned.

[1] Rivero and Tschudi, *Peruvian Antiquities*, p. 162, after J. Acosta.

[2] Loskiel, *Ges. der Miss. der evang. Brüder*, p. 60.

fire. The manner of this was " to place four logs in
the centre of the square, end to end, forming a cross,
the outer ends pointing to the cardinal points; in the
centre of the cross the new fire is made." [1] This is
the precise form of the cross which was, " without
any doubt," affirms Las Casas, an object of worship
on the coast near Cumana, before the Christians
came there.[2]

As the emblem of the winds who dispense the
fertilizing showers it is emphatically the tree of our
life, our subsistence, and our health. It never had any
other meaning in America, and if, as has been said, [3]
the tombs of the Mexicans were cruciform, it was perhaps with reference to a resurrection and a future life
as portrayed under this symbol, indicating that the
buried body would rise by the action of the four

[1] Hawkins, *Sketch of the Creek Country*, p. 75. Lapham and
Pidgeon mention that in the State of Wisconsin many low
mounds are found in the form of a cross with the arms directed
to the cardinal points. They contain no remains. Were they
not altars built to the Four Winds? In the mythology of the
Dakotas, who inhabited that region, the winds were always
conceived as birds, and for the cross they have a native name
literally signifying "the musquito hawk spread out" (Riggs,
Dict. of the Dakota, s. v.) Its Maya name is *vahom che*, the tree
erected or set up, the adjective being drawn from the military
language and implying as a defence or protection, as the warrior lifts his lance or shield (Landa, *Rel. de las Cosas de Yucatan*, p. 65).

[2] *Historia Apologetica*, MSS. cap. 125. He gives two figures
of it, the first, two equal lines crossed at right angles; the
second, an oblong parallelogram, its opposite angles united by
straight lines. The natives of Cumana were Caribs.

[3] Squier, *The Serpent Symbol in America*, p. 98.

spirits of the world, as the buried seed takes on a new existence when watered by the vernal showers. There is nothing far-fetched in such an explanation. We positively know that the Mayas placed the entrails of their dead in jars, in groups of four, and which were called *bacabs* from the four rain gods.[1]

The cross frequently recurs in the ancient Egyptian writings, where it is interpreted *life;* doubtless, could we trace the hieroglyph to its source, it would likewise prove to be derived from the four winds; that it represented the "Nile Key" is now rarely maintained.

While thus recognizing the natural origin of this consecrated symbol, while discovering that it is based on the sacredness of numbers, and this in turn on the structure and necessary relations of the human body, thus disowning the meaningless mysticism that Joseph de Maistre and his disciples have advocated, let us on the other hand be equally on our guard against accepting the material facts which underlie these beliefs as their deepest foundation and their exhaustive explanation. That were but withered fruit for our labors, and it might well be asked, where is here the divine idea said to be dimly prefigured in mythology? The universal belief in the sacredness of numbers is an instinctive faith in an immortal truth. The laws of chemical combination, of the various modes of motion, of all organic growth, show that simple numerical relations govern all the properties and are inherent to the very constitution of matter. In view of such facts is it presumptuous to predict

[1] H. de Charencey, *Le Mythe de Votan*, p. 39.

that experiment itself will prove the truth of Kepler's beautiful saying : " The universe is a harmonious whole, the soul of which is God ; numbers, figures, the stars, all nature, indeed, are in unison with the mysteries of religion? "

CHAPTER IV.

THE SYMBOLS OF THE BIRD AND THE SERPENT.

Relations of man to the lower animals.—Two of these, the BIRD and the SERPENT, chosen as symbols beyond all others.—The Bird throughout America the symbol of the Clouds and Winds.—Meaning of certain species.—The symbolic meaning of the Serpent derived from its mode of locomotion, its poisonous bite, and its power of charming.—Usually the symbol of the Lightning and the Waters.—The Rattlesnake the symbolic species in America.—The war charm.—The Cross of Palenque.—The god of riches.—Both symbols devoid of moral significance.

THOSE stories which the Germans call *Thierfabeln*, wherein the actors are different kinds of brutes, seem to have a particular relish for children and uncultivated nations. Who cannot recall with what delight he nourished his childish fancy on the pranks of Reynard the Fox, or the tragic adventures of Little Red Riding Hood and the Wolf? The question has been raised whether the human traits thus ascribed to animals were at first taken literally, or were intended merely as agreeable figures of speech for classes of men. We cannot doubt but that the former was the case. Going back to the dawn of civilization, we find these relations not as amusing fictions, but as myths, embodying religious tenets, and the brute heroes held up as the ancestors of mankind, even as rightful claimants of man's prayers and praises.

The effort has been made to trace early faiths to an

animal worship exclusively, but it has failed, as such
a narrow theory must. The " totems " employed to
designate the clans among the North American tribes
have been called in to aid the theory. But it is now
generally conceded that the totemic badge had a
political or social rather than a religious significance.
Nevertheless there **are** instances, and many of
them, where superstitious honors were paid the lower
animals. The Lower Creeks, like the ancient Egyptians, venerated the alligator, and never destroyed
one.[1] The jaguar was worshipped by the Moxos,
and they appointed as priests those who had escaped
from its claws.[2] Christians as they are, the Quichés
of Guatemala yet believe that each of them has a
beast as a patron and protector.[3]

Man praying to the beast is a spectacle so humil-
iating that it prompts us to seek the explanation of
it least disparaging to the dignity of reason. We
may remember that as a hunter the primitive man
was always matched against the wild creatures of the
woods, so superior to him in their dumb certainty
of instinct, their swift motion, their muscular force,
their permanent and sufficient clothing. Their ways
were guided by a wit beyond his divination, and
they gained a living with little toil or trouble. They
did not mind the darkness so terrible to him, but
through the night called one to the other in a tongue
whose meaning he could not fathom, but which, he

---

[1] B. Roman, *Nat. and Civ. Hist. of Florida*, p. 101.

[2] D'Orbigny, *L'Homme Américain*, ii. p. 235.

[3] Karl Scherzer, *Die Indianer von Santa Catalana, Istlávacan*,
p. 11. (Vienna, 1856).

doubted not, was as full of purport as his own. He did not recognize in himself those god-like qualities destined to endow him with the royalty of the world, while far more clearly than we do he saw the sly and strange faculties of his antagonists. They were to him, therefore, not inferiors, but equals—even superiors. He doubted not that once upon a time he had possessed their instinct, they his language, but that some necromantic spell had been flung on them both to keep them asunder. None but a potent sorcerer could break this charm, but such an one could understand the chants of birds and the howls of savage beasts, and on occasion transform himself into one or another animal, and course the forest, the air, or the waters, as he saw fit. Therefore, it was not the beast that he worshipped, but that share of the omnipresent deity which he thought he perceived under its form.[1]

Beyond all others, two subdivisions of the animal kingdom have so riveted the attention of men by their unusual powers, and enter so frequently into the myths of every nation of the globe, that a right understanding of their symbolic value is an essential preliminary to the discussion of the divine legends. They are the BIRD and the SERPENT. We shall not go amiss if we seek the reasons of their pre-eminence in the facility with which their peculiarities offered sensuous images under which to convey the idea of divinity, ever present in the soul of man, ever striving at articulate expression.

---

[1] That these were the real views entertained by the Indians in regard to the brute creation, see Heckewelder, *Acc. of the Ind. Nations,* p. 247 ; Schoolcraft, *Ind. Tribes,* iii. p. 520.

The bird has the incomprehensible power of flight; it floats in the atmosphere, it rides on the winds, it soars toward heaven where dwell the gods; its plumage is stained with the hues of the rainbow and the sunset; its song was man's first hint of music; it spurns the clods that impede his footsteps, and flies proudly over the mountains and moors where he toils wearily along. He sees no more enviable creature; he conceives the gods and angels must also have wings; and pleases himself with the fancy that he, too, some day will shake off this coil of clay, and rise on pinions to the heavenly mansions. All living beings, say the Eskimos, have the faculty of soul (*tarrak*), but especially the birds.[1] As messengers from the upper world and interpreters of its decrees, the flight and the note of birds have ever been anxiously observed as omens of grave import. "There is one bird especially," remarks the traveller Coreal, of the natives of Brazil, "which they regard as of good augury. Its mournful chant is heard rather by night than day. The savages say it is sent by their deceased friends to bring them news from the other world, and to encourage them against their enemies."[2] In Peru and in Mexico there was a College of Augurs, corresponding in purpose to the auspices of ancient Rome, who practised no other means of divination than watching the course and professing to interpret the songs of fowls. So natural and so general is such a superstition, and so widespread is the respect it still obtains in civilized and

[1] Egede, *Nachrichten von Grönland*, p. 156.
[2] *Voiages aux Indes Occidentales*, pt. ii. p. 203: Amst. 1722.

Christian lands, that it is not worth while to summon witnesses to show that it prevailed universally among the red race also. What imprinted it with redoubled force on their imagination was the common belief that birds were not only divine nuncios, but the visible spirits of their departed friends. The Powhatans held that a certain small wood bird received the souls of their princes at death, and they religiously refrained from doing it harm; [1] while the Aztecs and various other nations thought that all good people, as a reward of merit, were metamorphosed at the close of life into feathered songsters of the grove, and in this form passed a certain term in the umbrageous bowers of Paradise.

But the usual meaning of the bird as a symbol looks to a different analogy—to that which appears in such familiar expressions as " the wings of the wind," " the flying clouds." Like the wind, the bird sweeps through the aërial spaces, sings in the forests, and rustles on its course; like the cloud, it floats in mid-air and casts its shadow on the earth; like the lightning, it darts from heaven to earth to strike its unsuspecting prey. These tropes were truths to savage nations, and led on by that law of language which forced them to conceive everything as animate or inanimate, itself the product of a deeper law of thought which urges us to ascribe life to whatever has motion, they found no animal so appropriate for their purpose here as the bird. Therefore the Algonkins say that birds always make the winds, that they create the water spouts, and that the clouds are the

[1] Beverly, *Hist. de la Virginie*, liv. iii. chap. viii.

spreading and agitation of their wings;[1] the Navajos, that at each cardinal point stands a white swan, who is the spirit of the blasts which blow from its dwelling; and the Dakotas, that in the west is the house of the Wakinyan, the Flyers, the breezes that send the storms. So, also, they frequently explain the thunder as the sound of the cloud-bird flapping his wings, and the lightning as the fire that flashes from his tracks, like the sparks which the buffalo scatters when he scours over a stony plain.[2] The thunder cloud was also a bird to the Caribs, and they imagined it produced the lightning in true Carib fashion by blowing it through a hollow reed, just as they to this day hurl their poisoned darts.[3] Most of the natives of the Northwest coast explain the thunder as the flapping of the wings of a giant bird, the lightning as the flash of his eye.[4] Tupis, Iroquois, Athapascas, for certain, perhaps all the families of the red race, were the subject pursued, partook of this persuasion; among them all it would probably be found that the same figures of speech were used in comparing clouds and winds with the feathered species as among us, with however this most significant difference, that whereas among us they are figures and nothing more, to them they expressed literal facts.

---

[1] Schoolcraft, *Ind. Tribes*, v. p. 420.

[2] Mrs. Eastman, *Legends of the Sioux*, p. 191. New York, 1849. This is a trustworthy and meritorious book, which can be said of very few collections of Indian traditions. They were collected during a residence of seven years in our northwestern territories, and are usually verbally faithful to the native narrations.

[3] De La Borde, *Relation des Caraibes*, p. 7. Paris, 1674.

[4] M. Macfie, *Vancouver Island and British Columbia*, p. 456.

How important a symbol did they thus become! For the winds, the clouds, producing the thunder and the changes that take place in the ever-shifting panorama of the sky, the rain bringers, lords of the seasons, and not this only, but the primary type of the soul, the life, the breath of man and the world, these in their rôle in mythology are second to nothing. Therefore as the symbol of these august powers, as messenger of the gods, and as the embodiment of departed spirits, no one will be surprised if they find the bird figure most prominently in the myths of the red race.

Sometimes some particular species seems to have been chosen as most befitting these dignified attributes. No citizen of the United States will be apt to assert that their instinct led the indigenes of our territory astray, when they chose, with nigh unanimous consent, the great American eagle as that fowl beyond all others proper to typify the supreme control and the most admirable qualities. Its feathers composed the war flag of the Creeks, and its images carved in wood or its stuffed skin surmounted their council lodges (Bartram); none but an approved warrior dare wear it among the Cherokees (Timberlake); and the Dakotas allowed such an honor only to him who had first touched the corpse of the common foe (De Smet). The Natchez and Akanzas seem to have paid it even religious honors, and to have installed it in their most sacred shrines (Sieur de Tonty, Du Pratz); and very clearly it was not so much for ornament as for a mark of dignity and a recognized sign of worth that its plumes were so highly prized. The natives of Zuñi, in New Mexico, employed four of its feathers to represent the four winds in their invocations for rain (Whipple), and probably it was the eagle which a tribe in Upper California (the Acagchemem) worshipped under the name Panes. Father Geronimo Boscana describes it as a species of vulture, and relates that one of them was immolated yearly, with solemn ceremony, in the temple of each village. Not a drop of blood was spilled, and the body was burned. Yet with an amount of faith that staggered even the Romanist, the natives maintained and believed that it was the same individual bird they sacrificed each year; more than this, that the same bird was slain by each of the villages![1]

The owl was regarded by Aztecs, Quichés, Mayas, Peruvians, Araucanians, and Algonkins as sacred to the lord of the dead. "The Owl" was one of the names of the Mexican Pluto, whose realm was in the north,[2] and the wind from that quarter was supposed by the Chipeways to be made by the owl as the south by the butterfly. The same tribe called the bridge which they said the souls of the departed must cross to arrive at the land of spirits, the "Owl Bridge."[3] As

---

[1] *Acc. of the Inds. of California*, ch. ix. Eng. trans. by Robinson. New York, 1847. The Acagchemem were a branch of the Netela tribe, who dwelt near the mission San Juan Capistrano (see Buschmann, *Spuren der Aztek. Sprache*, etc., p. 548).

[2] Called in the Aztec tongue *Tecolotl*, night owl; literally, the stone scorpion. The transfer was mythological. The Christians prefixed to this word *tlaca*, man, and thus formed a name for Satan, which Prescott and others have translated "rational owl." No such deity existed in Ancient Anahuac (see Buschmann, *Die Voelker und Sprachen Neu Mexico's*, p. 262).

[3] Schoolcraft, *Ind. Tribes*, v. p. 420. Barraga, *Otchipwe Dict.* s. v. *Kakokajogan*.

the bird of night, it was the fit emissary of him who rules the darkness of the grave. Something in the looks of the creature as it sapiently stares and blinks in the light, or perhaps that it works while others sleep, got for it the character of wisdom. So the Creek priests carried with them as the badge of their learned profession the stuffed skin of one of these birds, thus modestly hinting their erudite turn of mind;[1] the Arickarees, according to Gen. J. M. Brown, place one above the "medicine stone" in their council lodge, and the culture hero of the Monquis of California was represented, like Pallas Athene, having one as his inseparable companion (Venegas).

As the associate of the god of light and air, and as the antithesis therefore of the owl, the Aztecs reverenced a bird called *quetzal*, which I believe is a species of parroquet. Its plumage is of a bright green hue, and was prized extravagantly as a decoration. It was one of the symbols and part of the name of Quetzalcoatl, their mythical civilizer, and the prince of all sorts of singing birds, myriads of whom were fabled to accompany him on his journeys.

The tender and hallowed associations that have so widely shielded the dove from harm, which for instance Xenophon mentions among the ancient Persians, were not altogether unknown to the tribes of the New World. Neither the Hurons nor Mandans would kill them, for they believed they were inhab-

[1] William Bartram, Travels, p. 504. Columbus found the natives of the Antilles wearing tunics with figures of these birds embroidered upon them. Prescott, *Conq. of Mexico*, i. p. 58, note.

ited by the souls of the departed,[1] and it is said, but on less satisfactory authority, that they enjoyed similar immunity among the Mexicans. Their soft and plaintive note and sober russet hue widely enlisted the sympathy of man, and linked them with his more tender feelings.

" As wise as the serpent, as harmless as the dove," is an antithesis that might pass current in any human language. They are the emblems of complementary, often contrasted qualities. Of all animals, the serpent is the most mysterious. No wonder it possessed the fancy of the observant child of nature. Alone of creatures it swiftly progresses without feet, fins, or wings. " There be three things which are too wonderful for me, yea, four which I know not," said wise King Solomon; and the chief of them were " the way of an eagle in the air, the way of a serpent upon a rock."

Its sinuous course is like to nothing so much as that of a winding river, which therefore we often call serpentine. The name Serpentine is borne by an English stream; a river in British America is called the Serpent; and in Arcadia the Greeks had the Ophis. So with the Indians. Kennebec, a stream in Maine, in the Algonkin means snake, and Antietam, the creek in Maryland of tragic celebrity, in an Iroquois dialect has the same significance. How easily might savages, construing the figure literally, make the serpent a river or water god! Many species being amphibious would confirm the idea. A lake

---

[1] *Rel. de la Nouv. France*, An 1636, ch. ix. Catlin, *Letters and Notes*, Lett. 22.

watered by innumerable tortuous rills wriggling into
it, is well calculated for the fabled abode of the king
of the snakes. Whether from this or not we may
not say, but certain it is that both Algonkins and
Iroquois had a myth that in the great lakes dwelt a
monster serpent, of irascible temper, who unless ap-
peased by meet offerings raised a tempest or broke the
ice beneath the feet of those venturing on his domain,
and swallowed them down.[1]

The rattlesnake was the species almost exclusively
honored by the red race. It is slow to attack, but
venomous in the extreme, and possesses the power of
the basilisk to attract within reach of its spring small
birds and squirrels. Probably this much talked of
fascination is nothing more than by its presence near
their nests to incite them to attack, and to hazard
near and nearer approaches to their enemy in hope
to force him to retreat, until once within the compass
of his fell swoop, they fall victims to their temerity.
I have often watched a cat act thus. Whatever explanation may be received, the fact cannot be questioned, and is ever attributed by the unreflecting to
some diabolic spell cast upon them by the animal.
They have the same strange susceptibility to the
influence of certain sounds as the vipers, in which
lies the secret of snake charming. Most of the Indian magicians were familiar with this singularity.
They employed it with telling effect to put beyond
question their intercourse with the unseen powers,

---

[1] *Rel. de la Nouv. France*, An 1648, p. 75 ; Cusic, *Trad. Hist.
of the Six Nations*, pt. iii. The latter is the work of a native
Tuscarora chief. It is republished in Schoolcraft's Indian
Tribes, but is of little value.

and to vindicate the potency of their own guardian spirits who thus enabled them to handle with impunity the most venomous of reptiles.[1] The well-known antipathy of these serpents to certain plants, for instance the hazel, which bound around the ankles is an efficient protection against their attacks, and perhaps some antidote to their poison used by the magicians, led to their frequent introduction in religious ceremonies. Such exhibitions must have made a profound impression on the spectators, and redounded in a corresponding degree to the glory of the performer. "Who is a manito?" asked the mystic meda chant of the Algonkins. "He," is the reply, "he who walketh with a serpent, walking on the ground, he is a manito."[2] And the intimate alliance of this symbol with the mysteries of the Unknown, is reflected in some dialects of their language, and also in that of their neighbors the Dakotas, where the same words *manito, wakan,* which express the conception of the supernatural, are also used as names of this species of animals. This curious fact is not without parallel, for in both Arabic and Hebrew the

[1] For example, in Brazil, Müller, *Amer. Urrelig.*, p. 277; in Yucatan, Cogolludo, *Hist. de Yucathan*, lib. iv. cap. 4; among the western Algonkins, *Hennepin, Decouverte dans l'Amer. Septen.* chap. 33. Dr. Hammond has expressed the opinion that the North American Indians enjoy the same immunity from the virus of the rattlesnake that certain African tribes do from some vegetable poisons (*Hygiene*, p. 73). But his observation must be at fault, for many travellers mention the dread these serpents inspired, and the frequency of death from their bites, e. g. *Rel. Nouv. France*, 1667, p. 22.

[2] *Narrative of the Captivity and Adventures of John Tanner*, p. 356.

word for serpent has many derivatives, meaning to
have intercourse with demoniac powers, to practise
magic, and to consult familiar spirits.[1]

The pious founder of the Moravian brotherhood,
the Count of Zinzendorf, owed his life on one ôcca-
sion to this deeply rooted superstition. He was
visiting a missionary station among the Shawnees, in
the Wyoming valley. Recent quarrels with the
whites had unusually irritated this unruly folk, and
they resolved to make him their first victim. After
he had retired to his secluded hut, several of their
braves crept upon him, and cautiously lifting the
corner of the lodge, peered in. The venerable man was
seated before a little fire, a volume of the Scriptures
on his knees, lost in the perusal of the sacred words.
While they gazed, a huge rattlesnake, unnoticed by
him, trailed across his feet, and rolled itself into a
coil in the comfortable warmth of the fire. Immediately
the would-be murderers forsook their purpose and
noiselessly retired, convinced that this was indeed a
man of God.

A more unique trait than any of these is its habit
of casting its skin every spring, thus as it were re-
newing its life. In temperate latitudes the rattle-

---

[1] In Arabic *dzann* is serpent ; *dzanan* a spirit, a soul, or the
heart. So in Hebrew *nachas,* serpent, has many derivatives
signifying to hold intercourse with demons, to conjure, a
magician, etc. See Nöldeke in the *Zeitschrift für Voelkerpsycho-
logie und Sprachwissenschaft,* i. p. 413. The dialects of the
Algonkin referred to are the Shawnee and Saukie (Gallatin's
Vocabularies). In Otoe *Waka,* or according to an earlier vocab-
ulary *Wacong,* is snake. Roehrig gives another example where
the terminal *n* of *wakan* is dropped. (*Language of the Dakota,*
p. 14). In the Crow dialect of Dakota, *iah'ise* snake, and *isah'e*
spirit, deity, present similarity (Hayden's Vocabularies).

snake, like the leaves and flowers, retires from sight during the cold season, and at the return of kindly warmth puts on a new and brilliant coat. Its cast-off skin was carefully collected by the savages and stored in the medicine bag as possessing remedial powers of high excellence. Itself thus immortal, they thought it could impart its vitality to them. So when the mother was travailing in sore pain, and the danger neared that the child would be born silent, the attending women hastened to catch some serpent and give her its blood to drink.[1]

It is well known that in ancient art this animal was the symbol of Æsculapius, and to this day, Professor Agassiz found that the Maues Indians, who live between the upper Tapajos and Madeira Rivers in Brazil, whenever they assign a form to any "remedio," give it that of a serpent.[2]

Probably this notion that it was annually rejuvenated led to its adoption as a symbol of Time among the Aztecs; or, perchance, as they reckoned by suns, and the figure of the sun, a circle, corresponds to nothing animate but a serpent with its tail in its mouth, eating itself, as it were, this may have been its origin. Either of them is more likely than that the symbol arose from the recondite reflection that time is "never ending, still beginning, still creating, still destroying," as has been suggested.

Only, however, within the last few years has the significance of the serpent symbol in its length and breadth been satisfactorily explained, and its frequent recurrence accounted for. By a searching

---

[1] Alexander Henry, *Travels*, p. 117.
[2] *Bost. Med. and Surg. Journal*, vol. 76, p. 21.

analysis of Greek and German mythology, Dr. Schwarz, of Berlin, has shown that the meaning which is paramount to all others in this emblem is *the lightning;* a meaning drawn from the close analogy which the serpent in its motion, its quick spring, and mortal bite, has to the zigzag course, the rapid flash, and sudden stroke of the electric discharge. He even goes so far as to imagine that by this resemblance the serpent first acquired the veneration of men. But this is an extravagance not supported by more thorough research. He has further shown with great aptness of illustration how, by its dread effects, the lightning, the heavenly serpent, became the god of terror and the opponent of such heroes as Beowulf, St. George, Thor, Perseus, and others, mythical representations of the fearful war of the elements in the thunder storm; how from its connection with the advancing summer and fertilizing showers it bore the opposite character of the deity of fruitfulness, riches, and plenty; how, as occasionally kindling the woods where it strikes, it was associated with the myths of the descent of fire from heaven, and as in popular imagination where it falls it scatters the thunderbolts in all directions, the flint-stones which flash when struck were supposed to be these fragments, and gave rise to the stone worship so frequent in the old world; and how, finally, the prevalent myth of a king of serpents crowned with a glittering stone or wearing a horn is but another type of the lightning.[1] Without accept-

[1] Schwarz, *Der Ursprung der Mythologie dargelegt an Griechischer und Deutscher Sage :* Berlin, 1860, *passim.*

ing unreservedly all these conclusions, I shall show how correct they are in the main when applied to the myths of the New World, and thereby illustrate how the red race is of one blood and one faith with our own remote ancestors in heathen Europe and Central Asia.

It asks no elaborate effort of the imagination to liken the lightning to a serpent. It does not require any remarkable acuteness to guess the conundrum of Schiller :—

> " Unter allen Schlangen ist eine
> Auf Erden nicht gezeugt,
> Mit der an Schnelle keine,
> An Wuth sich keine vergleicht."

When Father Buteux was a missionary among the Algonkins, in 1637, he asked them their opinion of the nature of lightning. " It is an immense serpent," they replied, "which the Manito is vomiting forth; you can see the twists and folds that he leaves on the trees which he strikes; and underneath such trees we have often found huge snakes." " Here is a novel philosophy for you ! " exclaims the Father.[1] So the Shawnees called the thunder "the hissing of the great snake ; "[2] and Tlaloc, the Toltec thunder god, held in his hand a serpent of gold to represent the

[1] *Rel de la Nouv. France :* An 1637, p. 53. Later versions of this belief are given by the Rev. Peter Jones, *Hist. of the Ojebway Indians,* pp. 86, 87 ; in them the thunder bird eats the serpents.

[2] *Sagen der Nord-Amer. Indianer,* p. 21. This is a German translation of part of Jones's *Legends of the N. Am. Inds. :* London, 1820. Their value as mythological material is very small.

lightning.[1] For this reason the Caribs spoke of the god of the thunder storm as a great serpent dwelling in the fruit forests,[2] and in the Quiché legends other names for Hurakan, the hurricane or thunder-storm, are the Strong Serpent, He who hurls below, referring to the lightning.[3]

Among the Hurons, in 1648, the Jesuits found a legend current that there existed somewhere a monster serpent called Onniont, who wore on his head a horn that pierced rocks, trees, hills, in short, everything he encountered. Whoever could get a piece of this horn was a fortunate man, for it was a sovereign charm and bringer of good luck. The Hurons confessed that none of them had had the good hap to find the monster and break his horn, nor indeed had they any idea of his whereabouts; but their neighbors, the Algonkins, furnished them at times small fragments for a large consideration.[4] Clearly the myth had been taught them for venal purposes by their trafficking visitors. Now among the Algonkins, the Shawnee tribe did more than all others combined to introduce and carry about religious legends and ceremonies. From the earliest times they seem to have had peculiar aptitude for the ecstasies, deceits, and fancies that made up the spiritual life of their associates. Their constantly roving life brought them in contact with the myths of many nations. And it is extremely probable that they first brought the tale of the horned serpent from the Creeks and Cherokees.

---

[1] Torquemada, *Monarquia Indiana*, lib. vi. cap. 37.

[2] De la Borde, *Relation des Caraibes*, p. 7.

[3] *Le Livre Sacré des Quichés*, p. 3.

[4] *Rel. de la Nouv. France*, 1648, p. 75.

It figured extensively in the legends of both these tribes.

The latter related that once upon a time among the glens of their mountains dwelt the prince of rattlesnakes. Obedient subjects guarded his palace, and on his head glittered in place of a crown a gem of marvellous magic virtues. Many warriors and magicians tried to get possession of this precious talisman, but were destroyed by the poisoned fangs of its defenders. Finally, one more inventive than the rest hit upon the bright idea of encasing himself in leather, and by this device marched unharmed through the hissing and snapping court, tore off the shining jewel, and bore it in·triumph to his nation. They preserved it with religious care, brought it forth on state occasions with solemn ceremony, and about the middle of the last century, when Captain Timberlake penetrated to their towns, told him its origin.[1]

The charm which the Creeks presented their young men when they set out on the war path was of very similar character. It was composed of the bones of the panther and the horn of the fabulous horned snake. According to a legend taken down by an unimpeachable authority toward the close of the last century, the great snake dwelt in the waters; the old people went to the brink and sang the sacred songs. The monster rose to the surface. The sages recommenced the mystic chants. He rose a little out of the water. Again they repeated the songs. This time he showed his horns and they cut one off. Still

[1] *Memoirs of Lieut. Henry Timberlake*, p. 48. London, 1765. This little book gives an account of the Cherokees at an earlier date than is elsewhere found.

a fourth time did they sing, and as he rose to listen cut off the remaining horn. A fragment of these in the " war physic " protected from inimical arrows and gave success in the conflict.[1]

But we must not be hasty in assigning historical grounds for the prevalence of this myth. It recurs where no such can be imagined, proving that it is a creation of the fancy, produced by similar associations of ideas. In the central region of the volcanic island of Dominica is a deep vale, wherein, alleged the Carib natives, dwelt a monstrous serpent; " upon its head is a very sparkling stone, like a carbuncle, which is commonly covered with a thin moving skin, like a man's eyelid; but when he drank and sported himself in that deep bottom, it was plainly discovered, the rocks about the place receiving a wondrous lustre from the fire issuing out of that precious crown." [2] This was probably the great serpent Racumon, brother of Savacon, the elemental bird who, according to De La Borde, these islanders believed to be lord of the hurricane and maker of the winds.[3]

In these myths, which attribute good fortune to the horn of the snake, that horn which pierces trees and rocks, which rises from the waters, which glitters as a gem, which descends from the ravines of the mountains, we shall not overstep the bounds of prudent reasoning if we see the thunderbolt, sign of the fructifying rain, symbol of the strength of the lightning, horn

---

[1] Hawkins, *Sketch of the Creek Country*, p. 80.

[2] Blomes, *State of His Majestie's Territories in America*, p. 73. London, 1687.

[3] *Relation des Caraibes*, p. 7. Paris, 1674.

of the heavenly serpent. They are strictly meteorological in their meaning. And when in later Algonkin tradition the hero Michabo appears in conflict with the shining prince of serpents who lives in the lake and floods the earth with its waters, and destroys the reptile with a dart, and further when the conqueror clothes himself with the skin of his foe and drives the rest of the serpents to the south where in that latitude the lightnings are last seen in the autumn ;[1] or when in the traditional history of the Iroquois we hear of another great horned serpent rising out of the lake and preying upon the people until a similar hero-god destroys it with a thunderbolt,[2] we cannot be wrong in rejecting any historical or ethical interpretation, and in construing them as allegories which at first represented the atmospheric changes which accompany the advancing seasons and the ripening harvests. They are narratives conveying under agreeable personifications the tidings of that unending combat which the Dakotas said is ever waged with varying fortunes by Unktahe against Wauhkeon, the God of Waters against the Thunder Bird.[3] They are the same stories which in the old world have been elaborated into the struggles of Ormuzd and Ahriman,

[1] Schoolcraft, *Algic Researches*, i. p. 179 sq. ; compare ii. p. 117.

[2] Morgan, *League of the Iroquois*, p. 159 ; Cusic, *Trad. Hist. of the Six Nations*, pt. ii.

[3] Mrs. Eastman, *Legends of the Sioux*, pp. 161, 212. In this explanation I depart from Prof. Schwarz, who has collected various legends almost identical with these of the Indians (with which he was not acquainted), and interpreted the precious crown or horn to be the summer sun, brought forth by the early vernal lightning. *Ursprung der Mythologie*, p. 27, note.

of Thor and Midgard, of St George and the Dragon,
and a thousand others.

Yet it were but a narrow theory of natural religion
that allowed no other meaning to these myths. Many
another elemental warfare is being waged around us,
and applications as various as nature herself lie in
these primitive creations of the human fancy. Let
it only be remembered that there was never any moral,
never any historical purport in them in the infancy
of religious life.

In snake charming as a proof of proficiency in
magic, and in the symbol of the lightning, which
brings both fire and water, which in its might controls victory in war, and in its frequency plenteous
crops at home, lies the secret of the serpent symbol.
As the " war physic " among the tribes of the United
States was a fragment of a serpent, and as thus signifying his incomparable skill in war the Iroquois
represent their mythical king Atatarho clothed in nothing but black snakes, so that when he wished to don a
new suit he simply drove away one set and ordered another to take their places, [1] so, by a precisely similar
mental process, the myth of the Nahuas assigns as a
mother to their war god Huitzilopochtli, Coatlicue,
the robe of serpents ; her dwelling place Coatepec,
the hill of serpents ; and at her lying-in say that she
brought forth a serpent. Her son's image was surrounded by serpents, his sceptre was in the shape of
one, his great drum was of serpents' skins, and his
statue rested on four vermiform caryatides.

As the symbol of the fertilizing summer showers

[1] Cusic, u. s., pt. ii.

the lightning serpent was the god of fruitfulness. Born in the atmospheric waters, it was an appropriate attribute of the ruler of the winds. But we have already seen that the winds were often spoken of as great birds. Hence the union of these two emblems in such names as Quetzalcoatl, Gucumatz, Kukulkan, all titles of the god of the air in the languages of Central America, all signifying the "Bird-serpent." Here also we see the solution of that monument which has so puzzled American antiquaries, the cross at Palenque. It is a tablet on the wall of an altar representing a cross surmounted by a bird, its lateral arms terminating in profiles of the rattle-snake head. The descending arm rests upon a skull, possibly that of a serpent, but more probably human. The cross I have previously shown was the symbol of the four winds, and the bird and serpent are simply the rebus of the air god, their ruler.[1] Quetzalcoatl, called also Yolcuat, the rattlesnake, was no less intimately associated with serpents than with birds. The entrance to his temple at Mexico represented the jaws of one of these reptiles, and he finally disappeared in the province of Coatzacoalco, the hiding-place of the serpent, sailing towards the

---

[1] This remarkable relic has been the subject of a long and able article in the *Revue Américaine* (tom. ii. p. 69), by the venerable traveller De Waldeck. Like myself—and I had not seen his opinion until after the above was written—he explains the cruciform design as indicating the four cardinal points, but offers the explanation merely as a suggestion, and without referring to these symbols as they appear in so many other connections. See also, Allen, *Analysis of the Life Form in Art*, pp. 37 (fig. 85) and 67.

east in a bark of serpents' skins. All this refers to his power over the lightning serpent.

He was also said to be the god of riches and the patron consequently of merchants. For with the summer lightning come the harvest and the ripening fruits, come riches and traffic. Moreover " the golden color of the liquid fire," as Lucretius expresses it, naturally led where this metal was known, to its being deemed the product of the lightning. Thus originated many of those tales of a dragon who watches a treasure in the earth, and of a serpent who is the dispenser of riches, such as were found among the Greeks and ancient Germans.[1] So it was in Peru where the god of riches was worshipped under the image of a rattlesnake horned and hairy, with a tail of gold. It was said to have descended from the heavens in the sight of all the people, and to have been seen by the whole army of the Inca.[2] Whether it was in reference to it, or as emblems of their prowess, that the Incas themselves chose as their arms two serpents with their tails interlaced, is uncertain; possibly one for each of these significations.

Because the rattlesnake, the lightning serpent, is thus connected with the food of man, and itself seems never to die but annually to renew its youth, the Algonkins called it "grandfather" and "king of snakes;" they feared to injure it; they believed it

---

[1] Schwarz, *Ursprung der Mythologie*, pp. 62 sqq.

[2] "I have examined many Indians in reference to these details," says the narrator, an Augustin monk writing in 1554, "and they have all confirmed them as eye-witnesses" (*Lettre sur les Superstitions du Pérou*, p. 106, ed. Ternaux-Compans. This document is very valuable).

could grant prosperous breezes, or raise disastrous tempests; crowned with the lunar crescent it was the constant symbol of life in their picture writing; and in the meda signs the mythical grandmother of mankind *me suk kum me go kwa* was indifferently represented by an old woman or a serpent.[1] For like reasons Cihuacoatl, the Serpent Woman, in the myths of the Nahuas was also called Tonantzin, our mother.[2]

The prominence of the rattlesnake as a peculiarly American symbol indicated by these references has received most ingenious and abundant illustration from indigenous art through the studies of Dr. Harrison Allen. Commencing with the suggestive remark that the serpent is the "only animal facile to the purposes of the pattern maker," he has traced its variant forms in the picture writing, the phonetic signs and the architectural ornaments of the red race, and shown the remarkable preference they had for the line representing the profile of the head of the rattlesnake, to the radical of which he has applied the term "the Crotalean curve."[3]

The serpent symbol in America has, however, met with frequent misinterpretation. It had such an ominous significance in Christian art, and one which chimed so well with the favorite proverb of the early missionaries — "the gods of the heathens are devils"—that wherever they saw a carving or picture of a serpent they at once recognized the

---

[1] *Narrative of John Tanner*, p. 355; Henry, *Travels*, p. 176.

[2] Torquemada, *Monarquia Indiana*, lib. vi. cap. 31.

[3] An Analysis of "The Life Form in Art." Phila., 1875.

sign manual of the Prince of Darkness, and inscribed the fact in their note-books as proof positive of their cherished theory. After going over the whole ground, I am convinced that none of the tribes of the red race attached to this symbol any ethical significance whatever, and that as employed to express atmospheric phenomena, and the recognition of divinity in natural occurrences, it far more frequently typified what was favorable and agreeable than the reverse.

CHAPTER V.

THE MYTHS OF WATER, FIRE, AND THE THUNDER-STORM, AND THE RELIGION OF SEX.

Water the oldest element.—Its use in purification.—Holy water.—The Rite of Baptism.—The Water of Life.—Its symbols.—The Vase.—The Moon.—The latter the goddess of love and agriculture, but also of sickness, night, and pain.—Often represented by a dog.—Fire worship under the form of Sun worship.—The perpetual fire.—The new fire.—Burning the dead.—The worship of the passions.—The religion of Sex in America.—Synthesis of the worship of Fire, Water, and the Winds in the THUNDER-STORM, personified as Haokah, Tupa, Catequil, Contici, Heno, Tlaloc, Mixcoatl, and other deities, many of them triune.

THE primitive man was a brute in everything but the susceptibility to culture ; the chief market of his time was to sleep, fight, and feed ; his bodily comfort alone had any importance in his eyes; and his gods were nothing, unless they touched him here. Cold, hunger, thirst, these were the hounds that were ever on his track ; these were the fell powers he saw constantly snatching away his fellows, constantly aiming their invisible shafts at himself. Fire, food, and water were the gods that fought on his side ; they were the chief figures in his pantheon, his kindliest, perhaps his earliest, divinities.

With a nearly unanimous voice mythologies assign the priority to water. It was the first of all things, the parent of all things. Even the gods themselves were born of water, said the Greeks and the Aztecs.

Cosmogonies reach no further than the primeval ocean that rolled its shoreless waves through a timeless night.

" Omnia pontus erant, deerant quoque litora ponto."

Earth, sun, stars, lay concealed in its fathomless abysses. " All of us," ran the Mexican baptismal formula, " are children of Chalchihuitlycue, Goddess of Water," and the like was said by the Peruvians of Mama Cocha, by the Botocudos of Taru, by the natives of Darien of Dobayba, by the Iroquois of Ataensic—all of them mothers of mankind, all personifications of water.

How account for such unanimity ? Not by supposing some ancient intercourse between remote tribes, but by the uses of water as the originator and supporter, the essential prerequisite of life. Leaving aside the analogy presented by the motherly waters which nourish the unborn child, nor emphasizing how indispensable it is as a beverage, the many offices this element performs in nature lead easily to the supposition that it must have preceded all else. By quenching thirst, it quickens life ; as the dew and the rain it feeds the plant, and when withheld the seed perishes in the ground, and forests and flowers alike wither away ; as the fountain, the river, and the lake, it enriches the valley, offers safe retreats, and provides store of fishes ; as the ocean, it presents the most fitting type of the infinite. It cleanses, it purifies ; it produces, it preserves. " Bodies, unless dissolved, cannot act," is a maxim of the earliest chemistry. Very plausibly, therefore, was it assumed as the source of all things.

The adoration of streams, springs, and lakes, or

9

rather of the spirits their rulers, prevailed everywhere; sometimes avowedly because they provided
food, as was the case with the Moxos, who called
themselves children of the lake or river on which
their village was, and were afraid to migrate lest their
parent should be vexed;[1] sometimes because they
were the means of irrigation, as in Peru, or on more
general mythical grounds. A grove by a fountain is
in all nature worship the ready-made shrine of the
sylphs who live in its limpid waves and chatter mysteriously in its shallows. On such a spot in our Gulf
States one rarely fails to find the sacrificial mound of
the ancient inhabitants, and on such the natives of
Central America were wont to erect their altars
(Ximenes). Lakes are the natural centres of civilization. Like the lacustrine villages which the Swiss
erected in ante-historic times, like ancient Venice, the
city of Mexico was first built on piles in a lake, and
for the same reason—protection from attack. Security
once obtained, growth and power followed. Thus we
can trace the earliest rays of Aztec civilization rising
from lake Tezcuco, of the Peruvian from Lake Titicaca, of the Muysca from Lake Guatavita. These
are the centres of legendary cycles. Their waters
were hallowed by venerable reminiscences. From
the depths of Titicaca rose Viracocha, mythical
civilizer of Peru. Guatavita was the bourne of many
a foot-sore pilgrim in the ancient empire of the Zac.
Once a year the high priest poured the collective
offerings of the multitude into its waves, and anointed
with oils and glittering with gold dust, dived deep in

---

[1] A. D'Orbigny, *L'Homme Américain*, i. p. 240.

its midst, professing to hold communion with the goddess who there had her home.[1]

Not only does the life of man depend on water, but his well-being also. As an ablution it invigorates him bodily and mentally. No institution was in higher honor among the North American Indians than the sweat-bath followed by the cold douche. It was popular not only as a remedy in every and any disease, but as a preliminary to a council or an important transaction. Its real value in cold climates is proven by the sustained fondness for the Russian bath in the north of Europe. The Indians, however, with their usual superstition attributed its good effects to some mysterious healing power in water itself. Therefore, when the patient was not able to undergo the usual process, or when his medical attendant was above the vulgar and routine practice of his profession, it was administered on the infinitesimal system. The quack muttered a formula over a gourd filled from a neighboring spring and sprinkled it on his patient, or washed the diseased part, or sucked out the evil spirit and blew it into a bowl of water, and then scattered the liquid on the fire or earth.[2] At appointed seasons the Tupi priests assembled the people, filled large jars with water, spoke certain words over them, and dipping in palm branches sprinkled their hearers.[3]

---

[1] Rivero and Tschudi, *Peruvian Antiquities,* 162, after J. Acosta.

[2] Narrative of *Oceola Nikkanoche, Prince of Econchatti,* p. 141 ; Schoolcraft, *Ind. Tribes,* iv. p. 650.

[3] Le Père Ives d'Evreux, *Histoire de Maragnan,* p. 306.

The use of such " holy water " astonished the Romanist missionaries, and they at once detected Satan parodying the Scriptures. But their astonishment rose to horror when they discovered among various nations a rite of baptism of appalling similarity to their own, connected with the imposing of a name, done avowedly for the purpose of freeing from inherent sin, believed to produce a regeneration of the spiritual nature, nay, in more than one instance called by an indigenous word signifying " to be born again." [1] Such a rite was of immemorial antiquity among the Cherokees, Aztecs, Mayas, and Peruvians. Had the missionaries remembered that it was practised in Asia with all these meanings long before it was chosen as the sign of the new covenant, they need have invoked neither Satan nor Saint Thomas to explain its presence in America.

As corporeal is near akin to spiritual pollution, and cleanliness to godliness, ablution preparatory to engaging in religious acts came early to have an emblematic as well as a real significance. The water freed the soul from sin as it did the skin from stain. We should come to God with clean hands and a clean heart. As Pilate washed his hands before the multitude to indicate that he would not accept the moral responsibility of their acts, so from a similar motive a Natchez chief, who had been persuaded against his sense of duty not to sacrifice himself on the pyre of his ruler, took clean water, washed his hands, and threw it upon live coals. [2] When an

[1] The term in Maya is *caput zihil*, corresponding exactly to the Latin *renasci*, to be re-born, Landa, *Rel. de Yucatan*, p. 144.

[2] Dumont, *Mems. Hist. sur la Louisiane*, i. p. 233.

ancient Peruvian had laid bare his guilt by confession, he bathed himself in a neighboring river and
repeated this formula :—

" O thou River, receive the sins I have this day
confessed unto the Sun, carry them down to the sea,
and let them never more appear." [1]

The Navajo who has been deputed to carry a dead
body to burial, holds himself unclean until he has
thoroughly washed himself in water prepared for the
purpose by certain ceremonies.[2] When a Bri-Bri has
touched a corpse or a pregnant woman he takes a calabash of water to purify himself.[3] A bath was an
indispensable step in the mysteries of Mithras, the
initiation at Eleusis, the meda worship of the Algonkins, the Busk of the Creeks, the ceremonials of
religion everywhere. Baptism was at first always
immersion. It was a bath meant to solemnize the
reception of the child into the guild of mankind,
drawn from the prior custom of ablution at any
solemn occasion. In both the object is greater purity,
bodily and spiritual. As certainly as there is a law
of conscience, as certainly as our actions fall short of
our volitions, so certainly is man painfully aware of
various imperfections and shortcomings. What he
feels he attributes to the infant. Avowedly to free
themselves from this sense of guilt, the Delawares
used an emetic (Loskiel), the Cherokees a potion
cooked up by an order of female warriors (Timberlake), the Takahlies of Washington Territory, the

---

[1] Acosta, *Hist. of the New World*, lib. v. cap. 25.

[2] *Senate Report on Condition of Indian Tribes*, p. 358. Washington, 1867.

[3] Gabb, *Ind. Tribes of Costa Rica*, p. 505.

Aztecs, Mayas, and Peruvians, auricular confession. Formulize these feelings and we have the dogmas of " original sin," and of " spiritual regeneration." The order of baptism among the Aztecs commenced, " O child, receive the water of the Lord of the world, which is our life ; it is to wash and to purify ; may these drops remove the sin which was given to thee before the creation of the world, since all of us are under its power ;" and concluded, "Now he liveth anew and is born anew, now is he purified and cleansed, now our mother the Water again bringeth him into the world." [1]

A name was then assigned to the child, usually that of some ancestor, who it was supposed would thus be induced to exercise a kindly supervision over the little one's future. In after life should the person desire admittance to a superior class of the population and had the wealth to purchase it—for here as in more enlightened lands nobility was a matter of money—he underwent a second baptism and received another name, but still ostensibly from the goddess of water. [2]

In Peru the child was immersed in the fluid, the priest exorcised the evil and bade it enter the water, which was then buried in the ground. [3] In either country sprinkling could take the place of immersion. The Cherokees believe that unless the rite is punctually performed when the child is three days old, it will inevitably die. [4]

---

[1] Sahagun, *Hist. de la Nueva España*, lib. vi. cap. 37.

[2] Ternaux-Compans, *Pièces rel. à la Conq. du Mexique*, p. 233.

[3] Velasco, *Hist. de la Royaume de Quito*, p. 106, and others.

[4] Whipple, *Rep. on the Indian Tribes*, p. 35. I am not sure

As thus curative and preservative, it was imagined
that there was water of which whoever should drink
would not die, but live forever. I have already
alluded to the Fountain of Youth, supposed long
before Columbus saw the surf of San Salvador to exist
in the Bahama Islands or Florida. It seems to have
lingered long on that peninsula. Not many years ago,
Coacooche, a Seminole chieftain, related a vision
which had nerved him to a desperate escape from the
Castle of St. Augustine. "In my dream," said he,
" I visited the happy hunting grounds and saw my
twin sister, long since gone. She offered me a cup
of pure water, which she said came from the spring
of the Great Spirit, and if I should drink of it, I should
return and live with her forever." [1] Some such mys-

that this practice was of native growth to the Cherokees. This
people had many customs and traditions strangely similar to
those of Christians and Jews. Their cosmogony is a paraphrase
of that of Genesis (Payne's MSS.) ; the number seven is as
sacred with them as it was with the Chaldeans (Whipple, u. s.);
and they have improved and increased by contact with the whites.
Significant in this connection is the remark of Bartram, who
visited them in 1773, that some of their females were "nearly
as fair and blooming as European women," and generally that
their complexion was lighter than their neighbors (*Travels*, p.
485). Two explanations of these facts may be suggested.
Payne says they had villages near Savannah and the English
in Carolina. More probably they derived their peculiarities
from the Spaniards of Florida. Mr. Shea is of opinion that missions were established among them as early as 1566 and 1643
(*Hist. of Catholic Missions in the U. S.*, pp. 58, 73). Certainly in
the latter half of the seventeenth century the Spaniards were
prosecuting mining operations in their territory (See *Am. Hist.
Mag.*, x. p. 137).

[1] Sprague, *Hist. of the Florida War*, p. 328.

tical respect for the element, rather than as a mere outfit for his spirit home, probably induced the earlier tribes of the same territory to place the conch-shell which the deceased had used for a cup conspicuously on his grave,[1] and the Mexicans and Peruvians to inter a vase filled with water with the corpse, or to sprinkle it with the liquid, baptizing it, as it were, into its new associations.[2] It was an emblem of the hope that should cheer the dwellings of the dead, a symbol of the resurrection which is in store for those who have gone down to the grave.

The vase or the gourd as a symbol of water, the source and preserver of life, is a conspicuous figure in the myths of ancient America. As Akbal or Huecomitl, the great or original vase, in Aztec and Maya legends it plays important parts in the drama of creation; as Tici (Ticcu) in Peru it is the symbol of the rains, and as a gourd it is often mentioned by the Caribs and Tupis as the parent of the atmospheric waters.

As the MOON is associated with the dampness and dews of night, an ancient and wide-spread myth identified her with the Goddess of Water. Moreover in spite of the expostulations of the learned, the common people the world over persist in attributing to her a marked influence on the rains. Whether false or true, this familiar opinion is of great antiquity, and was decidedly approved by the Indians, who were all, in the words of an old author, "great observers

---

[1] Basanier, *Histoire Notable de la Floride,* p. 10.

[2] Sahagun, *Hist. de la Nueva España,* lib. iii. app. cap. i.; Meyen, *Ueber die Ureinwohner von Péru,* p. 29.

of the weather by the moon." [1] They looked upon her not only as forewarning them by her appearance of the approach of rains and fogs, but as being their actual cause.

Isis, her Egyptian title, literally means moisture; Ataensic, whom the Hurons said was the moon, is derived from the word for water; in Hidatsa *midi* is moon, *mi'di* water, and Citatli and Atl, moon and water, are constantly confounded in Aztec theology. Their attributes were strikingly alike. They were both the mythical mothers of the race, and both protect women in child-birth, the babe in the cradle, the husbandman in the field, and the youth and maiden in their tender affections. As the transfer of legends was nearly always from the water to its lunar goddess, by bringing them in at this point their true meaning will not fail to be apparent.

We must ever bear in mind that the course of mythology is from many gods toward one, that it is a synthesis, not an analysis, and that in this process the tendency is to blend in one the traits and stories of originally separate divinities. As has justly been observed by the Mexican antiquarian Gama: "It was a common trait among the Indians to worship many gods under the figure of one, principally those whose activities lay in the same direction, or those in some way related among themselves." [2]

The time of full moon was chosen both in Mexico and Peru to celebrate the festival of the deities of

---

[1] Gabriel Thomas, *Hist. of West New Jersey*, p. 6. London, 1698.

[2] Gama, *Des. de las dos Piedras*, etc., i. p. 36.

water, the patrons of agriculture,[1] and very generally the ceremonies connected with the crops were regulated by her phases. The Nicaraguans said that the god of rains, Quiateot, rose in the east,[2] thus hinting how this connection originated. At a lunar eclipse the Orinoco Indians seized their hoes and labored with exemplary vigor on their growing corn, saying the moon was veiling herself in anger at their habitual laziness;[3] and a description ot the New Netherlands, written about 1650, remarks that the savages of that land "ascribe great influence to the moon over crops."[4] This venerable superstition, common to all races, still lingers among our own farmers, many of whom continue to observe " the signs of the moon" in sowing grain, setting out trees, cutting timber, and other rural avocations.

As representing water, the universal mother, the moon was the protectress of women in child-birth, the goddess of love and babes, the patroness of marriage. To her the mother called in travail, whether by the name of "Diana, diva triformis" in pagan Rome, by that of Mama Quilla in Peru, or of Meztli in Anahuac. Under the title of Yohualticitl, the Lady of Night, she was also in this latter country the guardian of babes, and as Teczistecatl, the cause of generation.[5]

---

[1] Garcia, *Or. de los Indios*, p. 109.

[2] Oviedo, *Rel. de la Prov. de Nicaragua*, p. 41. The name is a corruption of the Aztec *Quiauhteotl*, Rain-God.

[3] Gumilla, *Hist. del Orinoco*, ii. cap. 23.

[4] *Doc. Hist. of New York*, iv. p. 130.

[5] Gama, *Des. de las dos Piedras*, ii. p. 41; Gallatin, *Trans. Am. Ethnol. Soc.*, i. p. 343.

Very different is another aspect of the moon goddess, and well might the Mexicans paint her with two colors. The beneficent dispenser of harvests and offspring, she nevertheless has a portentous and terrific phase. She is also the goddess of the night, the dampness, and the cold; she engenders the miasmatic poisons that rack our bones; she conceals in her mantle the foe who takes us unawares; she rules those vague shapes which fright us in the dim light; the causeless sounds of night, or its more oppressive silence are familiar to her; she it is who sends dreams wherein gods and devils have their sport with man, and slumber, the twin brother of death. In the occult philosophy of the middle ages she was "Chief over the Night, Darkness, Rest, Death, and the Waters;"[1] in the language of the Algonkins, her name is identical with the words for night, death, old, sleep, and water.[2]

She is the evil minded woman who thus brings diseases upon men, who at the outset introduced pain and death in the world—our common mother, yet

[1] Adrian Van Helmont, *Workes*, p. 142, fol. London, 1662.

[2] The moon is *nipa*, or *nipaz; nipa*, I sleep; *nipawi*, night; *nip*, I die; *nepua*, dead; *nipanoue*, cold. This odd relationship was first pointed out by Volney (Duponceau, *Langues de l'Amérique du Nord*, p. 317). But the kinship of these words to that for water, *nip, nipi, nepi*, has not before been noticed. This proves the association of ideas on which I lay so much stress in mythology. A somewhat similar relationship exists in the Aztec and cognate languages, *miqui*, to die, *micqui* dead, *mictlan*, the realm of death, *te-miqui*, to dream, *cec-miqui*, to freeze. Would it be going too far to connect these with *metzli* moon? (See Buschmann, *Spuren der Aztekischen Sprache im Nördlichen Mexico*, p. 80.)

the cruel cause of our present woes. Sometimes it is the moon, sometimes water, of whom this is said.

" We are all of us under the power of evil and sin, *because* we are children of the Water," says the Mexican baptismal formula. That Unktahe, spirit of water, is the master of dreams and witchcraft, is the belief of the Dakotas.[1] A female spirit, wife of the great manito whose heart is the sun, the ancient Algonkins believed brought death and disease to the race; " it is she who kills men, otherwise they would never die; she eats their flesh and knaws their vitals, till they fall away and miserably perish." [2] Who is this woman? In the legend of the Muyscas it is Chia, the moon, who was also goddess of water and flooded the earth out of spite.[3] Her reputation was notoriously bad. Did she appear in a dream to a Sauk warrior, he dressed himself and served as a woman to avoid her blows.[4] The Brazilian mother carefully shielded her infant from the lunar rays, believing that they would produce sickness; [5] the hunting tribes of our own country will not sleep in its light, nor leave their game exposed to its action. We ourselves have not outgrown such words as lunatic, moonstruck, and the like. Where did we get these ideas? The philosophical historian of medicine, Kurt Sprengel, traces them to the primitive and popular medical theories of ancient Egypt, in accordance with

1 Schoolcraft, *Ind. Tribes*, vol. iii. p. 485.

2 *Rel. de la Nouv. France*, 1634, p. 16.

3 Humboldt, *Vues des Cordélleres*, p. 21.

4 Keating, *Narrative*, i. p. 216, in Waitz.

5 Spix and Martius, *Travels in Brazil*, ii. p. 247.

which all maladies were the effects of the anger of the goddess Isis, the Moisture, the Moon.[1]

We have here the key to many myths. Take that of Centeotl, the Aztec goddess of Maize. She was said at times to appear as a woman of surpassing beauty, and allure some unfortunate to her embraces, destined to pay with his life for his brief moments of pleasure. Even to see her in this shape was a fatal omen. She was also said to belong to a class of gods whose home was in the west, and who produced sickness and pains.[2] Here we see the evil aspect of the moon reflected on another goddess, who was at first solely the patroness of agriculture.

As the goddess of sickness, it was supposed that persons afflicted with certain diseases had been set apart by the moon for her peculiar service. These diseases were those of a humoral type, especially such as are characterized by issues and ulcers. As in Hebrew the word *accursed* is derived from a root meaning *consecrated to God*, so in the Aztec, Quiché, and other tongues, the word for *leprous, eczematous*, or *syphilitic*, means also *divine*. This bizarre change of meaning is illustrated in a very ancient myth of their family. It is said that in the absence of the sun all mankind lingered in darkness. Nothing but a human sacrifice could hasten his arrival. Then Metzli, the moon, led forth one Nanahuatl, the leprous, and building a pyre, the victim threw himself in its midst. Straightway Metzli followed his example, and as she disappeared in the bright flames the sun rose over the

---

[1] *Hist. de la Médecine*, i. p. 34.

[2] Gama, *Des. de las dos Piedras*, etc., ii. pp. 100–102. Compare Sahagun, *Hist. de la Nueva España*, lib. i. cap. vi.

horizon.[1] Is not this a reference to the kindling rays of the aurora, in which the dank and baleful night is sacrificed, and in whose light the moon presently fades away, and the sun comes forth ?

Another reaction in the mythological laboratory is here disclosed. As the good qualities of water were attributed to the goddess of night, sleep, and death, so her malevolent traits were in turn reflected back on this element. Other thoughts aided the transfer. In primitive geography the Ocean Stream coils its infinite folds around the speck of land we inhabit, biding its time to swallow it wholly. Unwillingly did it yield the earth from its bosom, daily does it steal it away piece by piece. Every evening it hides the light in its depths, and Night and the Waters resume their ancient sway. The word for ocean (*mare*) in the Latin tongue means by derivation a desert, and the Greeks spoke of it as " the barren brine." Water is a treacherous element. Man treads boldly on the solid earth, but the rivers and lakes constantly strive to swallow those who venture within their reach. As streams run in tortuous channels, and as rains accompany the lightning serpent, this animal was occasionally the symbol of the waters in their dangerous manifestations. The Huron magi-

---

[1] Codex Chimalpopoca, in Brasseur, *Hist. du Mexique* i. p.183. Gama and others translate Nanahuatl by *el buboso*. Brasseur by *le syphilitique*, and the latter founds certain medical speculations on the word. It is entirely unnecessary to say to a surgeon that it could not possibly have had the latter meaning, inasmuch as the diagnosis between secondary or tertiary syphilis and other similar diseases was unknown. That it is so employed now is nothing to the purpose. The same or a similar myth was found in Central America and on the Island of Haiti.

cians fabled that in the lakes and rivers dwelt one of vast size called *Angont*, who sent sickness, death, and other mishaps, and the least mite of whose flesh was a deadly poison. They added—and this was the point of the tale—that they always kept on hand portions of the monster for the benefit of any who opposed their designs.[1] The legends of the Algonkins mention a rivalry between Michabo, creator of the earth, and the Spirit of the Waters, who was unfriendly to the project.[2] In later tales this antagonism becomes more and more pronounced, and borrows an ethical significance which it did not have at first. Taking, however, American religions as a whole, water is far more frequently represented as producing beneficent effects than the reverse.

Dogs were supposed to stand in some peculiar relation to the moon, probably because they howl at it and run at night, uncanny practices which have cost them dear in reputation. The custom prevailed among tribes so widely asunder as Peruvians, Tupis, Creeks, Iroquois, Algonkins, and Greenland Eskimos to thrash the curs most soundly during an eclipse.[3] The Creeks explained this by saying that the big dog was swallowing the sun, and that by whipping the little ones they could make him desist. What the big dog was they were not prepared to say. We

[1] *Rel. de la Nouv. France*, 1648, p. 75.

[2] Charlevoix is in error when he identifies Michabo with the Spirit of Waters, and may be corrected from his own statements elsewhere. Compare his *Journal Historique*, pp. 281 and 344 ; ed. Paris, 1740.

[3] Bradford, *American Antiquities*, p. 333 ; Martius, *Von dem Rechtszustande unter den Ureinwohnern Brasiliens*, p. 32 ; Schoolcraft, *Ind. Tribes*, i. p. 271.

know. It was the night goddess, represented by the
dog, who was thus shrouding the world at midday.
The ancient Romans sacrificed dogs to Hecate and
Diana; in Egypt they were sacred to Isis, and thus as
traditionally connected with night and its terrors,
the Prince of Darkness, in the superstition of the middle ages, preferably appeared under the form of a cur,
as that famous poodle which accompanied Cornelius
Agrippa, or that which grew to such enormous size
behind the stove of Dr. Faustus. In a better sense,
they represented the more agreeable characteristics
of the lunar goddess. Xochiquetzal, most fecund of
Aztec divinities, patroness of love, of sexual pleasure,
and of childbirth, was likewise called *Itzcuinan*,
which, literally translated, is *bitch-mother*. This
strange and to us so repugnant title for a goddess
was not without parallel elsewhere. When in his
wars the Inca Pachacutec carried his arms into the
province of Huanca, he found its inhabitants had installed in their temples the figure of a dog as their
highest deity. They were accustomed also to select
one as his living representative, to pray to it and
offer it sacrifice, and when well fattened, to serve it
up with solemn ceremonies at a great feast, eating
their god *substantialiter*. The priests in this province
summoned their attendants to the temples by blowing
through an instrument fashioned from a dog's skull.[1]
This canine canonization explains why in some parts
of Peru a priest was called by way of honor *allco*,
dog![2] And why in many tombs both there and in
Mexico their skeletons are found carefully interred

[1] La Vega, *Hist. des Incas*, liv. vi. cap. 9.
[2] *Lett. sur les Superstitions du Pérou*, p. 111.

with the human remains. Many tribes on the Pacific coast united in the adoration of a wild species, the coyote, the *canis latrans* of naturalists. The Shoshonees of New Mexico call it their progenitor,[1] and with the Nahuas it was in such high honor that it had a temple of its own, a congregation of priests devoted to its service, statues carved in stone, an elaborate tomb at death, and is said to be meant by the god Chantico, whose audacity caused the destruction of the world. The story was that he made a sacrifice to the gods without observing a preparatory fast, for which he was punished by being changed into a dog. He then invoked the god of death to deliver him, which attempt to evade a just punishment so enraged the divinities that they immersed the world in water.[2]

During a storm on our northern lakes the Indians think no offering so likely to appease the angry wa-

[1] Schoolcraft, *Ind. Tribes*, iv. p. 224. Other modern coyote myths in Bancroft, *Native Races*, iii. ch. ii. iii.

[2] Chantico, according to Gama, means "Wolf's Head," though I cannot verify this from the vocabularies within my reach. He is sometimes called Cohuaxolotl Chantico, the snake-servant Chantico, considered by Gama as one, by Torquemada as two deities (see Gama, *Des. de las dos Piedras*, etc., i. p. 12; ii. p. 66). The English word *cantico* in the phrase, for instance, "to cut a cantico," though an Indian word, is not from this, but from the Algonkin Delaware *gentkehn*, to dance a sacred dance. The Dutch describe it as "a religious custom observed among them before death" (*Doc. Hist. of New York*, iv. p. 63). William Penn says of the Lenape, "their worship consists of two parts, sacrifice and cantico," the latter "performed by round dances, sometimes words, sometimes songs, then shouts; their postures very antic and differing." (*Letter to the Free Society of Traders*, 1683, sec. 21.)

ter god who is raising the tempest as a dog. Therefore they hasten to tie the feet of one and toss him
overboard.[1] One meets constantly in their tales and
superstitions the mysterious powers of the animals,
and the distinguished actions he has at times performed bear usually a close parallelism to those attributed to water and the moon.

Hunger and thirst were thus alleviated by water.
Cold remained, and against this *fire* was the shield.
It gives man light in darkness and warmth in winter;
it shows him his friends and warns him of his foes;
the flames point toward heaven and the smoke makes
the clouds. Around it social life begins. For his
home and his hearth the savage has but one word,
and what of tender emotion his breast can feel, is
linked to the circle that gather around his fire. The
council fire, the camp fire, and the war fire, are so
many epochs in his history. By its aid many arts
become possible, and it is a civilizer in more ways
than one. In the figurative language of the red race,
it is constantly used as " an emblem of peace, happiness, and abundance." [2] To extinguish an enemy's

[1] Charlevoix, *Hist. Gen. de la Nouv. France*, i. p. 394:
Paris, 1740. On the different species of dogs indigenous to
America, see a note of Alex. von Humboldt, *Ansichten der Natur*,
i. p. 194. It may be noticed that Chichimec, properly Chichi-
mecatl, the name of the Aztec tribe who succeeded the ancient
Toltecs in Mexico, means literally " people of the dog," and
probably was derived from some mythological fable connected
with that animal.

[2] *Narr. of the Captiv. of John Tanner*, p. 362. From the word
for fire in many American tongues is formed the adjective *red*.
Thus, Algonkin, *skoda*, fire, *miskoda*, red; Kolosch, *kan*, fire,
kan, red; Ugalentz, *takak*, fire, *takak-uete*, red; Tahkali, *cŭn*,

fire is to slay him; to light a visitor's fire is to bid him welcome. It may also be terrible and painful. The prairie fire, the forest conflagration, the volcano and the lightning show that its mood is not always kind. Fire worship was closely related to that of the sun, and so much has been said of sun worship among the aborigines of America that it is well at once to assign it its true position.

A generation ago it was a fashion very much approved to explain all symbols and myths by the action of this orb on nature. This short and easy method with mythology has, in Carlylian phrase, had its bottom pulled from under it in these later times. Nowhere has it manifested its inefficiency more palpably than in America. One writer, while thus explaining the religions of the tribes of colder regions, and higher latitudes, denies sun worship among the natives of hot climates; another asserts that only

---

fire, *tenil-cŭn*, red ; Quiche, *cak*, fire, *cak*, red, etc. From the adjective *red* comes often the word for *blood*, and in symbolism the color red may refer to either of these ideas. It was the royal color of the Incas, brothers of the sun, and a llama swathed in a red garment was the Peruvian sacrifice to fire (Garcia, *Or. de los Indios*, lib. iv. caps. 16, 19). On the other hand the war Quipus, the war wampum, and the war paint were all of this hue, boding their sanguinary significance. The word for fire in the language of the Delawares, Nanticokes, and neighboring tribes puzzles me. It is *tarnda* cr *tinda*. This is the Swedish word *taenda*, from whose root comes our *tinder*. Yet it is found in vocabularies as early as 1650, and is universally current to-day. It has no resemblance to the word for fire in pure Algonkin. Was it adopted from the Swedes ? Was it introduced by wandering Vikings in remote centuries? Or is it only a coincidence ?

among the latter did it exist at all; while a third lays down the maxim that the religion of the red race everywhere " was but a modification of Sun or Fire worship." [1] All such sweeping generalizations are untrue, and must be so. No one key can open all the arcana of symbolism. Man devised means as varied as nature herself to express the idea of God within him. The sun was but one of these, and not the first nor the most important. Fear, said the wise Epicurean, first made the gods. Gratitude has no power to make one. The sun with its regular course, its kindly warmth, its beneficent action, nowise inspires terror, but the reverse. It conjures no phantasms to appal the superstitious fancy, and its place in primitive mythology is conformably inferior. The myths of the Eskimos and northern Athapascas omit its action altogether. The Algonkins by no means imagined it the highest god, and at most but one of his emblems.[2] That it often appears in their prayers is true, but this arose from the fact that in many of their dialects, as well as in the language of the Mayas and others, the word for heaven or sky was identical with that for sun, and the former, as J have shown, was the supposed abode

[1] Compare D'Orbigny, *L'Homme Américain*, i. p. 242; Müller, *Amer. Urreligionen*, p. 51, and Squier, *Serpent Symbol in America*, p. 111. This is a striking instance of the confusion of ideas introduced by false systems of study, and also of the considerable misapprehension of American mythology which has hitherto prevailed.

[2] La Hontan, *Voy. dans l'Amér. Sept.*, p. ii. 127; *Rel. Nouv. France*, 1637, p. 54.

of deity, " the wigwam of the Great Spirit."[1] The alleged sun worship of the Cherokees rests on testimony modern, doubtful, and unsupported.[2] The Blackfeet pray to Natose, the sun. " I have seen them do so hundreds of times," writes Gen. J. M. Brown ; " yet in every instance when questioned they explained that they prayed not to the sun but to the Old Man who lives there." In North America the Natchez alone were avowed worshippers of this luminary. Yet they adored it under the name Great Fire (*wah sil*), clearly pointing to a prior adoration of that element. The heliolatry organized principally for political ends by the Incas of Peru, stands alone in the religions of the red race. Those shrewd legislators at an early date officially announced that Inti, the sun, their own elder brother, was ruler of the cohorts of heaven by like divine right that they were of the four corners of the earth.

This scheme ignominiously failed, as every attempt to fetter the liberty of conscience must and should. The later Incas finally indulged publicly in heterodox remarks, and compromised the matter by acknowledging a divinity superior even to their brother, the sun, as we have seen in a previous chapter.

Further to illustrate this peculiarity of American religions,—for it is an important one—I would refer

[1] Copway, *Trad. Hist. of the Ojibway Nation*, p. 165. *Kesuch* in Algonkin signifies both sky and sun (Duponceau, *Langues de l'Amér. du Nord*, p. 312). So apparently does *kin* in the Maya.

[2] Payne's manuscripts, compiled within this century, from which Mr. Squier drew this assertion, are of doubtful value. They are in the Pa. Hist. Soc. Library.

to the Choctaw sayings regarding fire and the Sun. They term the former *shahli miko*, " more a chief," and *hashe ittiapa* " he who accompanies the sun and the sun him." Their language has a " war or fire particle " with many curious significations, as to wage war. On going to war they call for aid to the Sun and the fire, his companion. But except as fire they do not address the Sun, nor does that body stand in any relation to their religious thought other than as a fire.[1]

The myths of creation never represent the sun as anterior to the world, but as manufactured by the " old people" (Navajos), as kindled and set going by the first of men (Algonkins), or as freed from some cave by a kindly deity (Haitians). It is always spoken of as a fire; only in Peru and Mexico had the precession of the equinoxes been observed, and without danger of error we can merge the consideration of its worship almost altogether in that of this element, and in that of Light.[2]

The institutions of a perpetual fire, of obtaining new fire, and of burning the dead, prevailed extensively in the New World. In the present discussion the origin of such practices, rather than the ceremonies with which they attended, has an interest. The savage knew that fire was necessary to his life. Were

[1] See Byington, *Grammar of the Choctaw Language*, p. 43 ; Rev. Alfred Wright, *Missionary Herald*, vol. 24, 1828.

[2] The words for fire and sun in American languages are usually from distinct roots, but besides the example of the Natchez I may instance to the contrary the Kolosch of British America, in whose tongue fire is *kan*, sun, *kakan* (*gake*, great), and the Tezuque of New Mexico, who use *tah* for both sun and fire.

it lost, he justly foreboded dire calamities and the ruin of his race. Therefore at stated times with due solemnity he produced it anew by friction or the flint, or else was careful to keep one fire constantly alive. These not unwise precautions soon fell to mere superstitions. If the Aztec priest at the stated time failed to obtain a spark from his pieces of wood, if the sacred fire by chance became extinguished, the end of the world or the destruction of mankind was apprehended. "You know it was a saying among our ancestors," said an Iroquois chief in 1753, "that when the fire at Onondaga goes out, we shall no longer be a people."[1] So deeply rooted was this notion, that the Catholic missionaries in New Mexico were fain to wink at it and perform the sacrifice of the mass in the same building where the flames were perpetually burning, that were not to be allowed to die until Montezuma and the fabled glories of ancient Anahuac with its heathenism should return.[2] Thus fire became the type of life. "Know that the life in your body and the fire on your hearth are one and the same thing, and that both proceed from one source," said a Shawnee prophet.[3] Such an expression was wholly in the spirit of his race. The greatest feast of the Delawares was that to their "grandfather, the fire."[4] "Their fire burns forever," was the Algonkin figure of speech to express the immortality of their gods.[5] "The ancient God, the Father and Mother of all

---

[1] *Doc. Hist. of New York*, ii. p. 634.

[2] Emory, *Milt'y. Reconnoissance of New Mexico*, p. 30.

[3] *Narrative of John Tanner*, p. 161.

[4] Loskiel, *Ges. der Miss. der evang. Brüder*, p. 55.

[5] *Narrative of John Tanner*, p. 351.

Gods," says an Aztec prayer, "is the God of the Fire which is in the centre of the court with four walls, and which is covered with gleaming feathers like unto wings;" [1] dark sayings of the priests, referring to the glittering lightning fire borne from the four sides of the earth.

As the path to a higher life hereafter, the burning of the dead was first instituted. It was a privilege usually confined to a select few. Among the Algonkin Ottawas, only those of the distinguished totem of the Great Hare, among the Nicaraguans none but the caciques, among the Caribs exclusively the priestly caste, were entitled to this peculiar honor. [2] The first gave as the reason for such an exceptional custom, that the members of so illustrious a clan as that of Michabo, the Great Hare, should not rot in the ground as common folks, but rise to the heavens on the flames and smoke. Those of Nicaragua seemed to think it the sole path to immortality, holding that only such as offered themselves on the pyre of their chieftain should escape annihilation at death; [3] and the tribes of upper California were persuaded that such as were not burned at death were liable to be transformed into the lower orders of brutes. [4] Strangely enough, we thus find a sort of baptism by fire deemed essential to a higher life beyond the grave.

Another analogy strengthened the symbolic force

---

[1] Sahagun, *Hist. Nueva España*, lib. vi. cap. 4.

[2] *Letts. Edifiantes et Curieuses*, iv. p. 104 ; Oviedo, *Hist. du Nicaragua*, p. 49 ; Gumilla, *Hist. del Orinoco*, ii. cap. 2.

[3] Oviedo, *Hist. Gen. de las Indias*, p. 16, in Barcia's *Hist. Prim.*

[4] *Presdt's Message and Docs.* for 1851, pt. iii. p. 506.

of fire as life. This is that which exists between the sensation of warmth and those passions whose physiological end is the perpetuation of the species. We see how native it is to the mind from such coarse expressions as "hot lust," "to burn," "to be in heat," "stews," and the like, figures not of the poetic, but the vulgar tongue. They occur in all languages, and hint how readily the worship of fire glided into that of the reproductive principle, into extravagances of chastity and lewdness, into the orgies of the so-called phallic worship.

Some have supposed that a sexual dualism pervades all natural religions, and this too has been assumed as the solution of all their myths. It has been said that the action of heat upon moisture, of the sun on the waters, the mysteries of reproduction, and the satisfaction of the sexual instincts, are the unvarying themes of primitive mythology. Like other exclusive theories, this falls before comprehensive criticism. It derives little support from American mythology.

There existed, indeed, a worship of the passions, which was at times grafted upon or rose out of that of fire by the analogy I have pointed out. Thus the Mexican god of fire was supposed to govern the generative proclivities,[1] and there is good reason to believe that the sacred fire watched by unspotted virgins among the Mayas had decidedly such a signification. Certainly it was so, if we can depend upon the authority of a ballad translated from the original immediately after the conquest, cited by the vener-

[1] Sahagun, *Hist. de la Nueva España*, i. cap. 13.

able traveller and artist Count de Waldeck. It purports to be from the lover of one of these vestals, and referring to her occupation asks with a fine allusion to its mystic meaning—

> " O vierge, quand pourrai-je te posséder pour ma compagne chérie?
> Combien de temps faut-il encore que tes vœux soient accomplis?
> Dis-moi le jour qui doit dévancer la belle nuit où tous deux,
> Alimenterons le feu qui nous fit naître et que nous devons perpétuer." [1]

There is a bright as well as a dark side even to such a worship. In Mexico, Peru, and Yucatan, the women who watched the flames must be undoubted virgins; they were usually of noble blood, and must vow perpetual chastity, or at least were free to none but the ruler of the realm. As long as they were consecrated to the fire, so long any carnal ardor was degrading to their lofty duties. The theory of sacrifice led to the belief that to forego fleshly pleasures was a peculiarly meritorious act in the eyes of the gods.

The whole subject of what has incorrectly been called " phallic worship " requires to be re-studied in the light of a higher science of religion than has hitherto been in vogue. This cult is one of several expressions of the religious sentiment, not primarily derived from the observation of nature in production, nor yet from mere lust, but from the promptings of reason and the emotion of love. As practised in early days at Lampsacus, or now among the Lingayets of India, it is pure, even austere. I would call the

---

[1] *Voyaye Pittoresque dans le Yucatan*, p. 49.

influence of the sex difference, as seen in myth and rite, the *religion of sex*, and would embrace under it not merely the worship of the phallus and the abstract generative principle, but the whole sexual relations so far as religion takes cognizance of them, not omiting the Comtist's adoration of woman.

I shall briefly sketch the ramifications of the religion of sex in the red race, as displayed toward the woman, toward the man, and toward their sexual relation.

The woman's share in reproduction is much more prominent and prolonged than the man's. What mystery there is in it—and there is much—belongs to her; and as the mysterious is the fear-inspiring, so superstition very early and very generally threw its terrors around her special physiological functions. The earliest of these is menstruation, and nearly everywhere in America we find that when this first appeared the girl fasted in seclusion, and was held unclean until it disappeared. Among our western tribes she still goes apart and builds her lonely fire; if a hunter touch her, he will kill no game, and the very dish she eats from will bring him ill fortune if he handle it.

In many tribes the formality of marriage was attended with ceremonies to guard against the imagined dangers which surround the *arcana mulieris*. Among the Mundrucus and Guaycurus of Brazil the bridegroom remains in an adjacent lodge under arms all night. In Cuba, Nicaragua and among the Caribs and Tupis the bride yielded herself first to another, lest her husband should come to some ill-luck by exercising a priority of possession;[1] a superstition repeatedly paralleled in the Old World.

Pregnancy was very generally considered to make a woman unclean. In many northern tribes the husband refrained from all relations during its continuance. Among the Costa Ricans, writes Mr. Gabb,[1] the worst *bukuru* (uncleanness) of all is that of a woman in her first pregnancy. "She infects the whole neighborhood. All the deaths and misfortunes in the vicinity are laid to her charge."[2] In many South American tribes both husband and wife begin a severe fast as soon as the latter discovers she is with child.[3]

Not less portentous was the mystery of childbirth. The Cunas of Darien would put to death a man who aided a woman in labor, though it were to save her life.[4] Among the Ottawas and neighboring tribes, a woman dare not enter the cabin of her husband nor eat with any man for one moon after her confinement.[5] But the most extraordinary of all customs was *la couvade*, common throughout the Tupi-Guaranay stem, and not confined to them. This was, that when the wife was delivered, the *husband* went to bed and was waited upon and treated as the really sick one! This act, so often spoken of as the most ridiculous of usages, as also the fast at the

[1] Martius, *Von dem Rechtzustande*, etc., p. 113 ; Oviedo, *Hist. de las Indias*, lib. xvii., cap. 4 ; Navarrete, *Viages.* iii. p. 414. This *jus primæ noctis* was exercised by the priests.

[2] The *Ind. Tribes and Langs. of Costa Rica*, p. 505.

[3] Martius, *Die Ind. Völkerschaften in Brasilien*, p. 402.

[4] De Puydt, *Jour. Roy. Geog. Soc.*, 1868, p. 97.

[5] Nic. Perrot, *Mem. de l'Am. Sept.* (1665,) p. 12.

commencement of pregnancy, I explain as propitiatory acts by the man to the mysterious forces he saw in reproduction.

The secret, superstitious fear which woman thus inspired did not desert her when the function of parturition ceased. The Fates, the Norns, the witches in Macbeth indicate how prevalent was the belief that woman holds the threads of our life in her age as in our infancy. So not only the myths but the customs of many tribes paid a frightened respect to old women, fearing them as powerful with the spirits, of strong " medicine," dangerous if angered.[1]

The marvellous power of production woman has, it was at times supposed she could impart to grains and seeds. When Father Gumilla asked the men of an Orinoco tribe why they did not help the women to plant corn, they replied, " because women know how to bring forth, and can tell the grain ; but we do not know how they do it, and cannot teach it." [2]   The wife of a Sioux, after she has planted her corn patch, will rise in the night, strip herself naked, and walk around it, thus to impart to the grains the magic of her own fecundity.[3]   The Pawnees were wont to moisten their seed corn with the blood of a woman, choosing a female prisoner to supply it.[4]   The simple faith here shown has no profound relations to nature's reproductive powers, but solely to the feminine functions.

Such in brief was the position of woman in the re-

---

[1] Compare Waitz, *Anthropologie*, iii., s. 101.

[2] Gumilla, *Hist. Orinoco*, ii. p. 237.

[3] Schoolcraft, *Ind. Tribes*, v. p. 70.

[4] Schoolcraft, *Oneota*, p. 20.

ligion of sex as found in the red race. What now was that of man?

The change which takes place at puberty was the signal for him to undergo a fast, and seek his guardian spirit. In North and South America this custom was general. From that time on he took a new name, but it was sacred and known but to his intimates.

That circumcision, in its proper sense of abscission of the fore skin, was anywhere in use, I have not satisfied myself; but that some sort of mutilation of the member was very widely practised, and for some superstitious notion, there can be no doubt.[1] That it had any reference beyond a vague one to the general mystery of sex remains to be shown. The same may be said of the scarification of the genitals and painful mutilations common among the Mandans, Aztecs, Mayas, and many other tribes, and the complete discerption of the part they occasionally practised.

The phallus was not an uncommon design in American art. I have seen several, well cut in stone, which have been found in the Mississippi valley; it appears often enough in Mexican and Yucatecan remains; very prominently in Incarian designs; and not rarely in the picture writings of savage tribes. But there seems no sufficient evidence that it anywhere was a

---

[1] Gumilla asserts this of tribes on the Apure and Orinoco (*Hist. del Orinoco*, p. 119); of Peruvian tribes, Coreal (*Voiages*, i. 291); of Nicaraguans, Oviedo (*Hist. Nic.* ii. p. 48); of Mayas, Coreal (i. p. 73); of Guaycurus and others, Garcia (*Or. de los Indios*, p. 124); of Hares and Dogribs, Mackenzie (*Voyage*, p. 27), etc.

symbol of the reproductive power of nature. That it was at times regarded as a fetich — as what was not?—is indeed true; the women of a tribe in Paraguay wore an image of it as an amulet,[1] as did the ladies of Pompeii; the soldiers of Cortes saw it in the reliefs of Panuco; and other examples are given. But this is not phallic worship in its real sense. The serpent, which in the Old World so often is the symbol of the phallus, was probably never so in America; although its similarity in form is so obvious that in various tongues—the Bri-bri of Costa Rica,[2] for example—the same word is applied to the animal and the organ.

As to the licentiousness in sexual relations which was presented at many of their religious ceremonies, it is not to be denied.

Miscellaneous congress very often terminated their dances and festivals. Such orgies were of common occurrence among the Algonkins and Iroquois at a very early date, and are often mentioned in the Jesuit Relations; Venegas describes them as frequent among the tribes of Lower California; and Oviedo refers to certain festivals of the Nicaraguans, during which the women of all rank extended to whosoever wished just such privileges as the matrons of ancient Babylon, that mother of harlots and all abominations, used to grant even to slaves and strangers in the temple of Melitta, as one of the duties of religion. But in fact there is no ground to invest these de-

[1] Lafitau, p. 72, after Ruis.

[2] Gabb, *Ind. Tribes and Langs. of Costa Rica,* p. 564 ; *Kebe*, snake, and also penis.

bauches with any recondite meaning. They are simply indications of the thorough immorality which prevailed throughout the race.

They were on a par with the revelries in the sacred grove of Aphaka, a fane which the discerning and liberal emperor Constantine razed to the ground, not out of intolerance, but because these orgies had nothing to do with religion except to wear it as a cloak for profligacy.

Any one who has listened to Indian tales, not as they are recorded in books, but as they are told by the camp-fire, will bear witness to the abounding obscenity they deal in.[1] That the same vulgarity shows itself in their arts and life, no genuine observer need doubt. And that it should be absent from their myths and cult were surprising; but its presence there is not to be construed in the sense of phallus worship.

The confounding of the attributes of sex in one person, common in Oriental religions, seems not to have been unknown in Aztec myths. The Abbé Brasseur and Mr. Bancroft quote several examples of these androgynous deities; but I think it probable that the votaries regarded such gods as of either sex, not of both at once.[2] That in many tribes, men

[1] The late George Gibbs will be acknowledged as an authority here. He was at the time of his death about preparing a Latin translation of the tales he had collected, as they were too erotic to print in English. He wrote me, " Schoolcraft's legends are emasculated to a degree that they become no longer Indian."

[2] The Mexican gods who are alleged to have united both sexes in one person are Ometeuctli and Omecihuatl (literally " two men" and " two women"), otherwise known as Citlalicue

dressed as women, yielded themselves to sodomitic
vices, is beyond question, and also that at times this
was done directly out of religious motives.[1]

On the other hand, not only was chastity in the
female and celibacy in the male held in superstitious
esteem, but it seems to have been at times enforced
by a mutilation of the parts.[2] The Aztec goddess
Suchiquetzal was a virgin,[3] and others could be
named. Very many of the great gods of the race,
Quetzalcoatl, Viracocha, Ioskeha, were at times said
to have been born of a virgin. Even among the
Indians of Paraguay the missionaries were startled
to find this tradition of the maiden mother of the
god.[4] I have already referred to the vestals of the
semi-civilized states.

Celibacy was very general among the priesthood.
The "medicine men" of an Algonkin tribe who lived
near Manhattan Island were so uncompromising on
this point that they never so much as partook of food
prepared by a married woman.[5] The same class
among the Rio Negro tribes of South America must
renounce marriage if they expect to exercise the
higher offices of their calling. Medicines, say they,

and Citlalatonac (literally " shining star " and " star skirt ") ;
and Chalchihuitlicue and Chalchihuitlatonac. Mr. Bancroft
seems to me to accept the arrenothele character of these deities
on insufficient evidence. See his *Native Races*, vol. ii. p. 273,
vol. iii. pp. 58, 373, etc.

[1] Waitz, *Anthropologie*, iii. p. 113.
[2] Davila Padilla, *Hist. de Santiago de Mexico*, lib. ii. cap. 88.
[3] *Cod. Tell. Remensis*, p. 197.
[4] *Letts. Ed. et Curieuses*, v. p. 309.
[5] *Doc. Hist. of New York*, iv. p. 28.

lose all efficacy if administered by a married man.[1] Among the hunting tribes east of the Mississippi, continence was observed when on the war-path, as they feared indulgence would be of evil omen.

By a flight of fancy inspired by a study of oriental mythology, the worship of the reciprocal principle in America has been connected with that of the sun and moon, as the primitive pair from whose fecund union all creatures proceeded. It is sufficient to say if such a myth exists among the Indians—which is questionable—it justifies no such deduction; that the moon is often mentioned in their languages merely as the "night sun;" and that in such important stocks as the Iroquois, Athapascas, Cherokees, Mbocobis and Tupis, the sun is represented as feminine; while the myths speak of them more frequently as brother and sister than as man and wife; nor did at least the northern tribes regard the sun as the cause of fecundity in nature at all, but solely as giving light and warmth.[2]

In contrast to this, so much the more positive was their association of the THUNDER-STORM as that which brings both warmth and rain with the renewed vernal life of vegetation. The impressive phenomena which characterize it, the prodigious noise, the awful flash, the portentous gloom, the blast, the rain, have left a profound impression on the myths of every land. Fire from water, warmth and moisture from the destructive breath of the tempest, this was the riddle

---

[1] Martius, *Völkerschaften Brasiliens*, p. 587.

[2] Schoolcraft, *Ind. Tribes*, v. pp. 416, 417; Waitz, *Anthropologie*, iii. p. 472.

of riddles to the untutored mind. "Out of the eater came forth meat, out of the strong came forth sweetness." It was the visible synthesis of all the divine manifestations, the winds, the water, and the flames.

The Dakotas conceived it as a struggle between the god of waters and the thunder bird for the command of their nation,[1] and as a bird, one of those which make a whirring sound with their wings, the turkey, the pheasant, or the nighthawk, it was very generally depicted by their neighbors, the Athapascas, Iroquois, and Algonkins.[2] As the herald of the summer it was to them a good omen and a friendly power. It was the voice of the Great Spirit of the four winds speaking from the clouds and admonishing them that the time of corn planting was at hand.[3] The flames kindled by the lightning were of a sacred nature, proper to be employed in lighting the fires of the religious rites, but on no account to be profaned by the base uses of daily life. When the flash entered the ground it scattered in all directions these stones, such as the flint, which betray their supernal origin by a gleam of fire when struck. These were the thunderbolts, and from such an one, significantly painted red, the Dakotas averred their race had proceeded.[4] For are we not all in a sense indebted for

[1] Mrs. Eastman, *Legends of the Sioux*, p. 161.

[2] *Rel. de la Nouv. France*, 1634, p. 27 ; Schoolcraft, *Algic Researches*, ii. p. 116 ; *Ind. Tribes*, v. p. 420.

[3] De Smet, *Western Missions*, p. 135 ; Schoolcraft, *Ind. Tribes*, i. p. 319.

[4] Mrs. Eastman, *Legends of the Sioux*, p. 72. By another legend they claimed that their first ancestor obtained his fire from

our lives to fire? " There is no end to the fancies entertained by the Sioux concerning thunder," observes Mrs. Eastman. They typified the paradoxical nature of the storm under the character of the giant Haokah. To him cold was heat, and heat cold; when sad he laughed, when merry groaned; the sides of his face and his eyes were of different colors and expressions; he wore horns or a forked headdress to represent the lightning, and with his hands he hurled the meteors. His manifestations were fourfold, and one of the four winds was the drum-stick he used to produce the thunder.[1]

Omitting many others, enough that the sameness of this conception is illustrated by the myth of Tupa, highest god and the first man of the Tupis of Brazil. During his incarnation, he taught them agriculture, gave them fire, the cane, and the pisang, and now in the form of a huge bird sweeps over the heavens, watching his children and watering their crops, admonishing them of the presence by the mighty sound of his voice, the rustling of his wings, and the flash of his eye. These are the thunder, the lightning, and the roar of the tempest. He is depicted with horns; he was one of four brothers, and only after a desperate struggle did he drive his fraternal rivals from the field. In his worship, the priests place pebbles in a dry gourd, deck it with feathers and arrows, and

t'ie sparks which a friendly panther struck from the rocks as he scampered up a stony hill (McCoy, *Hist. of Baptist Indian Missions,* p. 364).

[1] Mrs. Eastman, ubi sup., p. 158; Schoolcraft, *Ind. Tribes,* vi. p. 645.

rattling it vigorously, reproduce in miniature the tremendous drama of the storm.[1]

As nations rose in civilization these fancies put on a more complex form and a more poetic fulness. Throughout the realm of the Incas the Peruvians venerated as creator of all things, maker of heaven and earth, and ruler of the firmament, the god Ataguju. The legend was that from him proceeded the first of mortals, the man Guamansuri, who descended to the earth and there seduced the sister of certain Guachemines, rayless ones, or Darklings, who then possessed it. For this crime they destroyed him, but their sister proved pregnant, and died in her labor, giving birth to two eggs. From these emerged the twin brothers, Apocatequil and Piguerao. The former was the more powerful. By touching the corpse of his mother he brought her to life, he drove off and slew the Guachemines, and, directed by Ataguju, released the race of Indians from the soil by turning it up with a spade of gold. For this reason they adored him as their maker. He it was, they thought, who produced the thunder and the lightning by hurling stones with his sling; and the thunderbolts that fall, said they, are his children. Few villages were willing to be without one or more of these. They were in appearance small, round, smooth stones, but had the admirable properties of securing fertility to the fields, protecting from lightning, and, by a transition easy to understand, were also adored as gods of the Fire, as well as material of the

[1] Waitz, *Anthropologie*, iii. p. 417 ; Müller, *Am. Urrelig.*, p. 271.

passions, and were capable of kindling the dangerous flames of desire in the most frigid bosoms. Therefore they were in great esteem as love charms.

Apocatequil's statue was erected on the mountains, with that of his mother on one hand, and his brother on the other. " He was Prince of Evil and the most respected god of the Peruvians. From Quito to Cuzco not an Indian but would give all he possessed to conciliate him. Five priests, two stewards, and a crowd of slaves served his image. And his chief temple was surrounded by a very considerable village whose inhabitants had no other occupation than to wait on him." In memory of these brothers, twins in Peru were always deemed sacred to the lightning, and when a woman or even a llama brought them forth, a fast was held and sacrifices offered to the two pristine brothers, with a chant commencing : *A chuchu cachiqui*, O Thou who causest twins, words mistaken by the Spaniards for the name of a deity.[1]

---

[1] On the myth of Catequil see particularly the *Lettre sur les Superstitions du Pérou*, p. 95 sqq., and compare Montesinos, *Ancien Pérou*, chaps. ii., xx. The letters g and j do not exist in Quichua, therefore Ataguju should doubtless read *Ata-chuchu*, which means lord, or ruler of the twins, from *ati* root of *atini*, I am able, I control, and *chuchu*, twins. The change of the root *ati* to *ata*, though uncommon in Quichua, occurs also in *atahualpa*, cock, from *ati* and *hualpa*, fowl. Apo-Catequil, or as given by Arriaga, another old writer on Peruvian idolatry, Apocatequilla, I take to be properly *apu-ccatec-quilla*, which literally means *chief of the followers of the moon*. Acosta mentions that the native name for various constellations was *cata-chillay* or *catuchillay*, doubtless corruptions of *ccatec quilla*, literally " following the moon." Catequil, therefore, the dark spirit of the storm rack, was also appropriately enough, and

Garcilasso de la Vega, a descendant of the Incas, has preserved an ancient indigenous poem of his nation, presenting the storm myth in a different form, which as undoubtedly authentic and not devoid of poetic beauty I translate, preserving as much as possible the trochaic tetrasyllabic verse of the original Quichua :—

> "Beauteous princess,
> Lo, thy brother
> Breaks thy vessel
> Now in fragments.
> From the blow come
> Thunder, lightning,
> Strokes of lightning.
> And thou, princess,
> Tak'st the water,
> With it rainest,
> And the hail, or
> Snow dispensest.
> Viracocha,
> World constructor,

perhaps primarily, lord of the night and stars. Piguerao, where the g appears again, is probably a compound of *piscu*, bird, and *uira*, white. Guachemines seems clearly the word *huachi*, a ray of light or an arrow, with the negative suffix *ymana*, thus meaning rayless, as in the text, or *ymana* may mean an excess as well as a want of anything beyond what is natural, which would give the signification " very bright shining." (Holguin, *Arte de la Lengua Quichua*, p. 106 : Cuzco, 1607.) Is this sister of theirs the Dawn, who, as in the Rig Veda, brings forth at the cost of her own life the white and dark twins, the Day and the Night, the latter of whom drives from the heavens the far-shooting arrows of light, in order that he may restore his mother again to life ? The answer may for the present be deferred. It is a coincidence perhaps worth mentioning that the Augustin monk who is our principal authority for this legend mentions two other twin deities Yamo and Yama, whose names are almost identical with the twins Yama and Yami of the Veda.

> World enliv'ner,
> To this office
> Thee appointed,
> Thee created." [1]

In this pretty waif that has floated down to us
from the wreck of a literature now forever lost, there
is more than one point to attract the notice of the
antiquary. He may find in it a hint to decipher those
names of divinities so common in Peruvian legends,
Contici and Illatici. Both mean " the Thunder Vase,"
and both doubtless refer to the conception here displayed of the phenomena of the thunder-storm.[2]

Again, twice in this poem is the triple nature of
the storm adverted to. This is observable in many
of the religions of America. It constitutes a sort of
Trinity, not in any point resembling that of Christianity, nor yet the Trimurti of India, but the only
one in the New World the least degree authenticated,
and which, as half seen by ignorant monks, has caused
its due amount of sterile astonishment. Thus, in the

---

[1] *Hist. des Incas*, liv. ii. cap. 28, and corrected in Markham's *Quichua Grammar*.

[2] The latter is a compound of *tici* or *ticcu*, a vase, and *ylla*, the
root of *yllani*, to shine, *yllapantac*, it thunders and lightens.
The former is from *tici* and *cun* or *con*, whence by reduplication
cun-un-un-an, it thunders. From *cun* and *tura*, brother, is probably derived *cuntur*, the condor, the flying thunder-cloud
being looked upon as a great bird also. Dr. Waitz has pointed
out that the Araucanians call by the title *con*, the messenger
who summons their chieftains to a general council. The Cunas, a Carib tribe, still live in the province of Darien. Las
Casas says the chief god there was Chicūn=principio de todo.
(*Hist. Apologet.* MSS. cap. 125). The *Dict. Galib.* gives as
Carib for thunder *cono-merou*. The syllable again appears in
the Carib, Savacon, the thunder God.

Quiché legends we read : " The first of Hurakan is the lightning, the second the track of the lightning, and the third the stroke of the lightning ; and these three are Hurakan, the Heart of the Sky." [1] It reappears with characteristic uniformity of outline in Iroquois mythology. Heno, the thunder, gathers the clouds and pours out the warm rains. Therefore he was the patron of husbandry. He was invoked at seed time and harvest ; and as purveyor of nourishment he was addressed as grandfather, and his worshippers styled themselves his grandchildren. He rode through the heavens on the clouds, and the thunderbolts which split the forest trees were the stones he hurled at his enemies. *Three* assistants were assigned him, whose names have unfortunately not been recorded, and whose offices were apparently similar to those of the three companions of Hurakan. [2]

So also the Aztecs supposed that Tlaloc, god of rains and the waters, ruler of the terrestrial paradise and the season of summer, manifested himself under the three attributes of the flash, the thunderbolt, and the thunder. [3]

But this conception of three in one was above the comprehension of the masses, and consequently these deities were also spoken of as fourfold in nature, three *and* one. Moreover, as has already been pointed out, the thunder god was usually ruler of the winds, and thus another reason for his quadruplicate nature

[1] *Le Livre Sacré*, p. 9. The name of the lightning in Quiché is *cak ul ha*, literally, " fire coming from water."

[2] Morgan, *League of the Iroquois*, p. 158.

[3] " El rayo, el relámpago, y el trueno." Gama, *Des. de las dos Piedras*, etc., ii. p. 76: Mexico, 1832.

was suggested. Hurakan, Haokah, Tlaloc, and probably Heno, are plural as well as singular nouns, and are used as nominatives to verbs in both numbers. Tlaloc was appealed to as inhabiting each of the cardinal points and every mountain top. His statue rested on a square stone pedestal, facing the east, and had in one hand a serpent of gold. Ribbons of silver, crossing to form squares, covered the robe, and the shield was composed of feathers of four colors, yellow, green, red, and blue. Before it was a vase containing all sorts of grain; and the clouds were called his companions, the winds his messengers.[1] As elsewhere, the thunderbolts were believed to be flints, and thus, as the emblem of fire and the storm, this stone figures conspicuously in their myths. Tohil, the god who gave the Quichés fire by shaking his sandals, was represented by a flint-stone.[2] Such a stone, in the beginning of things, fell from heaven to earth, and broke into 1600 pieces, each of which sprang up a god;[3] an ancient legend, which-shadows forth the subjection of all things to him who gathers the clouds from the four corners of the earth, who thunders with his voice, who satisfies with his rain " the desolate and waste ground, and causes the tender herb to spring forth." This is the germ of the adoration of stones as emblems of the fecundating rains. This is why, for example, the Navajos use as their charm for rain certain long round stones,

---

[1] Torquemada, *Monarquia Indiana*, lib. vi. cap. 23. Gama, ubi sup. ii. 76, 77.

[2] Brasseur, *Le Livre Sacré*, Introd. p. cxxii.

[3] Torquemada, ibid., lib. vi. cap. 41.

which they think fall from the cloud when it thunders.[1]

Mixcoatl, the Cloud Serpent, or Iztac-Mixcoatl, the White or Gleaming Cloud Serpent, said to have been the only divinity of the ancient Chichimecs, held in high honor by the Nahuas, Nicaraguans, and Otomis, and identical with Taras, supreme god of the Tarascos and Camaxtli, god of the Teo-Chichimecs, is another personification of the thunder-storm. To this day this is the familiar name of the tropical tornado in the Mexican language.[2] He was represented, like Jove, with a bundle of arrows in his hand, the thunderbolts. Both the Nahuas and Tarascos related legends in which he figured as father of the race of man. Like other lords of the lightning he was worshipped as the dispenser of riches and the patron of traffic; and in Nicaragua his image is described as being "engraved stones,"[3] probably the supposed products of the thunder.

[1] *Senate Report on the Indian Tribes,* p. 358 : Washington, 1867.

[2] Brasseur, *Hist. du Mexique,* i. p. 201, and on the extent of his worship, Waitz, *Anthropol.,* iv. p. 144.

[3] Oviedo, *Hist. du Nicaragua,* p. 47.

CHAPTER VI.

THE SUPREME GODS OF THE RED RACE.

Analysis of American culture myths.—The Manibozho or Michabo of the Algonkins shown to be an impersonation of LIGHT, a hero of the Dawn, and their highest deity.—The myths of Ioskeha of the Iroquois, Viracocha of the Peruvians, and Quetzalcoatl of the Toltecs essentially the same as that of Michabo.—Other examples.—Ante-Columbian prophecies of the advent of a white race from the east as conquerors.—Rise of later culture myths under similar forms.

THE philosopher Machiavelli, commenting on the books of Livy, lays it down as a general truth that every form and reform has been brought about by a single individual. Since a remorseless criticism has shorn so many heroes of their laurels, our faith in the maxim of the great Florentine wavers, and the suspicion is created that the popular fancy which personifies under one figure every social revolution is an illusion. It springs from that tendency to hero worship, ineradicable in the heart of the race, which leads every nation to have an ideal, the imagined author of its prosperity, the father of his country, and the focus of its legends. As has been hinted, research is not friendly to their renown, and dissipates them altogether into phantoms of the brain, or sadly dims the lustre of their fame. Arthur, bright star of chivalry, dwindles to a Welsh subaltern; the Cid Campeador, defender of the faith, sells his sword as often to Moslem as to Christian, and *sells* it ever; while Siegfried and Feridun vanish into nothings.

Such a conclusion will not at first be accepted without a struggle. The historian will cling to what he has been used to regard as the *fact;* he will defend it as that which alone is fruitful and of lasting power; he will maintain that "the ideal is drawn originally from examples;" that nations may not obtain lofty conceptions of moral truth without living embodiments thereof.[1] But the philosopher who has closely sifted the nature of mind comes to a different conclusion; he finds the ideal is drawn from within, not given from without; he says with the Apostle "In the beginning was the Thought," Εν αρχη ην ὁ Λογος; and he lays down the maxim that "imitation has no place in morals." [2] Scrutinizing closely the ideals of history, he discovers these heroes to be lords of the realms of pious or patriotic fancy only.

As elsewhere the world over, so in America, many tribes had to tell of such a personage, some such august character, who taught them what they knew, the tillage of the soil, the properties of plants, the art of picture writing, the secrets of magic; who founded their institutions and established their religions, who governed them long with glory abroad and peace at home; finally, did not die, but like Frederick Barbarossa, Charlemagne, King Arthur, and all great heroes, vanished mysteriously, and still lives somewhere, ready at the right moment to return to his beloved people and lead them to victory and happiness. Such to the Algonkins was Michabo or

[1] See Mr. Kirk's remarks in his edition of Prescott's *Conquest of Mexico*, i. p. 63.

[2] Kant, *The Metaphysic of Ethics*, p. 19.

Manibozho, to the Iroquois Ioskeha, Wasi to the Cherokees, Tamoi to the Caribs; so the Mayas had Zamna, the Toltecs Quetzalcoatl, the Muyscas Nemqueteba; such among the Quichuas was Viracocha, among the Mandans Numock-muckenah, among the Hidatsa Itamapisa, and among the natives of the Orinoko Amalivaca; and the catalogue could be extended indefinitely.

It is not always easy to pronounce upon these heroes, whether they belong to history or mythology, their nation's poetry or its prose. In arriving at a conclusion we must remember that a fiction built on an idea is infinitely more tenacious of life than a story founded on fact. Further, that if a striking similarity in the legends of two such heroes be discovered under circumstances which forbid the thought that one was derived from the other, then both are probably mythical. If this is the case in not two but in half a dozen instances, then the probability amounts to a certainty, and the only task remaining is to explain such narratives on consistent mythological principles. If after sifting out all foreign and later traits, it appears that when first known to Europeans, these heroes were assigned all the attributes of highest divinity, were the imagined creators and rulers of the world, and mightiest of spiritual powers, then their position must be set far higher than that of deified men. They must be accepted as the supreme gods of the red race, the analogues in the western continent, of Jupiter, Osiris, and Odin in the eastern, and whatever opinions contrary to this may have been advanced by writers and travellers must be set down to the account of that prevailing ignorance of

American mythology which has fathered so many other blunders. To solve these knotty points I shall choose for analysis the culture myths of the Algonkins, the Iroquois, the Toltecs of Mexico, and the Quichuas or Peruvians, guided in my choice by the fact that these four families are the best known, and, in many points of view, the most important on the continent.

From the remotest wilds of the northwest to the coast of the Atlantic, from the southern boundaries of Carolina to the cheerless swamps of Hudson Bay, the Algonkins were never tired of gathering around the winter fire and repeating the story of Manibozho or Michabo, the Great Hare. With entire unanimity their various branches, the Powhatans of Virginia, the Lenni Lenape of the Delaware, the warlike hordes of New England, the Ottawas of the far north, and the western tribes perhaps without exception, spoke of " this chimerical beast," as one of the old missionaries calls it, as their common ancestor. The totem or clan which bore his name was looked up to with peculiar respect. In many of the tales which the whites have preserved of Michabo he seems half a wizard, half a simpleton. He is full of pranks and wiles, but often at a loss for a meal of victuals ; ever itching to try his arts magic on great beasts and often meeting ludicrous failures therein ; envious of the powers of others, and constantly striving to outdo them in what they do best; in short, little more than a malicious buffoon delighting in practical jokes, and abusing his superhuman powers for selfish and ignoble ends. But this is a low, modern, and corrupt version of the character of Michabo, bearing no more resemblance to his real and ancient one than the language and acts of our Saviour and the apostles in the coarse Mystery Plays of the Middle Ages do to those recorded by the Evangelists.

What he really was we must seek in the accounts of older travellers, in the invocations of the jossa-keeds or prophets, and in the part assigned to him in the solemn mysteries of religion. In these we find him portrayed as the patron and founder of the meda worship,[1] the inventor of picture writing, the father and guardian of their nation, the ruler of the winds, even the maker and preserver of the world and creator of the sun and moon. From a grain of sand brought from the bottom of the primeval ocean, he fashioned the habitable land and set it floating on the waters, till it grew to such a size that a strong young wolf, running constantly, died of old age ere he reached its limits. Under the name Michabo Ovi-saketchak, the Great Hare who created the Earth, he was originally the highest divinity recognized by them, " powerful and beneficent beyond all others, maker of the heavens and the world." He was founder of the medicine hunt in which after appro-priate ceremonies and incantations the Indian sleeps, and Michabo appears to him in a dream, and tells him where he may readily kill game. He himself was a mighty hunter of old; one of his footsteps

---

[1] The *meda* worship is the ordinary religious ritual of the Algonkins. It consists chiefly in exhibitions of legerdemain, and in conjuring and exorcising demons. A *jossakeed* is an inspired prophet who derives his power directly from the higher spirits, and not as the *medawin*, by instruction and practice.

measured eight leagues, the Great Lakes were the beaver dams he built, and when the cataracts impeded his progress he tore them away with his hands. Attentively watching the spider spread its web to trap unwary flies, he devised the art of knitting nets to catch fish, and the signs and charms he tested and handed down to his descendants are of marvellous efficacy in the chase. In the autumn, in " the moon of the falling leaf," ere he composes himself to his winter's sleep, he fills his great pipe and takes a godlike smoke. The balmy clouds float over the hills and woodlands, filling the air with the haze of the " Indian summer."

Sometimes he was said to dwell in the skies with his brother the snow, or, like many great spirits, to have built his wigwam in the far north on some floe of ice in the Arctic Ocean ; while the Chipeways localized his birthplace and former home to the Island Michilimakinac at the outlet of Lake Superior. But in the oldest accounts of the missionaries he was alleged to reside toward the east, and in the holy formulæ of the meda craft, when the winds are invoked to the medicine lodge, the east is summoned in his name, the door opens in that direction, and there, at the edge of the earth, where the sun rises, on the shore of the infinite ocean that surrounds the land, he has his house and sends the luminaries forth on their daily journey.[1]

---

[1] For these particulars see the *Rel. de la Nouv. France*, 1667, p. 12, 1670, p. 93 ; Charlevoix, *Journal Historique*, p. 344 ; Schoolcraft, *Indian Tribes*, v. pp. 420 sqq., and Alex. Henry, *Travs. in Canada and the Ind. Territories*, pp. 212 sqq. These are decidedly the best references of the many that could be

It is passing strange that such an insignificant creature as the rabbit should have received this apotheosis. No explanation of it in the least satisfactory has ever been offered. Some have pointed it out as a senseless, meaningless, brute worship. It leads to the suspicion that there may lurk here one of those confusions of words which have so often led to confusion of ideas in mythology. Manibozho, Nanibojou, Missibizi, Michabo, Messou, all variations of the same name in different dialects rendered according to different orthographies, scrutinize them closely as we may, they all seem compounded according to well ascertained laws of Algonkin euphony from the words corresponding to *great* and *hare* or *rabbit*, or the first two perhaps from *spirit* and *hare* (*michi*, great, *wabos*, hare, *manito wabos*,spirit hare, Chipeway dialect), and so they have invariably been translated even by the Indians themselves. But looking more narrowly at the word, it is clearly capable of another and very different interpretation, of an interpretation which discloses at once the origin and the secret meaning of the whole story of Michabo, in the light of which it appears no longer the incoherent fable of savages, but a true myth, instinct with nature, pregnant with matter, nowise inferior to those which fascinate in the chants of the Rig Veda, or the weird pages of the Edda.

On a previous page I have emphasized with what might have seemed superfluous force, how prominent in primitive mythology is the east, the source of the morning, the day-spring on high, the cardinal point

furnished. Peter Jones' *History of the Ojibway Indians*, p. 35; Nic. Perrot, *Mem. sur l'Amér. Sept.* (1665), pp, 12, 19, 339, and Blomes, *State of his Maj. Terr.*, p. 193.

which determines and controls all others. But I did
not lay so much stress on it as others have. " The
whole theogony and philosophy of the ancient
world," says Max Müller, " centred in the Dawn,
the mother of the bright gods, of the Sun in his
various aspects, of the morn, the day, the spring;
herself the brilliant image and visage of immortality." [1]
Now it appears on attentively examining the Algonkin root *wab*, that it gives rise to words of very
diverse meaning, that like many others in all languages while presenting but one form it represents
ideas of wholly unlike origin and application, that in
fact there are two distinct roots having this sound.
One is the initial syllable of the word translated hare
or rabbit, but the other means *white*, and from it is
derived the words for the east, the dawn, the light,
the day, and the morning.[2] Beyond a doubt this is
the compound in the names Michabo and Manibozho
which therefore mean the Great Light, the Spirit of
Light, of the Dawn, or the East, and in the literal
sense of the word the Great White One, as indeed he
has sometimes been called.

In this sense all the ancient and authentic myths

---

[1] *Science of Language*, Second series, p. 518.

[2] Dialectic forms in Algonkin for white, are *wabi, wape, wompi,
waubish, oppai;* for morning, *wapan, wapaneh, opah;* for east
wapa, waubun, waubamo; for dawn, *wapa, waubun;* for day
wompan, oppan; for light, *oppung;* and many others similar.
In the Abnaki dialect, *wanbighen*, it is white, is the customary
idiom to express the breaking of the day (Vetromile, *The Abnakis and their History*, p. 27: New York, 1866). The loss in
composition of the vowel sound represented by the English w,
and in the French writers by the figure 8, is supported by
frequent analogy.

concerning him are plain and full of meaning. They divide themselves into two distinct cycles. In the one Michabo is the spirit of light who dispels the darkness ; in the other as chief of the cardinal points he is lord of the winds, prince of the powers of the air, whose voice is the thunder, whose weapon the lightning, the supreme figure in the encounter of the air currents, in the unending conflict which the Dakotas described as waged by the waters and the winds.

In the first he is grandson of the moon, his father is in the West Wind, and his mother, a maiden, dies in giving him birth at the moment of conception. For the moon is the goddess of night, the Dawn is her daughter, who brings forth the morning and perishes herself in the act, and the West, the spirit of darkness as the East is of light, proceeds and as it were begets the latter, as the evening does the morning. Straightway, however, continues the legend, the son sought the unnatural father to revenge the death of his mother, and then commenced a long and desperate struggle. " It began on the mountains. The West was forced to give ground. Manibozho drove him across rivers and over mountains and lakes, and at last he came to the brink of this world. 'Hold,' cried he, 'my son, you know my power and that it is impossible to kill me.' " [1]   What is this but the diurnal combat of light and darkness, carried on from what time " the jocund morn stands tiptoe on the misty mountain tops," across the wide world to the sunset, the struggle that knows no end, for both the opponents are immortal ?

[1] Schoolcraft, *Algic Researches*, i. pp. 135–142.

In the second, and evidently to the native mind more important cycle of legends, he was represented as one of four brothers, the North, the South, the East, and the West, all born at a birth, whose mother died in ushering them into the world;[1] for hardly has the kindling orient served to fix the cardinal points ere it is lost and dies in the advancing day. Yet it is clear that he was something more than a personification of the east or the east wind, for it is repeatedly said that it was he who assigned their duties to all the winds, to that of the east as well as the others. This is a blending of his two characters. Here too his life is a battle. No longer with his father, indeed, but with his brother Chakekenapok, the flint-stone, whom he broke in pieces and scattered over the land, and changed his entrails into fruitful vines. The conflict was long and terrible. The face of nature was desolated as by a tornado, and the gigantic boulders and loose rocks found on the prairies are the missiles hurled by the mighty com-

---

[1] The names of the four brothers, Wabun, Kabun, Kabibo-nokka, and Shawano, express in Algonkin both the cardinal points and the winds which blow from them. In another version of the legend, first reported by Father de Smet and quoted by Schoolcraft without acknowledgment, they are Nanaboojoo Chipiapoos, Wabosso, and Chakekenapok. Lederer gives the names in the Oenock dialect in Virginia as Pash, Sepoy, Aska-rin and Maraskarin (*Discoveries*, p. 4). He calls them igno-rantly "four women." When Captain Argoll visited the Po-tomac in 1610 a chief told him : " We have five gods in all; our chief god appears often unto us in the form of a mighty great hare ; the other four have no visible shape, but are in-deed the four winds which keep the four corners of the earth." (Wm. Strachey, *Historie of Travaile into Virginia*, p. 98.)

batants. Or else his foe was the glittering prince
of serpents whose abode was the lake; or was the
shining Manito whose home was guarded by fiery
serpents and a deep sea; or was the great king of
fishes; all symbols of the atmospheric waters, all
figurative descriptions of the wars of the elements.
In these affrays the thunder and lightning are at his
command, and with them he destroys his enemies.
For this reason the Chipeway pictography represents
him brandishing a rattlesnake, the symbol of the
electric flash,[1] and sometimes they called him the
Northwest Wind, which in the region they inhabit
usually brings the thunder-storms.

As ruler of the winds he was, like Quetzalcoatl,
father and protector of all species of birds, their
symbols.[2] He was patron of hunters, for their course
is guided by the cardinal points. Therefore, when
the medicine hunt has been successful, the prescribed
sign of gratitude to him was to scatter a handful of
the animal's blood towards each of these.[3] As daylight brings vision, and to see is to know, it was no
fable that gave him as the author of their arts, their
wisdom and their institutions.

In effect, his story is a world-wide truth, veiled
under a thin garb of fancy. It is but a variation of
that narrative which every race has to tell, out of
gratitude to the beneficent Father who everywhere
has cared for His children. Michabo, giver of life
and light, creator and preserver, is no apotheosis of a

---

[1] *Narrative of John Tanner*, p. 351.
[2] Schoolcraft, *Algic Res.*, i. p. 216.
[3] *Narrative of John Tanner*, p. 354.

prudent chieftain, still less the fabrication of an idle fancy or a designing priestcraft, but in origin, deeds, and name the not unworthy personification of the purest conceptions they possessed concerning the Father of All. To Him at early dawn the Indian stretched forth his hands in prayer ; and to the sky or the sun as his homes, he first pointed the pipe in his ceremonies, rites often misinterpreted by travellers as indicative of sun worship. As later observers tell us to this day the Algonkin prophet builds the medicine lodge to face the sunrise, and in the name of Michabo, who there has his home, summons the spirits of the four quarters of the world and Gizhigooke, the day maker, to come to his fire and disclose the hidden things of the distant and the future ; so the earliest explorers relate that when they asked the native priests who it was they invoked, what demons or familiars, the invariable reply was " the Kichigouai, the genii of light, those who make the day." [1]

Our authorities on Iroquois traditions, though numerous enough, are not so satisfactory. The best, perhaps is Father Brebeuf, a Jesuit missionary, who resided among the Hurons in 1626. Their culture myth, which he has recorded, is strikingly similar to that of the Algonkins. Two brothers appear in it, Ioskeha and Tawiscara, names which find their meaning in the Oneida dialect as the White one and the Dark one.[2] They were twins, born of a virgin mother,

[1] Compare the *Rel. de la Nouv. France,* 1634, p. 14, 1637, p. 46, with Schoolcraft, *Ind. Tribes,* v. p. 419. *Kichigouai* is the same word as *Gizhigooke,* according to a different orthography.

[2] The names *18skeha* and *Ta8iscara* I venture to identify with the Oneida *owisske* or *owiska,* white, and *tetiucalas* (*tyokaras,*

who died in giving them life. Their grandmother
was the moon, called by the Hurons Ataensic, a word
which signifies literally *she bathes herself,* and which,
in the opinion of Father Bruyas, a most competent
authority, is derived from the word for water.[1]

The brothers quarrelled, and finally came to blows;
the former using the horns of a stag, the latter the
wild rose. He of the weaker weapon was very
naturally discomfited and sorely wounded. Fleeing
for life, the blood gushed from him at every step,
and as it fell turned into flint-stones. The victor
returned to his grandmother, and established his lodge
in the far east, on the borders of the great ocean,
whence the sun comes. In time he became the father
of mankind, and special guardian of the Iroquois.
The earth was at first arid and sterile, but he destroyed the gigantic frog which had swallowed all

tewhgar'ars Mohawk), dark or darkness. The prefix i to *owisske*
is the impersonal third person singular; the suffix *ha* gives a
future sense, so that *i-owisske-ha* or *iouskeha* means "it is going
to become white." Brebeuf gives a similar example of *gaon,*
old; *a-gaon-ha, il va devenir vieux* (*Rel. Nouv. France,* 1636, p.
99). But "it is going to become white," meant to the Iroquois
that the dawn was about to appear, just as *wanbighen,* it is white,
did to the Abnakis (see note on page 179), and as the Eskimos
say, *kau ma wok,* it is white, to express that it is daylight
(Richardson's Vocab. of Labrador Eskimo in his *Arctic Expedition*). Therefore, that Ioskeha is an impersonation of the light
of the dawn admits of no dispute.

[1] The orthography of Brebeuf is *aataentsic.* This may be
analyzed as follows: root *aouen,* water; prefix *at, il y a quelque
chose là dedans; ataouen, se baigner;* from which comes the
form *ataouensere.* (See Bruyas, *Rad. Verb. Iroquæor.,* pp. 30, 31.)
Here again the mythological role of the moon as the goddess of
water comes distinctly to light.

the waters, and guided the torrents into smooth streams and lakes.[1] The woods he stocked with game; and having learned from the great tortoise, who supports the world, how to make fire, taught his children, the Indians, this indispensable art. He it was who watched and watered their crops; and indeed, without his aid, says the old missionary, quite out of patience with such puerilities, " they think they could not boil a pot." Sometimes they spoke of him as the sun, but this only figuratively.[2]

From other writers of early date we learn that the essential outlines of this myth were received by the Tuscaroras and the Mohawks, and as the proper names of the two brothers are in the Oneida dialect, we cannot err in considering this the national legend of the Iroquois stock. There is strong likelihood that the Taronhiawagon, he who comes from the Sky, of the Onondagas, who was their supreme God, who spoke to them in dreams, and in whose honor the chief festival of their calendar was celebrated about the winter solstice, was, in fact, Ioskeha under another name.[3] As to the legend of the Good and

---

[1] This offers an instance of the uniformity which prevailed in symbolism in the New World. The Aztecs adored the goddess of water under the figure of a frog carved from a single emerald; or of human form, but holding in her hand the leaf of a water lily ornamented with frogs. (Brasseur, *Hist. de Mexique,* i. p. 324.)

[2] *Rel. de la Nouv. France,* 1636, p. 101.

[3] *Rel. de la Nouv. France,* 1671, p. 17. Cusic spells it *Taren-yawagon,* and translates it Holder of the Heavens. But the name is evidently a compound of *garonhia,* sky, softened in the Onondaga dialect to *taronhia* (see Gallatin's Vocabs. under the word sky), and *wagin,* I come.

Bad Minds given by Cusic, to which I have referred in a previous chapter, and the later and wholly spurious myth of Hiawatha, first made public by Mr. Clark in his History of Onondaga (1849), and which, in the graceful poem of Longfellow, is now familiar to the world, they are but pale and incorrect reflections of the early native traditions.

So strong is the resemblance Ioskeha bears to Michabo, that what has been said in explanation of the latter will be sufficient for both. Yet I do not imagine that the one was copied or borrowed from the other. We cannot be too cautious in adopting such a conclusion. The two nations were remote in everything but geographical position. I call to mind another similar myth. In it a mother is also said to have brought forth twins, or a pair of twins, and to have paid for them with her life. Again the one is described as the bright, the other as the dark twin ; again it is said that they struggled one with the other for the mastery. Scholars, likewise, have interpreted the mother to mean the Dawn, the twins either Light and Darkness, or the Four Winds. Yet this is not Algonkin theology; nor is it at all related to that of the Iroquois. It is the story of Sarama in the Rig Veda, and was written in Sanscrit, under the shadow of the Himalayas, centuries before Homer.

Such uniformity points not to a common source in history, but in psychology. Man, chiefly cognizant of his existence through his senses, thought with an awful horror of the night which deprived him of the use of one and foreshadowed the loss of all. Therefore *light* and *life* were to him synonymous; therefore all religions promise to lead

> " From night to light,
> From night to heavenly light ; "

therefore He who rescues is ever the Light of the World; therefore it is said " to the upright ariseth light in darkness ; " therefore everywhere the kindling East, the pale Dawn, is the embodiment of his hopes and the centre of his reminiscences. Who shall say that his instinct led him here astray ? For is not, in fact, all life dependent on light ? Do not all those marvellous and subtle forces known to the older chemists as the imponderable elements, without which not even the inorganic crystal is possible, proceed from the rays of light ? Let us beware of that shallow science so ready to shout Eureka, and reverently acknowledge a mysterious intuition here displayed, which joins with the latest conquests of the human mind to repeat and emphasize that message which the Evangelist heard of the Spirit and declared unto men, that " God is Light." [1]

Both these heroes, let it be observed, live in the uttermost east ; both are the mythical fathers of the

---

[1] 'O Θεος φως εστι, The First Epistle General of John, i. 5. In curious analogy to these myths is that of the Eskimos of Greenland. In the beginning, they relate, were two brothers, one of whom said : " There shall be night and there shall be day, and men shall die, one after another." But the second said, " There shall be no day, but only night all the time, and men shall live forever." They had a long struggle, but here once more he who loved darkness rather than light was worsted, and the day triumphed. (*Nachrichten von Grönland aus einem Tagebuche vom Bischof Paul Egede*, p. 157 : Kopenhagen, 1790. The date of the entry is 1738.)

race. To the east, therefore, should these nations have pointed as their original dwelling place. This they did in spite of history. Cusic, who takes up the story of the Iroquois a thousand years before the Christian era, locates them first in the most eastern region they ever possessed ; while the Algonkins with one voice called those of their tribes living nearest the rising sun *Abnakis*, our ancestors at the east, or at the dawn ; literally our *white* ancestors.[1] I designedly emphasize this literal rendering. It reminds one of the white twin of Iroquois legend, and illustrates how the color white came to be intimately associated with the morning light and its beneficent effects. Moreover, color has a specific effect on the mind; there is a music to the eye as well as to the ear; and white, which holds all hues in itself, disposes the soul to all pleasant and elevating emotions.[2] Not fashion alone bids the bride wreathe her brow with orange flowers, nor was it a mere figure of speech that led the inspired poet to call his love " fairest among women," and to prophecy a Messiah " fairer than the children of men," fulfilled in that day when He appeared " in garments so white as no fuller on earth could white them."

No nation is free from the power of this law. " White," observed Adair of the southern Indians,

---

[1] I accept without hesitation the derivation of this word, proposed and defended by that accomplished Algonkin scholar, the Rev. Eugene Vetromile, from *wanb*, white or east, and *naghi* ancestors (*The Abnakis and their History*, p. 29: New York, 1866).

[2] White light, remarks Goethe, has in it something cheerful and ennobling; it possesses " eine heitere, muntere, sanft reizende Eigenschaft." *Farbenlehre*, sec's. 766, 770.

" is their fixed emblem of peace, happiness, prosperity, purity, and holiness." [1] Their priests dressed in white robes, as did those of Peru and Mexico ; the kings of the various species of animals were all supposed to be white ; [2] the cities of refuge established as asylums for alleged criminals by the Cherokees in the manner of the Israelites were called " white towns," and for sacrifices animals of this color were ever most highly esteemed. All these sentiments were linked to the dawn. Language itself is proof of it. Many Algonkin words for east, morning, dawn, day, light, as we have already seen, are derived from a radical signifying *white*. Or we can take a tongue nowise related, the Quiché, and find its words for east, dawn, morning, light, bright, glorious, happy, noble, all derived from *zak*, white. We read in their legends of the earliest men that they were " white children," " white sons," leading " a white life beyond the dawn," and the creation itself is attributed to the Dawn, the White one, the White sacrificer of of Blood.[3] But why insist upon the point when in European tongues we find the daybreak called *l'aube*, *alva*, from *albus*, white ? Enough for the purpose if the error of those is manifest who, in such expressions, would seek support for any theory of ancient

---

[1] *Hist. of the N. Am. Indians*, p. 159.

[2] La Hontan, *Voy. dans l'Amér. Sept.*, ii. p. 42.

[3] " Blanco pizote," Ximenes, p. 4. *Vocabulario Quiché*, s. v. *zak*. In the far north the Eskimo tongue presents the same analogy. Day, morning, bright, light, lightning, all are from the same root (*kau*), signifying white (Richardson, Vocab. of Labrador Eskimo). So in Hidatsa, from *hati*, to grow light, come *ohati* white, *amahati* to shine, etc. (Matthews, *Hidatsa Grammar*).

European immigration; enough if it displays the true meaning of those traditions of the advent of benevolent visitors of fair complexions in ante-Columbian times, which both Algonkins and Iroquois [1] had in common with many other tribes of the western continent. Their explanation will not be found in the annals of Japan, the triads of the Cymric bards, nor the sages of Icelandic skalds, but in the propensity of the human mind to attribute its own origin and culture to that white-shining orient where sun, moon, and stars, are daily born in renovated glory, to that fair mother, who, at the cost of her own life, gives light and joy to the world, to the brilliant womb of Aurora, the glowing bosom of the Dawn.

She is the common mother whom the western Eskimos call Sidne, the daughter of their supreme being Anguta, and from her proceeded all things having life, while her father made inorganic matter.[2]

The Salish, Nesquallies and Yakimas on the Northwest Coast refer to her as "the daughter of the sun," the spouse of the primeval bird Yehl, the master of the winds, and appeal to her as mother of their race.[3]

In Haiti her name was Itaba-tahuana; she was a virgin who died in bringing into the world four brothers at a birth, who caused the Deluge, and marrying the four winds begat the nations of men.[4]

---

[1] Some fragments of them may be found in Campanius, *Acc. of New Sweden*, 1650, book iii. chap. 11, and in Byrd, *The Westover Manuscripts*, 1733, p. 82. They were in both instances alleged to have been white and bearded men, the latter probably a later trait in the legend.

[2] C. F. Hall, *Arctic Researches*, p. 571.

[3] M. Macfie, *Vancouver's Island*, &c., p. 454.

[4] D. G. Brinton, *The Arawack Language*, &c. p. 17. To the

And thus she meets us from the equator to the pole.

Even the complicated mythology of Peru yields to the judicious application of these principles of interpretation. Its peculiar obscurity arises from the policy of the Incas to blend the religions of conquered provinces with their own. Thus about 1350 the Inca Pachacutec subdued the country about Lima where the worship of Con and Pachacamà prevailed.¹ The local myth represented these as father and son, or brothers, children of the sun. They were without

student of mythology I would point out the similarity of these myths to those of the four dwarfs, Austri, Vestri, Sudri and Nordri, who support the sky, and the maiden Ostara (from whom comes our name of *Easter* Sunday), often associated with them in ancient German mythology. It is greatly to be regretted that the myth of Ostara remains so incomplete.

¹ *Con* or *Cun* I have already explained to mean thunder, *Con tici*, the mythical thunder vase. Pachacamà is doubtless, as M. Leonce Angrand has suggested, from *ppacha*, source, and *camà*, all, the Source of All things (Desjardins, *Le Pérou avant la Conq. Espagnole*, p. 23, note). But he and all other writers have been in error in considering this identical with *Pachacàmac*, nor can the latter mean *creator of the world*, as it has constantly been translated. It is a participial adjective from *pacha*, place, especially the world, and *camac*, present participle of *camani*, I animate, from which also comes *camakenc*, the soul, and means *animating the world*. It was never used as a proper name. The following trochaic lines from the Quichua poem translated in the previous chapter, show its true meaning and correct accent:

Pāchă rūrăc,	World creating.
Pāchă cāmăc,	World animating.
Viracocha,	Viracocha.
Camasunqui,	He animates thee.

The last word is the second transition, present tense, of *camani*, while *camac* is its present participle.

flesh or blood, impalpable, invisible, and incredibly swift of foot. Con first possessed the land, but Pachacamà attacked and drove him to the north. Irritated at his defeat he took with him the rain, and consequently to this day the sea-coast of Peru is largely an arid desert. Now when we are informed that the south wind, that, in other words, which blows to the north, is the actual cause of the aridity of the lowlands,[1] and consider the light and airy character of these antagonists, we cannot hesitate to accept this as a myth of the winds. The name of *Con tici*, the Thunder Vase, was indeed applied to Viracocha in later times, but they were never identical. Viracocha was the culture hero of the ancient Aymara-Quichua stock. He was more than that, for in their creed he was creator and possessor of all things. Lands and herds were assigned to other gods to support their temples, and offerings were heaped on their altars, but to him none. For, asked the Incas: "Shall the Lord and Master of the whole world need these things from us?" "To him," says Acosta, "they did attribute the chief power and commandement over all things;" and elsewhere "in all this realm the chief idoll they did worship was Viracocha, and *after him* the Sunne."[2]

Ere sun or moon was made, he rose from the bosom of Lake Titicaca, and presided over the erection of those wondrous cities whose ruins still dot its islands and western shores, and whose history is totally lost in the night of time. He himself constructed these luminaries and placed them in the sky, and then peopled

[1] Ulloa, *Mémoires Philosophiques sur l'Amérique*, i. p. 105.

[2] Acosta, *Hist. of the New World*, bk. v. chap. 4, bk. vi. chap. 19, Eng. trans., 1704.

the earth with its present inhabitants. From the lake he journeyed westward, not without adventures, for he was attacked with murderous intent by the beings whom he had created. When, however, scorning such unequal combat, he had manifested his power by hurling the lightning on the hill-sides and consuming the forests, they recognized their maker, and humbled themselves before him. He was reconciled, and taught them arts and agriculture, institutions and religion, meriting the title they gave him of *Pachay-achachic*, teacher of all things. At last he disappeared in the western ocean. Four personages, companions or sons, were closely connected with him. They rose together with him from the lake, or else were his first creations. These are the four mythical civilizers of Peru, who another legend asserts emerged from the cave Pacarin tampu, the Lodgings of the Dawn.[1] To these Viracocha gave the earth, to one the north, to another the south, to a third the east, to a fourth the west. Their names are very variously given, but as they have already been identified with the four winds, we can omit their consideration here.[2] Tradition, as

---

[1] The name is derived from *tampu*, corrupted by the Spaniards to *tambo*, an inn, and *paccari* morning, or *paccarin*, it dawns, which also has the figurative signification, it is born. It may therefore mean either Lodgings of the Dawn, or as the Spaniards usually translated it, House of Birth, or Production, *Casa de Producimiento.*

[2] The names given by Balboa (*Hist. du Pérou*, p. 4) and Montesinos (*Ancien Pérou*, p. 5) are Manco, Cacha, Auca, Uchu. The meaning of Manco is unknown. The others signify, in their order, messenger, enemy or traitor, and the little one. The myth of Viracocha is given in its most antique form by Juan de Betanzos, in the *Historia de los Ingas*, compiled in the first

13

has rightly been observed by the Inca Garcilasso de la Vega,[1] transferred a portion of the story of Viracocha to Manco Capac, first of the historical Incas. King Manco, however, was a real character, the Rudolph of Hapsburg of their reigning family, and flourished about the eleventh century.

There is a general resemblance between this story and that of Michabo. Both precede and create the sun, both journey to the west, overcoming opposition with the thunderbolt, both divide the world between the four winds, both were the fathers, gods, and teachers of their nations. Nor does it cease here. Michabo, I have shown, is the white spirit of the Dawn. Viracocha, all authorities translate "the fat or foam of the sea." The idea conveyed is of whiteness, foam being called fat from its color.[2] So true is this that to-day in Peru white men are called *viracochas*, and the early explorers constantly received the same epithet.[3] The name is a metaphor. The dawn rises above the horizon as the snowy foam on the surface of a lake. As the Algonkins spoke of the Abnakis, their white ancestors, as the Innuits

years of the conquest from the original songs and legends. It is quoted in Garcia, *Origen de los Indios*, lib. v. cap. 7. Balboa, Montesinos, Acosta, and others have also furnished me some incidents. Whether Atachuchu mentioned in the last chapter was not another name of Viracocha may well be questioned. It is every way probable. Las Casas (*Hist. Apol. de las Indias*, cap. 125) gives the names of the two contestants as Conditi-Viracocha and his son Taguapica-Viracocha.

[1] *Hist. des Incas*, liv. iii. chap. 25.

[2] It is compounded of *vira*, fat, foam (which perhaps is akin to *yurac*, white), and *cocha*, a pond or lake.

[3] See Desjardins, *Le Pérou avant la Conq. Espagnole*, p. 67.

assert the men first made were white but gave place to those of their own color,[1] as in Mexican legends the early Toltecs were of fair complexion, so the Aymaras sometimes called the first four brothers *viracochas,* white men.[2] It is the ancient story how

> " Light
> Sprung from the deep, and from her native east
> To journey through the airy gloom began."

The central figure of Toltec mythology is Quetzalcoatl. Not an author on ancient Mexico but has something to say about the glorious days when he ruled over the land. No one denies him to have been a god, the god of the air, highest deity of the Toltecs, in whose honor was erected the pyramid of Cholula, grandest monument of their race. But many insist that he was at first a man, some deified king. There were in truth many Quetzalcoatls, for his high priest always bore his name, but he himself is a pure creation of the fancy, and all his alleged history is nothing but a myth.

His emblematic name, the Bird-Serpent, and his rebus and cross at Palenque, I have already explained. Others of his titles were, Ehecatl, the air; Yolcuat, the rattlesnake; Tohil, the rumbler; Huemac, the strong hand; Nani he hecatle, lord of the four winds; Tlaviz calpan tecutli, lord of the light of the dawn.[3] The same dualism reappears in him that has been

---

[1] C. F. Hall, *Arctic Researches,* p. 566. These first men were called *Kaudluna,* from the root *Kau,* white, morning, etc.

[2] Gomara, *Hist. de las Indias,* cap. 119, in Müller.

[3] "Propriamente es la primera claridad que apareció en el mundo." *Codex Telleriano-Remensis,* p. 205. This codex appeared in the *Archives Paléographiques.*

noted in his analogues elsewhere. He is both lord
of the eastern light and the winds.

As the former, he was born of a virgin in the land
of Tula or Tlapallan, in the distant Orient, and was
high priest of that happy realm. The morning star
was his symbol, and the temple of Cholula was dedicated to him expressly as the author of light.[1] As
by days we measure time, he was the alleged inventor
of the calendar. Like all the dawn heroes, he too
was represented as of white complexion, clothed in
long white robes, and, as most of the Aztec gods, with
a full and flowing beard.[2] When his earthly work
was done he too returned to the east, assigning as a
reason that the sun, the ruler of Tlapallan, demanded
his presence. But the real motive was that he had
been overcome by Tezcatlipoca, otherwise called
Yoalliehecatl, the wind or spirit of night, who had descended from heaven by a spider's web and presented
his rival with a draught pretended to confer immortality, but, in fact, producing uncontrollable longing

---

[1] Brasseur, *Hist. de Mexique,* i. p. 302.

[2] There is no reason to lay any stress upon this feature.
Beard was nothing uncommon among the Aztecs and many
other nations of the New World. It was held to add dignity to
the appearance, and therefore Sahagun, in his description of
the Mexican idols, repeatedly alludes to their beards, and Müller
quotes various authorities to show that the priests wore them
long and full (*Amer. Urreligionen,* p. 429). Not only was Quetzalcoatl himself reported to have been of fair complexion—white
indeed—but the Creole historian Ixtlilxochitl says the old legends
asserted that all the Toltecs, natives of Tollan, or Tula, as their
name signifies, were so likewise. Still more, Aztlan, the traditional home of the Nahuas, or Aztecs proper, means literally the
white land, according to one of our best authorities (Buschmann,
Ueber die Aztekischen Ortsnamen, p. 612 : Berlin, 1852).

for home. For the wind and the light both depart when the gloaming draws near, or when the clouds spread their dark and shadowy webs along the mountains, and pour the vivifying rain upon the fields.

In his other character, he was begot of the breath of Tonacateotl, god of our flesh or subsistence,[1] or (according to Gomara) was the son of Iztac Mixcoatl, the white cloud serpent, the spirit of the tornado. It was he who created the world, and alone of the Aztec gods was supposed to possess a human body.[2] Messenger of Tlaloc, god of rains, he was figuratively said to sweep the road for him, since, in that country, violent winds are the precursors of the wet seasons. Wherever he went all manner of singing birds bore him company, emblems of the whistling breezes. When he finally disappeared in the far east, he sent back four trusty youths who had ever shared his fortunes, "incomparably swift and light of foot," with directions to divide the earth between them and rule it till he should return and resume his power. When he would promulgate his decrees, his herald proclaimed them from Tzatzitepec, the hill of shouting, with such a mighty voice that it could be heard a hundred leagues around. The arrows which he shot transfixed great trees, the stones he threw levelled forests, and when he laid his hands on the rocks the mark was indelible. Yet as thus emblematic of the thunder-storm, he possessed in full measure its

---

[1] Kingsborough, *Antiquities of Mexico*, v. p. 109.

[2] *Codex Telleriano-Remensis*, p. 199. This authority calls the creator Quetzalcoatl, "el primero," and distinguishes him from the "Quetzalcoatl de Tula, que es el que tomó nombre del primero Quetzalcoatl." p. 201.

better attributes. By shaking his sandals he gave
fire to men, and peace, plenty, and riches blessed his
subjects. Tradition says he built many temples to
Mictlanteuctli, the Aztec Pluto, and at the creation
of the sun that he slew all the other gods, for the
advancing dawn disperses the spectral shapes of night,
and yet all its vivifying power does but result in
increasing the number doomed to fall before the
remorseless stroke of death.[1]

His symbols were the bird, the serpent, the cross,
and the flint, representing the clouds, the lightning,
the four winds, and the thunderbolt. Perhaps, as
Huemac, the Strong Hand, he was god of the earth-
quakes. The Zapotecs worshipped such a deity under
the image of this member carved from a precious
stone,[2] calling to mind the " Kab ul," the Working
Hand, adored by the Mayas,[3] and said to be one of
the images of Zamna, their hero god.[4] The human
hand, " that divine tool, " as it has been called, might
well be regarded by the reflective mind as the teacher
of the arts and the amulet whose magic power has

---

[1] The myth of Quetzalcoatl I have taken chiefly from Sahagun,
Hist. de la Nueva España, lib. i. cap. 5 ; lib. iii. caps. 3, 13, 14 ;
lib. x. cap. 29; and Torquemada, *Monarquia Indiana*, lib. vi. cap.
24. It must be remembered that the Quiché legends identify
him positively with the Tohil of Central America (*Le Livre
Sacré*, p. 247).

[2] Padilla Davila, *Hist. de la Prov. de Santiago de Mexico*, lib.
ii. cap. 89.

[3] Cogolludo, *Hist. de Yucathan*, lib iv. cap. 8.

[4] Zamna, not Votan, corresponded in the Maya pantheon to
Michabo and his congeners. As M. de Charencey correctly says,
" Bien opposé à Votan. Zamnà aurait tous les traits d'un génie
atmosphérique" (*Le Mythe de Votan*, p. 36).

won for man what vantage he has gained in his long combat with nature and his fellows.

I might next discuss the culture myth of the Muyscas, whose hero Bochica or Nemqueteba bore the other name SUA, the White One, the Day, the East, an appellation they likewise gave the Europeans on their arrival. He had taught them in remotest times how to manufacture their clothing, build their houses, cultivate the soil, and reckon time. When he disappeared, he divided the land between four chiefs, and laid down many minute rules of government which ever after were religiously observed.[1] Or I might choose that of the Caribs, whose patron Tamu, called Grandfather, and Old Man of the Sky, was a man of light complexion, who in the old times came from the east, instructed them in agriculture and arts, and disappeared in the same direction, promising them assistance in the future, and that at death he would receive their souls on the summit of the sacred tree, and transport them safely to his home in the sky.[2] Or from the more fragmentary mythology of ruder

---

[1] He is also called Idacanzas and Nemterequetaba. Some have maintained a distinction between Bochica and Sua, which, however, has not been shown. The best authorities on the mythology of the Muyscas are Piedrahita, *Hist. de las Conq. del Nuevo Reyno de Granada*, 1668 (who is copied by Humboldt, *Vues des Cordillères*, pp. 246 sqq), and Simon, *Noticias de Tierra Firme*, Parte ii., in Kingsborough's *Mexico*.

[2] D'Orbigny, *L'Homme Américain*, ii. p. 319, and Rochefort, *Hist. des Isles Antilles*, p. 482 (Waitz). The name has various orthographies, Tamu, Tamöi, Tamou, Itamoulou, Tamoin, modern Tamuya, etc. Perhaps the Ama-livaca of the Orinoko Indians is another form. This personage corresponds even minutely in many points with the Tamu of the island Caribs.

nations, proof might be brought of the well nigh
universal reception of these fundamental views.   As,
for instance, when the Mandans of the Upper Missouri speak of their first ancestor as a son of the
West, who preserved them at the flood, and whose
garb was always of four milk-white wolf skins ; [1] and
when the Pimos, a people of the valley of the Rio
Gila, relate that their birthplace was where the sun
rises, that there for generations they led a joyous life,
until their beneficent first parent disappeared in the
heavens.   From that time, say they, God lost sight
of them, and they wandered west, and further west
till they reached their present seats.[2]   Or I might
instance the Tupis of Brazil, who were named after
the first of men, Tupa, he who alone survived the
flood, who was one of four brothers, who is described
as an old man of fair complexion, *un vieillard blanc*,[3]
and who is now their highest divinity, maker of all
things,[4] ruler of the lightning and the storm, whose

[1] Catlin, *Letters and Notes*, Letter 22.

[2] Journal of Capt. Johnson, in Emory, *Reconnoissance of New
Mexico*, p. 601.

[3] M. De Charencey, in the *Revue Américaine*, ii. p. 317.   *Tupa*
it may be observed means in Quichua, lord or royal.   Father
Holguin gives as an example *a tupa Dios*, O Lord God (*Vocabulario Quichua*, p. 348 : Ciudad de los Reyes, 1608).   In the
Quiché dialects *tepeu* is one of the common appellations of divinity and is also translated lord or ruler.   We are not yet sufficiently advanced in the study of American philology to draw
any inference from these resemblances, but they should not be
overlooked.

[4] "Il a fait tout " (Le Père Ives d'Evreux,   *Hist. de Marignan*,
p. 280).   Another Tupi myth is that of Timandonar and Aricoute.   They were brothers, one of fair complexion, the other
dark.   They were constantly struggling, and Aricoute, which

voice is the thunder, and who is the guardian of their
nation. But is it not evident that these and all such legends are but variations of those already analyzed?

In thus removing one by one the wrappings of
symbolism, and displaying at the centre and summit
of these various creeds He who is throned in the
sky, who comes with the dawn, who manifests himself in the light and the storm, and whose ministers
are the four winds, I set up no new god. The ancient
Israelites prayed to him who was seated above the
firmament, who commanded the morning and caused
the day-spring to know its place, who answered out
of the whirlwind, and whose envoys were the four
winds, the four cherubim described with such wealth
of imagery in the introduction to the book of Ezekiel.
The Mahometan adores "the clement and merciful
Lord of the Daybreak," whose star is in the east,
who rides on the storm, and whose breath is the
wind. The primitive man in the New World also
associated these physical phenomena as products of
an invisible power, conceived under human form,
called by name, worshipped as one, and of whom all
related the same myth differing but in unimportant
passages. This was the primeval religion. It was not
monotheism, for there were many other gods; it was
not pantheism, for there was no blending of the cause
with the effects; still less was it fetichism, an adoration of sensuous objects, for these were recognized as
effects. It teaches us that the idea of God neither
arose from the phenomenal world nor was sunk in
it, as is the shallow theory of the day, but is as

means the cloudy or stormy day, came out worst. See Denis,
Une Fête Bresilienne, etc., p. 88.

Kant long ago defined it, a conviction of a highest and first principle which binds all phenomena into one.

One point of these legends deserves closer attention for the influence it exerted on the historical fortunes of the race. The dawn heroes were conceived as of fair complexion, mighty in war, and though absent for a season, destined to return and claim their ancient power. Here was one of those unconscious prophecies, pointing to the advent of a white race from the east, that wrote the doom of the red man in letters of fire. Historians have marvelled at the instantaneous collapse of the empires of Mexico, Peru, the Mayas, and the Natchez, before a handful of Spanish filibusters. The fact was, wherever the whites appeared they were connected with these ancient predictions of the spirit of the dawn returning to claim his own. Obscure and ominous prophecies, "texts of bodeful song," rose in the memory of the natives, and paralyzed their arms.

" For a very long time," said Montezuma, at his first interview with Cortes, " has it been handed down that we are not the original possessors of this land, but came hither from a distant region under the guidance of a ruler who afterwards left us and never returned. We have ever believed that some day his descendants would come and resume dominion over us. Inasmuch as you are from that direction, which is toward the rising of the sun, and serve so great a king as you describe, we believe that he is also our natural lord, and are ready to submit ourselves to him." [1]

The gloomy words of Nezahualcoyotl, a former

1 Cortes, *Carta Primera*, pp. 113, 114.

prince of Tezcuco, foretelling the arrival of white
and bearded men from the east, who would wrest
the power from the hands of the rightful rulers and
destroy in a day the edifice of centuries, were ringing
in his ears. But they were not so gloomy to the
minds of his down-trodden subjects, for that day was
to liberate them from the thralls of servitude. Therefore when they first beheld the fair complexioned
Spaniards, they rushed into the water to embrace
the prows of their vessels, and dispatched messengers throughout the land to proclaim the return of
Quetzalcoatl.[1]

The noble Mexican was not alone in his presentiments. When Hernando de Soto on landing in Peru
first met the Inca Huascar, the latter related an
ancient prophecy which his father, Huayna Capac,
had repeated on his dying bed, to the effect that in
the reign of the thirteenth Inca, white men (*viracochas*) of surpassing strength and valor would come
from their father the Sun and subject to their rule
the nations of the world. "I command you," said
the dying monarch, "to yield them homage and obedi-
ence, for they will be of a nature superior to ours."[2]

The natives of Haiti told Columbus of similar predictions long anterior to his arrival.[3] The Maryland Indians said the whites were an old generation
revived, who had come back to kill their nation and
take their places.[4] And Father Lizana has preserved
in the original Maya tongue several such foreboding

---

[1] Sahagun, *Hist. de la Nueva España*, lib. xii. caps. 2, 3.

[2] La Vega, *Hist. des Incas*, lib. ix. cap. 15.

[3] Peter Martyr, *De Reb. Oceanicis*, Dec. iii. lib. vii.

[4] Blomes, *State of his Maj. Terr.*, p. 199.

chants. Doubtless he has adapted them somewhat to proselytizing purposes, but they seem very likely to be close copies of authentic aboriginal songs, referring to the return of Zamna or Kukulcan, lord of the dawn and the four winds, worshipped at Cozumel and Palenque under the sign of the cross. An extract will show their character :—

> "At the close of the thirteenth Age of the world,
> While the cities of Itza and Tancah still flourish,
> The sign of the Lord of the Sky will appear,
> The light of the dawn will illumine the land,
> And the cross will be seen by the nations of men.
> A father to you, will He be, Itzalanos,
> A brother to you, ye natives of Tancah ;
> Receive well the bearded guests who are coming,
> Bringing the sign of the Lord from the daybreak,
> Of the Lord of the Sky, so clement yet powerful." [1]

The older writers, Gomara, Cogolludo, Villagutierre, have taken pains to collect other instances of this presentiment of the arrival and domination of a race. Later white historians, fashionably incredulous of what they cannot explain, have passed them over in silence. That they existed there can be no doubt, and that they arose in the way I have stated, is almost proven by the fact that in Mexico, Bogota, and Peru, the whites were at once called from the proper names

---

[1] Lizana, *Hist. de Nuestra Señora de Itzamal*, lib. ii. cap. i. in Brasseur, *Hist. de Mexique*, ii. p. 605. The prophecies are of the priest who bore the title—not name—*chi'an ba'am*, and whose offices were those of divination and astrology. The verse claims to date from about 1450, and was very well known throughout Yucatan, so it is said. The number thirteen which in many of these prophecies is the supposed limit of the present order of things, is doubtless derived from the observation that thirteen moons complete one solar year.

of the heroes of the Dawn, *Suas, Viracochas,* and *Quet-zalcoatls.*

When the church of Rome had crushed remorse-lessly the religions of México and Peru, all hope of the return of Quetzalcoatl and Viracocha perished with the institutions of which they were the mythi-cal founders. But it was only to arise under new incarnations and later names. As well forbid the heart of youth to bud forth in tender love, as that of oppressed nationalities to cherish the faith that some ideal hero, some royal man, will yet arise, and break in fragments their fetters, and lead them to glory and honor.

When the name of Quetzalcoatl was no longer heard from the teocalli of Cholula, that of Monte-zuma took its place. From ocean to ocean, and from the river Gila to the Nicaraguan lake, nearly every aboriginal nation still cherishes the memory of Mon-tezuma, not as the last unfortunate ruler of a vanish-ed state, but as the prince of their golden era, their Saturnian age, lord of the winds and waters, and founder of their institutions. When, in the depth of the tropical forests, the antiquary disinters some statue of earnest mien, the natives whisper one to the other, "Montezuma! Montezuma!"[1] In the le-gends of New Mexico he is the founder of the pueblos, and intrusted to their guardianship the sacred fire. Departing, he planted a tree, and bade them watch it well, for when that tree should fall and the fire die out, then he would return from the far East, and lead his loyal people to victory and power. When

[1] Squier, *Travels in Nicaragua,* ii. p. 35.

the present generation saw their land glide, mile by
mile, into the rapacious hands of the Yankees—when
new and strange diseases desolated their homes—
finally, when in 1846 the sacred tree was prostrated,
and the guardian of the holy fire was found dead on
its cold ashes, then they thought the hour of deliver-
ance had come, and every morning at earliest dawn
a watcher mounted to the house-tops, and gazed long
and anxiously in the lightening east, hoping to descry
the noble form of Montezuma advancing through
the morning beams at the head of a conquering
army. [1]

Groaning under the iron rule of the Spaniards, the
Peruvians would not believe that the last of the
Incas had perished an outcast and a wanderer in the
forests of the Cordilleras.   For centuries they clung
to the persuasion that he had but retired to another
mighty kingdom beyond the mountains, and in due
time would return and sweep the haughty Castilian
back into the ocean.   In 1781, a mestizo, Jose Gabriel Condorcanqui, of the province of Tinta, took
advantage of this strong delusion, and binding
around his forehead the scarlet fillet of the Incas,
proclaimed himself the long lost Inca Tupac Amaru,
and a true child of the sun.   Thousands of Indians
flocked to his standard, and at their head he took

---

[1] Whipple, *Report on the Ind. Tribes*, p. 36.   Emory, *Recon.
of New Mexico*, p. 64.   The latter adds that among the Pueblo
Indians, the Apaches, and Navajos, the name of Montezuma is
" as familiar as Washington to us."   This is the more curious
as neither the Pueblo Indians nor either of the other tribes is in
any way related to the Aztec race by language, as has been shown
by Dr. Buschmann, *Die Voelker and Sprachen Neu Mexico's*, p.
262.

the field, vowing the extermination of every soul of the hated race. Seized at last by the Spaniards, and condemned to a public execution, so profound was the reverence with which he had inspired his followers, so full their faith in his claims, that, undeterred by the threats of the soldiery, they prostrated themselves on their faces before this last of the children of the sun, as he passed on to a felon's death.[1]

These fancied reminiscences, these unfounded hopes, so vague, so child-like, let no one dismiss them as the babblings of ignorance. Contemplated in their broadest meaning as characteristics of the race of man, they have an interest higher than any history, beyond that of any poetry. They point to the recognized discrepancy between what man is, and what he feels he should be, must be ; they are the indignant protests of the race against acquiescence in the world's evil as the world's law ; they are the incoherent utterances of those yearnings for nobler conditions of existence, which no savagery, no ignorance, nothing but a false and lying enlightenment can wholly extinguish.

[1] Humboldt, *Essay on New Spain,* bk. ii. chap. vi., Eng. trans.; *Ansichten der Natur,* ii. pp. 357, 386.

CHAPTER VII.

THE MYTHS OF THE CREATION, THE DELUGE, THE EPOCHS OF NATURE, AND THE LAST DAY.

Cosmogonies usually portray the action of the SPIRIT on the WATERS.—
Those of the Muscogees, Athapascas, Quichés, Mixtecs, Iroquois, Al-
gonkins, and others.—The Flood-Myth an unconscious attempt to re-
concile a creation in time with the eternity of matter.—Proof of this
from American mythology.—Characteristics of American Flood-Myths.
—The person saved usually the first man.—The number seven.—Their
Ararats.—The rôle of birds.—The confusion of tongues.—The Aztec,
Quiché, Algonkin, Tupi, and earliest Sanscrit flood myths.—The belief
in Epochs of Nature a further result of this attempt at reconciliation.—
Its forms among Peruvians, Mayas, and Aztecs.—The expectation of the
End of the World a corollary of this belief.—Views of various nations.

COULD the reason rest content with the belief
that the universe always was as it now is, it
would save much beating of brains. Such is the
comfortable condition of the Eskimos, the Rootdig-
gers of California, the most brutish specimens of humanity everywhere. Vain to inquire their story of
creation, for, like the knife-grinder of anti-Jacobin
renown, they have no story to tell. It never occurred to them that the earth had a beginning, or underwent any greater changes then those of the seasons. [1] But no sooner does the mind begin to reflect

[1] So far as this applies to the Eskimos, it might be questioned
on the authority of Paul Egede, whose valuable *Nachrichten
von Grönland* contains several flood-myths, &c. But these Eski-

the intellect to employ itself on higher themes than the needs of the body, than the law of casualty exerts its power, and the man, out of such materials as he has at hand, manufactures for himself a Theory of Things.

What these materials were has been shown in the last few chapters. A simple primitive substance, a divinity to mould it—these are the requirements of every cosmogony. Concerning the first no nation ever hesitated. All agree that before time began *water* held all else in solution, covered and concealed everything. The reasons for this assumed priority of water have been already touched upon. Did a tribe dwell near some great sea others can be imagined. The land is limited, peopled, stable; the ocean fluctuating, waste, boundless. It insatiably swallows all rains and rivers, quenches sun and moon in its dark chambers, and raves against its bounds as a beast of prey. Awe and fear are the sentiments it inspires; in Aryan tongues its synonyms are the *desert* and the *night*. [1] It produces an impression of immensity, infinity, formlessness, and barren changeableness, well suited to a notion of chaos. It is sterile, receiving all things, producing nothing. Hence the necessity of a creative power to act upon it, as it were to impregnate its barren germs. Some cosmo-

mos had had for generations intercourse with European missionaries and sailors, and as the other tribes of their stock were singularly devoid of corresponding traditions, it is likely that in Greenland they were of foreign origin.

[1] Pictet, *Origines Indo-Européennes* in Michelet, *La Mer.* The latter has many eloquent and striking remarks on the impressions left by the great ocean.

14

gonies find this in one, some in another personification of divinity. Commonest of all is that of the wind, or its emblem the bird, types of the breath of life.

Thus the venerable record in Genesis, translated in the authorized version "and the Spirit of God moved on the face of the waters," may with equal correctness be rendered "and a mighty wind brooded on the surface of the waters," presenting the picture of a primeval ocean fecundated by the wind as a bird.[1] The eagle that in the Finnish epic of Kalewala floated over the waves and hatched the land, the egg that in Chinese legend swam hither and thither until it grew to a continent, the giant Ymir, the rustler (as wind in trees), from whose flesh, says the Edda, our globe was made and set to float like a speck in the vast sea between Muspel and Niflheim, all are the same tale repeated by different nations in different ages. But why take illustrations from the old world when they are so plenty in the new.

Before the creation, said the Muscogees, a great body of water was alone visible. Two pigeons flew to and fro over its waves, and at last spied a blade of grass rising above the surface. Dry land gradually followed, and the islands and continents took their present shapes.[2] Whether this is an authentic aboriginal myth, is not beyond question. No such doubt attaches to that of the Athapascas. With singular

---

[1] " Spiritus Dei incubuit superficei aquarum " is the translation of one writer. The word for spirit in Hebrew, as in Latin, originally meant wind, as I have before remarked.

[2] Schoolcraft, *Ind. Tribes*, i. p. 266.

unanimity, most of the northwest branches of this stock trace their descent from a raven, " a mighty bird, whose eyes were fire, whose glances were lightning, and the clapping of whose wings was thunder. On his descent to the ocean the earth instantly rose, and remained on the surface of the water. This omnipotent bird then called forth all the variety of animals." [1]

Very similar, but with more of poetic finish, is the legend of the Quichés :—

" This is the first word and the first speech. There were neither men nor brutes ; neither birds, fish, nor crabs, stick nor stone, valley nor mountain, stubble nor forest, nothing but the sky. The face of the land was hidden. There was naught but the silent sea and the sky. There was nothing joined, nor any sound, nor thing that stirred ; neither any to do evil, nor to rumble in the heavens, nor a walker on foot ; only the silent waters, only the pacified ocean, only it in its calm. Nothing was but stillness, and rest, and darkness, and the night ; nothing but the Maker and Moulder, the Hurler, the Bird-Serpent. In the waters, in a limpid twilight, covered with green feathers, slept the mothers and fathers." [2]

Over this passed Hurakan, the mighty wind, and called out Earth ! and straightway the solid land was there.

The picture writings of the Mixtecs preserved

---

[1] Mackenzie, *Hist. of the Fur Trade,* p. 83 ; Richardson, *Arctic Expedition*, p. 236.

[2] Ximenes, *Or. de los Ind. de Guat.*, pp. 5–7. I translate freely, following Ximenes rather than Brasseur.

a similar cosmogony: " In the year and in the day of clouds, before ever were either years or days, the world lay in darkness; all things were orderless, and a water covered the slime and the ooze that the earth then was." By the efforts of two winds, called, from astrological associations, that of Nine Serpents and that of Nine Caverns, personified one as a bird and one as a winged serpent, the waters subsided and the land dried.[1]

In the birds that here play such conspicuous parts, we cannot fail to recognize the winds and the clouds; but more especially the dark thunder clouds, soaring in space at the beginning of things, most forcible emblem of the aërial powers. They are the symbols of that divinity which acted on the passive and sterile waters, the fitting result being the production of a universe. Other symbols of the divine could also be employed, and the meaning remain the same. Or were the fancy too helpless to suggest any, they could be dispensed with, and purely natural agencies take their place. Thus the unimaginative Iroquois narrated that when their primitive female ancestor was kicked from the sky by her irate spouse, there was as yet no land to receive her, but that it "suddenly bubbled up under her feet, and waxed bigger, so that ere long a whole country was perceptible."[2] Or that certain amphibious animals, the beaver, the otter, and the muskrat, seeing her descent, hastened to dive and bring up sufficient mud to construct an island for her residence.[3] The muskrat is also the simple machinery

---

[1] Garcia, *Or. de los Indios*, lib. v. cap. 4.

[2] *Doc. Hist. of New York*, iv. p. 130 (circ. 1650).

[3] *Rel. de la Nouv. France*, An. 1638, p. 101.

in the cosmogony of the Takahlis of the northwest coast, the Osages and some Algonkin tribes.

These latter were, indeed, keen enough to perceive that there was really no *creation* in such an account. Dry land was wanting, but earth was there, though hidden by boundless waters. Consequently, they spoke distinctly of the action of the muskrat in bringing it to the surface as a formation only. Michabo directed him, and from the mud formed islands and main land. But when the subject of creation was pressed, they replied they knew nothing of that, or roundly answered the questioner that he was talking nonsense.[1] Their myth, almost identical with that of their neighbors, was recognized by them to be not of a construction, but a reconstruction only ; a very judicious distinction, but one which has a most important corollary. A reconstruction supposes a previous existence. This they felt, and had something to say about an earth anterior to this of ours, but one without light or human inhabitants. A lake burst its bounds and submerged it wholly. This is obviously nothing but a mere and meagre fiction, invented to explain the origin of the primeval ocean. But mark it well, for this is the germ of those marvellous myths of the Epochs of Nature, the catastrophes of the universe, the deluges of water and of fire, which have laid such strong hold on the human fancy in every land and in every age.

The purpose for which this addition was made to the simpler legend is clear enough. It was to avoid the dilemma of a creation from nothing on the one

---

[1] *Rel. de la Nouv. France*, An. 1634, p. 13.

hand, and the eternity of matter on the other. *Ex nihilo nihil* is an apothegm indorsed alike by the profoundest metaphysicians and the rudest savages. But the other horn was no easier. To escape accepting the theory that the world has ever been as it now is, was the only object of a legend of its formation. As either lemma conflicts with fundamental laws of thought, this escape was eagerly adopted, and in the suggestive words of Prescott, men "sought relief from the oppressive idea of eternity by breaking it up into distinct cycles or periods of time." [1] Vain but characteristic attempt of the ambitious mind of man! The Hindoo philosopher reconciles to his mind the suspension of the world in space by imagining it supported by an elephant, the elephant by a tortoise, and the tortoise by a serpent. We laugh at the Hindoo, and fancy we diminish the difficulty by explaining that it revolves around the sun, and the sun around some far-off star. Just so the general mind of humanity finds some satisfaction in supposing a world or a series of worlds anterior to the present, thus escaping the insoluble enigma of creation by removing it indefinitely in time.

The support lent to these views by the presence of marine shells on high lands, or by faint reminiscences of local geologic convulsions, I estimate very low. Savages are not inductive philosophers, and by nothing short of a miracle could they preserve the remembrance of even the most terrible catastrophe beyond a few generations. Nor has any such occurred within the ken of history of sufficient magnitude to make a very permanent or wide-spread impression.

[1] *Conquest of Mexico*, i. p. 61.

Not physics, but metaphysics, is the exciting cause of these beliefs in periodical convulsions of the globe. The idea of matter cannot be separated from that of time, and time and eternity are contradictory terms. Common words show this connection. World, for example, in the old language *waereld*, from the root to wear, by derivation means an age or cycle (Grimm).

In effect, a myth of creation is nowhere found among primitive nations. It seems repugnant to their reason. Dry land and animate life had a beginning, but not matter. A series of constructions and demolitions may conveniently be supposed for these. The analogy of nature, as seen in the vernal flowers springing up after the desolation of winter, of the sapling sprouting from the fallen trunk, of life everywhere rising from death, suggests such a view. Hence arose the belief in Epochs of Nature, elaborated by ancient philosophers into the Cycles of the Stoics, the Great Days of Brahm, long periods of time rounded off by sweeping destructions, the Cataclysms and Ekpyrauses of the universe. Some thought in these all beings perished ; others that a few survived.[1] This latter and more common view is the origin of the myth of the deluge. How fa-

[1] For instance, Epictetus favors the opinion that at the solstices of the great year not only all human beings, but even the gods, are annihilated; and speculates whether at such times Jove feels lonely (*Discourses*, bk. iii. chap. 13). Macrobius, so far from coinciding with him, explains the great antiquity of Egyptian civilization by the hypothesis that that country is so happily situated between the pole and equator, as to escape both the deluge and conflagration of the great cycle. (*Somnium Scipionis*, lib. ii. cap. 10.)

miliar such speculations were to the aborigines of America there is abundant evidence to show.

The early Algonkin legends do not speak of an antediluvian race, nor of any family who escaped the waters. Michabo, the spirit of the dawn, their supreme deity, alone existed, and by his power formed and peopled it. Nor did their neighbors, the Dakotas, though firm in the belief that the globe had once been destroyed by the waters, suppose that any had escaped.[1] The same view was entertained by the Nicaraguans[2] and the Botocudos of Brazil. The latter attributed its destruction to the moon falling to the earth from time to time.[3]

Much the most general opinion, however, was that some few escaped the desolating element by one of those means most familiar to the narrator, by ascending some mountain, on a raft or canoe, in a cave, or even by climbing a tree. No doubt some of these legends have been modified by Christian teachings; but many of them are so connected with local peculiarities and ancient religious ceremonies, that no unbiased student can assign them wholly to that source, as Professor Vater has done, even if the authorities for many of them were less trustworthy than they are. There are no more common heirlooms in the traditional lore of the red race. Nearly every old author quotes one or more of them. They present great uniformity of outline, and rather than engage in repetitions of little interest, they can be

---

[1] Schoolcraft, *Ind. Tribes*, iii. p. 263, iv. p. 230.
[2] Oviedo, *Hist. du Nicaragua*, pp. 22, 27.
[3] Müller, *Amer. Urrelig.*, p. 254, from Max and Denis.

more profitably studied in the aggregate than in detail.

By far the greater number represent the last destruction of the world to have been by water. A few, however, the Takahlis of the North Pacific coast, the Yurucares of the Bolivian Cordilleras, and the Mbocobi of Paraguay, attribute it to a general conflagration which swept over the earth, consuming every living thing except a few who took refuge in a deep cave.[1] The more common opinion of a submersion gave rise to those traditions of a universal flood so frequently recorded by travellers, and supposed by many to be reminiscences of that of Noah.

There are, indeed, some points of striking similarity between the deluge myths of Asia and America. It has been called a peculiarity of the latter that in them the person saved is always the first man. This, though not without exception, is certainly the general rule. But these first men were usually the highest deities known to their nations, the only creators of the world, and the guardians of the race.[2]

Moreover, in the oldest Sanscrit legend of the flood in the Zatapatha Brahmana, Manu is also the first man, and by his own efforts creates offspring.[3]

[1] Morse, *Rep. on the Ind. Tribes*, App. p. 346; D' Orbigny, *Frag. d'un Voyage dans l'Amér. Mérid.*, p. 512.

[2] When, as in the case of one of the Mexican Noahs, Coxcox, this does not seem to hold good, it is probably owing to the loss of the real form of the myth.

[3] My knowledge of the Sanscrit form of the flood-myth is drawn principally from the dissertation of Professor Felix Nève, entitled *La Tradition Indienne du Deluge dans sa Forme la plus ancienne*, Paris, 1851. There is in the oldest versions no dis-

A later Sanscrit work assigns to Manu the seven Richis or shining ones as companions. Seven was also the number of persons in the ark with Noah. Curiously enough one Mexican and one early Peruvian myth give out exactly seven individuals as saved in their floods.[1] This coincidence arises from the mystic powers attached to the number seven, derived from its frequent occurrence in astrology. Proof of this appears by comparing the later and the older versions of this myth, either in the book of Genesis, where the latter is distinguished by the use of the word Elohim for Jehovah,[2] or the Sanscrit account in the Zatapatha Brahmana with those in the later Puranas.[3] In both instances the number seven hardly or at all occurs in the oldest version, while it is constantly repeated in those of later dates.

In Oriental astrology the seven planets are supposed to have conferred this sacredness on the heptad. In America it was the Pleiades. Gumilla informs us that the Orinoco tribes computed their year from the period these stars rise at sunset.[4] Father Venegas says of a nation of California that they reverence the seven stars to such a degree that to look at

tinct reference to an antediluvian race, and in India Manu is by common consent the Adam as well as the Noah of the legends.

[1] Prescott, *Conquest of Peru*, i. p. 88 ; *Codex Vaticanus*, No. 3776, in Kingsborough.

[2] And also various peculiarities of style and language lost in translation. The two accounts of the Deluge are given side by side in Dr. Smith's *Dictionary of the Bible* under the word Pentateuch.

[3] See the dissertation of Prof. Nève referred to above.

[4] *Hist. del. Orinoco*, ii. p. 281.

them carelessly is calamitous.[1] Their culmination
dated the commencement of the Mexican year. With
the Peruvians they were worshipped as first of the
starry host.[2]

As the mountain or rather mountain chain of Ara-
rat was regarded with veneration wherever the Semitic accounts were known, so in America heights
were pointed out with becoming reverence as those
on which the few survivors of the dreadful scenes of
the deluge were preserved. On the Red River near
the village of the Caddoes was one of these, a small
natural eminence, " to which all the Indian tribes for
a great distance around pay devout homage," according to Dr. Sibley.[3] The Cerro Naztarny on the Rio
Grande, the peak of Old Zuñi in New Mexico, that
of Colhuacan on the Pacific Coast, Mount Apoala in
Upper Mixteca, and Mount Neba in the province of
Guaymi, are some of many elevations asserted by the
neighboring nations to have been places of refuge
for their ancestors when the fountains of the great
deep broke forth.

One of the Mexican traditions related by Torquemada identified this with the mountain of Tlaloc in
the terrestrial paradise, and added that one of the
seven demigods who escaped commenced the pyramid
of Cholula in its memory. He intended that its
summit should reach the clouds, but the gods, angry
at his presumption, drove away the builders with
lightning. This has a suspicious resemblance to

---

[1] *Hist. of California*, p. 107.

[2] Balboa, *Hist. de Pérou*, pp. 57–8.

[3] *American State Papers*, Indian Affairs, i. p. 729. Date of
legend, 1801.

Bible stories. Equally fabulous was the retreat of
the Araucanians. It was a three-peaked mountain
which had the property of floating on water, called
Theg-Theg, the Thunderer. This they believed
would preserve them in the next as it did in the last
cataclysm, and as its only inconvenience was that it
approached too near the sun, they always kept on
hand wooden bowls to use as parasols.[1]

The intimate connection that once existed between
the myths of the deluge and those of the creation is
illustrated by the part assigned to birds in so many
of them. They fly to and fro over the waves ere any
land appears, though they lose in great measure the
significance of bringing it forth, attached to them in
the cosmogonies as emblems of the divine spirit.
The dove in the Hebrew account appears in that of
the Algonkins as a raven, which Michabo sent out
to search for land before the muskrat brought it to
him from the bottom. A raven also in the Athapascan myth saved their ancestors from the general
flood, and in this instance it is distinctly identified
with the mighty thunder bird, who at the beginning
ordered the earth from the depths. Prometheus-like,
it brought fire from heaven, and saved them from a
second death by cold.[2] Precisely the same beneficent actions were attributed by the Natchez to the
small red cardinal bird,[3] and by the Mandans and
Cherokees an active participation in the event was
assigned to wild pigeons. The Navajos and Aztecs
thought that instead of being drowned by the waters

[1] Molina, *Hist. of Chili*, ii. p. 82.
[2] Richardson, *Arctic Expedition*, p. 239.
[3] Dumont, *Mems. Hist. sur la Louisiane*, i. p. 163.

the human race were transformed into birds and thus escaped. In all these and similar legends, the bird is a relic of the cosmogonal myth which explained the origin of the world from the action of the winds, under the image of the bird, on the primeval ocean.

The Mexican Codex Vaticanus No. 3738 represents after the picture of the deluge a bird perched on the summit of a tree, and at its foot men in the act of marching. This has been interpreted to mean that after the deluge men were dumb until a dove distributed to them the gift of speech. The New Mexican tribes related that all except the leader of those who escaped to the mountains lost the power of utterance by terror,[1] and the Quichés that the antediluvian race were "puppets, men of wood, without intelligence or language." These stories, so closely resembling that of the confusion of tongues at the tower of Babel or Borsippa, are of doubtful authenticity. The first is an entirely erroneous interpretation, as has been shown by Señor Ramirez, director of the Museum of Antiquities at Mexico. The name of the bird in the Aztec tongue was identical with the word *departure*, and this is its signification in the painting.[2]

Stories of giants in the days of old, figures of mighty proportions looming up through the mist of ages, are common property to every nation. The Mexicans and Peruvians had them as well as others, but their connection with the legends of the flood and the creation is incidental and secondary. Were the case otherwise, it would offer no additional point

[1] Schoolcraft, *Ind. Tribes*, v. p. 686.

[2] Desjardins, *Le Pérou avant la Conq. Espagn.*, p. 27.

of similarity to the Hebrew myth, for the word rendered *giants* in the phrase, " and there were giants in
those days," has no such meaning in the original.
It is a blunder which crept into the Septuagint, and
has been cherished ever since, along with so many
others in the received text.

A few specimens will serve as examples of all these
American flood myths. The Abbé Brasseur has
translated one from the Codex Chimalpopoca, a work
in the Nahuatl language of Ancient Mexico, written
about half a century after the conquest. It is as
follows :—

" And this year was that of Ce-calli, and on the
first day all was lost. The mountain itself was submerged in the water, and the water remained tranquil
for fifty-two springs.

" Now towards the close of the year, Titlahuan
had forewarned the man named Nata and his wife
named Nena, saying, ' Make no more pulque, but
straightway hollow out a large cypress, and enter it
when in the month Tozoztli the water shall approach
the sky.' They entered it, and when Titlacahuan
had closed the door he said, ' Thou shalt eat but a
single ear of maize, and thy wife but one also.'

" As soon as they had finished [eating], they went
forth and the water was tranquil ; for the log did not
move any more ; and opening it they saw many fish.

" Then they built a fire, rubbing together pieces of
wood, and they roasted the fish. The gods Citlalli-
nicue and Citlallatonac looking below exclaimed,
' Divine Lord, what means that fire below? Why
do they they thus smoke the heavens? '

" Straightway descended Titlacahuan Tezcatlipoca,

and commenced to scold, saying, 'What is this fire doing here?' And seizing the fishes he moulded their hinder parts and changed their heads, and they were at once transformed into dogs." [1]

That found in the oft quoted legends of the Quichés is to this effect:—

"Then by the will of the Heart of Heaven the waters were swollen and a great flood came upon the manikins of wood. For they did not think nor speak of the Creator who had created them, and who had caused their birth. They were drowned, and a thick resin fell from heaven.

"The bird Xecotcovach tore out their eyes; the bird Camulatz cut off their heads; the bird Cotzbalam devoured their flesh; the bird Tecumbalam broke their bones and sinews, and ground them into powder." [2]

"Because they had not thought of their Mother and Father, the Heart of Heaven, whose name is Hurakan, therefore the face of the earth grew dark and a pouring rain commenced, raining by day, raining by night.

"Then all sorts of beings, little and great, gathered together to abuse the men to their faces; and all spoke, their mill-stones, their plates, their cups, their dogs, their hens.

"Said the dogs and hens, 'Very badly have you

[1] Cod. Chimalpopoca, in Brasseur, *Hist. du Mexique*, Pièces Justificatives.

[2] These four birds, whose names have lost their signification, represent doubtless the four winds, or the four rivers, which, as in so many legends, are the active agents in overwhelming the world in its great crises.

treated us, and you have bitten us. Now we bite you in turn.'

"Said the mill-stones, 'Very much were we tormented by you, and daily, daily, night and day, it was *squeak, squeak, screech, screech,* for your sake. Now yourselves shall feel our strength, and we will grind your flesh, and make meal of your bodies,' said the mill-stones. [1]

"And this is what the dogs said, 'Why did you not give us our food? No sooner did we come near than you drove us away, and the stick was always within reach when you were eating, because, forsooth, we were not able to talk. Now we will use our teeth and eat you,' said the dogs, tearing their faces.

"And the cups and dishes said, 'Pain and misery you gave us, smoking our tops and sides, cooking us over the fire, burning and hurting us as if we had no feeling. [2] Now it is your turn, and you shall burn,' said the cups insultingly.

"Then ran the men hither and thither in despair. They climbed to the roofs of the houses, but the houses crumbled under their feet; they tried to mount to the tops of the trees, but the trees hurled them far from them; they sought refuge in the caverns, but the caverns shut before them.

---

[1] The word rendered mill-stone, in the original means those larged hollowed stones on which the women were accustomed to bruise the maize. The imitative sounds for which I have substituted others in English, are in Quiché, *holi, holi, huqui, huqui.*

[2] Brasseur translates " quoique nous ne sentissions rien," but Ximenes " nos quemasteis, y sentimos el dolor." As far as I can make out the original, it is the negative conditional as I have given it in the text.

"Thus was accomplished the ruin of this race, destined to be destroyed and overthrown; thus were they given over to destruction and contempt. And it is said that their posterity are those little monkeys who live in the woods." [1]

The Algonkin tradition has often been referred to. Many versions of it are extant, the oldest and most authentic of which is that translated from the Montagnais dialect by Father Le Jeune, in 1634.

"One day as Messou was hunting, the wolves which he used as dogs entered a great lake and were detained there.

"Messou looking for them everywhere, a bird said to him, 'I see them in the middle of this lake.'

"He entered the lake to rescue them, but the lake overflowing its banks covered the land and destroyed the world.

"Messou, very much astonished at this, sent out the raven to find a piece of earth wherewith to rebuild the land, but the bird could find none; then he ordered the otter to dive for some, but the animal returned empty; at last he sent down the muskrat, who came back with ever so small a piece, which however was enough for Messou to form the land on which we are.

"The trees having lost their branches, he shot arrows at their naked trunks which became their limbs, revenged himself on those who had detained his wolves, and having married the muskrat, by it peopled the world."

Finally may be given the meagre legend of the

[1] *Le Livre Sacré*, p. 27; Ximenes, *Or. de los Indios*, p. 13.

Tupis of Brazil, as heard by Hans Staden, a prisoner among them about 1550, and Coreal, a later voyager. Their ancient songs relate that a long time ago a certain very powerful Mair, that is to say, a stranger, who bitterly hated their ancestors, compassed their destruction by a violent inundation. Only a very few succeeded in escaping—some by climbing trees, others in caves. When the water subsided the remnant came together, and by gradual increase populated the world. [1]

Or, it is given by an equally ancient authority as follows :—

" Monan, without beginning or end, author of all that is, seeing the ingratitude of men, and their contempt for him who had made them thus joyous, withdrew from them, and sent upon them *tata*, the divine fire, which burned all that was on the surface of the earth. He swept about the fire in such a way that in places he raised mountains, and in others dug valleys. Of all men one alone, Irin Magé, was saved, whom Monan carried into the heaven. He seeing

[1] The American nations among whom a distinct and well authenticated myth of the deluge was found are as follow : Athapascas, Algonkins, Iroquois, Cherokees, Chikasaws, Caddos, Natchez, Dakotas, Apaches, Navajos, Mandans, Pueblo Indians, Aztecs, Mixtecs, Zapotecs, Tlascalans, Mechoacans, Toltecs, Nahuas, Mayas, Quiches, Haitians, natives of Darien and Popoyan, Muyscas, Quichuas, Tuppinambas, Achaguas, Araucanians, and doubtless others. The article by M. de Charencey in the *Revue Américaine, Le Deluge, d'après les Traditions Indiennes de l'Amérique du Nord,* contains some valuable extracts, but is marred by lack of criticism of sources, and makes no attempt at analysis, nor offers for their existence a rational explanation.

all things destroyed, spoke thus to Monan : ' Wilt thou also destroy the heavens and their garniture? Alas ! henceforth where will be our home ? Why should I live, since there is none other of my kind ? ' Then Monan was so filled with pity that he poured a deluging rain on the earth which quenched the fire, and flowing from all sides, formed the ocean, which we called *parana*, the great waters." [1]

In these narratives I have not attempted to soften the asperities nor conceal the childishness which run through them. But there is no occasion to be astonished at these peculiarities, nor to found upon them any disadvantageous opinion of the mental powers of their authors and believers. We can go back to the cradle of our own race in Central Asia, and find traditions every whit as infantile. I cannot refrain from adding the earliest Aryan myth of the same great occurrence, as it is handed down to us in ancient Sanscrit literature. It will be seen that it is little, if at all, superior to those just rehearsed.

" Early in the morning they brought to Manu water to wash himself; when he had well washed, a fish came into his hands.

" It said to him these words : ' Take care of me; I will save thee.' ' What wilt thou save me from ? ' ' A deluge will sweep away all creatures ; I wish thee to escape.' ' But how shall I take care of thee ? '

" The fish said : ' While we are small there is more

---

[1] *Une Fête Brésilienne célèbre à Rouen en* 1550, *par M. Ferdinand Denis*, p. 82. The native words in this account guarantee its authenticity. In the Tupi language, *tata*, means fire ; *parana*, ocean ; Monan, from *moná* to construct, to build. The original authority is Thevet.

than one danger of death, for one fish swallows another. Thou must, in the first place, put me in a vase. Then, when I shall exceed it in size, thou must dig a deep ditch, and place me in it. When I grow too large for it, throw me in the sea, for I shall then be beyond the danger of death.'

"Soon it became a great fish; it grew, in fact, astonishingly. Then it said to Manu, 'In such a year the Deluge will come. Thou must build a vessel, and then pay me homage. When the waters of the Deluge mount up, enter the vessel. I will save thee.'

" When Manu had thus taken care of the fish, he put it in the sea. The same year that the fish had said, in this very year, having built the vessel, he paid the fish homage. Then the Deluge mounting, he entered the vessel. The fish swam near him. To its horn Manu fastened the ship's rope, with which the fish passed the Mountain of the North.

"The fish said: 'See! I have saved thee. Fasten the vessel to a tree, so that the water does not float thee onward when thou art on the mountain top. As the water decreases, thou wilt descend little by little.' Thus Manu descended gradually. Therefore to the mountain of the north remains the name, Descent of Manu. The Deluge had destroyed all creatures; Manu survived alone." [1]

Hitherto I have spoken only of the last convulsion which swept over the face of the globe, and of but one cycle which preceded the present. Most of the more savage tribes contented themselves with this,

---

[1] Professor Nève, *ubi supra*, from the Zatapatha Brahmana.

but it is instructive to observe how, as they advanced in culture, and the mind dwelt more intently on the great problems of Life and Time, they were impelled to remove further and further the dim and mysterious Beginning. The Peruvians imagined that *two* destructions had taken place, the first by a famine, the second by a flood—according to some a few only escaping—but, after the more widely accepted opinion, accompanied by the absolute extirpation of the race. Three eggs which dropped from heaven hatched out the present race; one of gold, from which came the priests; one of silver, which produced the warriors; and the last of copper, source of the common people.[1]

The Mayas of Yucatan increased the previous worlds by one, making the present the *fourth*. Two cycles had terminated by devastating plagues. They were called " the sudden deaths," for it was said so swift and mortal was the pest, that the buzzards and other foul birds dwelt in the houses of the cities, and ate the bodies of their former owners. The third closed either by a hurricane, which blew from all four of the cardinal points at once, or else, as others

[1] Avendano, *Sermones*, Lima, 1648, in Rivero and Tschudi, *Peruv. Antiqs.*, p. 114. In the year 1600, Oñate found on the coast of California a tribe whose idol held in one hand a shell containing three eggs, in the other an ear of maize, while before it was placed a cup of water. Vizcaino, who visited the same people a few years afterwards, mentions that they kept in their temples tame ravens, and looked upon them as sacred birds. (Torquemada, *Mon. Ind.*, lib. v. cap. 40 in Waitz). Thus, in all parts of the continent do we find the bird, as a symbol of the clouds, associated with the rains and the harvests.

said, by an inundation, which swept across the world, swallowing all things in its mountainous surges.[1]

As might be expected, the vigorous intellects of the Aztecs impressed upon this myth a fixity of outline nowhere else met with on the continent, and wove it intimately into their astrological reveries and religious theories. Unaware of its prevalence under more rudimentary forms throughout the continent, Alexander von Humboldt observed that, " of all the traits of analogy which can be pointed out between the monuments, manners, and traditions of Asia and America, the most striking is that offered by the Mexican mythology in the cosmogonical fiction of the periodical destructions and regenerations of the universe." [2] Yet it is but the same fiction that existed elsewhere, somewhat more definitely outlined. There exists great discrepancy between the different authorities, both as to the number of Aztec ages or Suns, as they were called, their durations, their terminations, and their names. The preponderance of testimony is in favor of *four* antecedent cycles, the present being the *fifth*. The interval from the first creation to the commencement of the present epoch, owing to the equivocal meaning of the numeral signs expressing it in the picture writings, may have been either 15228, 2316, or 1404 solar years. Why these

---

[1] The deluge was called *hun yecil*, which according to Cogolludo, means *the inundation of the trees*, for all the forests were swept away (*Hist. de Yucathan*, lib. iv. cap. 5). Bishop Landa adds, to substantiate the legend, that all the woods of the peninsula appear as if they had been planted at one time, and that to look at them one would say they had been trimmed with scissors. (*Rel. de las Cosas de Yucatan*, 58, 60.)

[2] *Vues des Cordillères*, p. 202.

numbers should have been chosen, no one has guessed. It has been looked for in combinations of numbers connected with the calendar, but so far in vain.

While most authorities agree as to the character of the destructions which terminated the suns, they vary much as to their sequence. Water, winds, fire, and hunger, are the agencies, and in one Codex (Vaticanus) occur in this order. Gama gives the sequence, hunger, winds, fire, and water; Humboldt, hunger, fire, winds, and water; Boturini, water, hunger, winds, fire. As the cycle ending by a famine is called the Age of Earth, Ternaux-Compans, the distinguished French *Américaniste*, has imagined that the four Suns correspond mystically to the domination exercised in turn over the world by its four constituent elements. But proof is wanting that Aztec philosophers knew the theory on which this explanation reposes.

Baron Humboldt suggested that the suns were "fictions of mythological astronomy, modified either by obscure reminiscences of some great revolution suffered by our planet, or by physical hypotheses, suggested by the sight of marine petrifactions and fossil remains;" [1] while the Abbé Brasseur, in his works on ancient Mexico, interprets them as exaggerated references to historical or geological events. As no solution can be accepted not equally applicable to the same myth as it appears in Yucatan, Peru, and the hunting tribes, and to the parallel teachings of the Voluspa, the Stoics, the Celts, and the Brahmans, both of these must be rejected.

[1] Ubi sup., p. 207.

And although the Hindoo legend is so close to the Aztec that it, too, defined four ages, each terminating by a general catastrophe, and each catastrophe exactly the same in both,[1] yet this is not at all indicative of a derivation from one original, but simply an illustration how the human mind, under the stimulus of the same intellectual cravings, produces like results. What the cravings are has already been shown.

The reason for adopting four ages, thus making the present the fifth, probably arose from the sacredness of that number in general; but directly, because this was the number of secular days in the Mexican week. A parallel is offered by the Hebrew narative. In it six epochs or days precede the seventh or present cycle, in which the creative power rests. This latter corresponded to the Jewish Sabbath, the day of repose; and in the Mexican calendar each fifth day was also a day of repose, employed in marketing and pleasure.

Doubtless the theory of the Ages of the world was long in vogue among the Aztecs before it received the definite form in which we now have it; and as this was acquired long after the calendar was fixed, it is every way probable that the latter was used as a guide to the former. Echevarria, a good authority on such matters, says the number of the Suns was agreed upon at a congress of astrologers,

---

[1] At least this is the doctrine of one of the Shastas. The race, it teaches, has been destroyed four times; first by water, secondly by winds, thirdly the earth swallowed them, and lastly fire consumed them. (Sepp, *Heidenthum und Christenthum*, i. p. 191.)

within the memory of a tradition.[1] Now in the calendar, these signs occur in the order, earth, air, water, fire, corresponding to the days distinguished by the symbols house, rabbit, reed, and flint, This sequence, commencing with Tochtli (rabbit, air), is that given as that of the Suns in the Codex Chimalpopoca, translated by Brasseur, though it seems a taint of European teaching when it is added that on the *seventh* day of the creation man was formed.[2]

Neither Jews nor Aztecs, nor indeed any American nation, appear to have supposed, with some of the old philosophers, that the present was an exact repetition of previous cycles,[3] but rather that each was an improvement on the preceding, a step in endless progress. Nor did either connect these beliefs with astronomical reveries of a great year, defined by the return of the heavenly bodies to one relative position in the heavens. The latter seems characteristic of the realism of Europe, the former of the idealism of the Orient; both inconsistent with the meagre astronomy and more scanty metaphysics of the red race.

The expectation of the end of the world is a natural complement to the belief in its periodical destructions. As at certain times past the equipoise of

[1] Echevarria y Veitia, *Hist. de la Nueva España*, lib. i. cap. 4, in Waitz.

[2] Brasseur, *Hist. du Mexique*, iii. p. 495.

[3] The contrary has indeed been inferred from such expressions of the writer of the book of Ecclesiastes as, " that which hath been is now, and that which is to be, hath already been " (chap. iii. 15), and the like, but they are susceptible of an application entirely subjective.

nature was lost, and the elements, breaking the chain of laws that bound them, ran riot over the universe, involving all life in one mad havoc and desolation, so in the future we have to expect that day of doom, when the ocean tides shall obey no shore, but overwhelm the continents with their mountainous billows or the fire, now chafing in volcanic craters and smoking springs, will leap forth on the forests and grassy meadows, wrapping all things in a winding sheet of flame, and melting the very elements with fervid heat. Then, in the language of the Norse prophetess, "shall the sun grow dark, the land sink in the waters, the bright stars be quenched, and high flames climb heaven itself." [1] These fearful forebodings have cast their shadow on every literature. The seeress of the north does but paint in wilder colors the terrible pictures of Seneca,[2] and the sibyl of the capitol only re-echoes the inspired predictions of Malachi. Well has the Christian poet said:—

> Dies iræ, dies illâ,
> Solvet sæclum in favillâ,
> Teste David cum Sibylâ.

Savage races, isolated in the impenetrable forests of another continent, could not escape this fearful looking for of destruction to come. It oppressed their souls like a weight of lead. On the last night of each cycle of fifty-two years, the Aztecs extinguished every fire, and proceeded, in solemn procession, to some sacred spot. Then the priests, with awe and trembling, sought to kindle a new fire by

---

[1] Voluspa, xiv. 51.
[2] *Natur. Quæstiones*, iii. cap. 27.

friction. Momentous was the endeavor, for did it fail, their fathers had taught them on the morrow no sun would rise, and darkness, death, and the waters would descend forever on this beautiful world. Quetzalcoatl, he who had made it, would destroy it.[1]

The same terror inspired the Peruvians at every eclipse, for some day, taught the Amautas, the shadow will veil the sun forever, and land, moon, and stars will be wrapt in a devouring conflagration to know no regeneration; or a drought will wither every herb of the field, suck up the waters, and leave the race to perish to the last creature; or the moon will fall from her place in the heavens and involve all things in her own ruin, a figure of speech meaning that the waters would submerge the land.[2] In that dreadful day, thought the Algonkins, when in anger Michabo will send a mortal pestilence to destroy the nations, or, stamping his foot on the ground, flames will burst forth to consume the habitable land, only a pair, or only, at most, those who have maintained inviolate the institutions he ordained, will he protect and preserve to inhabit the new world he will then fabricate. Therefore they do not speak of this catastrophe as the end of the world, but use one of those nice grammatical distinctions so frequent in American aboriginal languages, and which can only be imitated, not interpreted, in ours,

[1] *Codex Tell.-Remensis*, p. 199. Such expressions should place beyond all doubt the purely mythical character of Quetzalcoatl.

[2] Velasco, *Hist. du Royaume du Quito*, p. 105; Navarrete, *Viages*, iii. p. 444.

signifying " when it will be near its end," " when it will no longer be available for man." [1]

An ancient prophecy handed down from their ancestors warns the Winnebagoes that their nation shall be annihilated at the close of the thirteenth generation. Ten have already passed, and that now living has appointed ceremonies to propitiate the powers of heaven, and mitigate its stern decree.[2] Well may they be about it, for there is a gloomy probability that the warning came from no false prophet. Few tribes were destitute of such presentiments. The Chikasaws, the Mandans of the Missouri, the Pueblo Indians of New Mexico, the Muyscas of Bogota, the Botocudos of Brazil, the Araucanians of Chili, have been asserted on testimony that leaves no room for scepticism, to have entertained such forebodings from immemorial time. Enough for the purpose if the list is closed with the prediction of a Maya priest, cherished by the inhabitants of Yucatan long before the Spaniard desolated their stately cities. It is one of those preserved by Father Lizana, curé of Itzamal, and of which he gives the original. Other witnesses inform us that this nation " had a tradition that the world would end," [3] and probably, like the Greeks and Aztecs, they supposed the gods would perish with it.

> " At the close of the ages, it hath been decreed,
>   Shall perish and vanish each weak god of men,
>   And the world shall be purged with a ravening fire.

---

[1] *Rel. de la Nouv. France*, An. 1637, p. 54. Schoolcraft, *Ind. Tribes*, i. p. 319, iv. p. 420.

[2] Schoolcraft, ibid., iv. p. 240.

[3] Cogolludo, *Hist. de Yucathan*, lib. iv. cap. 7.

Happy the man in that terrible day,
Who bewails with contrition the sins of his life,[1]
And meets without flinching the fiery ordeal."

[1] The Spanish of Lizana is—

> " En la ultima edad, segun esta determinado,
> Avra fin el culto de dioses vanos ;
> Y el mundo sera purificado con fuego.
> El que esto viere sera llamado dichoso
> Si con dolor lloraré sus pecados."

(*Hist. de Nuestra Señora de Itzamal*, in Brasseur, *Hist. du Mexique*, ii. p. 603.) I have attempted to obtain a more literal rendering from the original Maya, but have not been successful.

CHAPTER VIII.

THE ORIGIN OF MAN.

Usually man is the EARTH-BORN, both in language and myths.—Illustrations from the legends of the Caribs, Apalachians, Iroquois, Quichuas, Aztecs, and others.—The underworld.—Man the product of one of the primal creative powers, the Spirit, or the Water, in the myths of the Athapascas, Eskimos, Moxos, and others.—Never literally derived from an inferior species.

NO man can escape the importunate question, whence am I? The first replies framed to meet it possess an interest to the thoughtful mind, beyond that of mere fables. They illustrate the position in creation claimed by our race, and the early workings of self-consciousness. Often the oldest terms for man are synopses of these replies, and merit a more than passing contemplation.

The seed is hidden in the earth. Warmed by the sun, watered by the rain, presently it bursts its dark prison-house, unfolds its delicate leaves, blossoms, and matures its fruit. Its work done, the earth draws it to itself again, resolves the various structures into their original mould, and the unending round recommences.

This is the marvellous process that struck the primitive mind. Out of the Earth rises life, to it it returns. She it is who guards all germs, nourishes all beings. The Aztecs painted her as a woman with countless breasts, the Peruvians called her Mama Allpa, *mother* Earth; in the Algonkin tongue the words for earth, mother, father, are from the same

root.[1]   *Homo, Adam, chamaigenēs,* what do all these
words mean but the earth-born, the son of the soil,
repeated in the poetic language of Attica in *anthropos,*
he who springs up as a flower ?

The word that corresponds to the Latin *homo* in
American languages has such singular uniformity in
so many of them that we might be tempted to regard
it as a fragment of some ancient and common tongue,
their parent stem.   In the Eskimo it is *inuk, innuk,*
plural *innuit ;* in Athapasca it is *dinni, tenné ;* in Algonkin, *inini, lenni, inwi ;* in Iroquois, *onwi, eniha ;*
in the Otomi of Mexico *n-aniche ;* in the Maya, *inic,
winic, winak ;* all in North America, and the number might be extended.   Of these only the last mentioned can plausibly be traced to a radical (unless
the Iroquois *onwi* is from *onnha* life, *onnhe* to live).
This Father Ximenes derives from *win,* meaning to
grow, to gain, to increase,[2] in which the analogy to
vegetable life is not far off, an analogy strengthened
by the myth of that stock which relates that the first
of men were formed of the flour of maize.[3]

[1] See Mr. Trumbull's note to Roger Williams' *Key into the
Languages of America,* p. 56.

[2] *Vocabulario Quiche,* s. v., ed. Brasseur, Paris, 1862.

[3] The Eskimo *innuk,* man, means also a possessor or owner ;
the yelk of an egg ; and the pus of an abscess (Egede, *Nachrichten von Grönland,* p. 106).   From it is derived *innuwok,* to
live, life.   Probably *innuk* also means the *semen masculinum,*
and in its identification with pus, may not there be the solution
of that strange riddle which in so many myths of the West In-
dies and Central America makes the first of men to be " the
purulent one?"   (See ante, p. 141.)   *Miniw* in Otchipwe means
" I have a running abscess, " and also " I bring forth, I produce,
beget."   Baraga, *Otchipwe Dict.* s. v.

In many other instances religious legend carries out this idea. The mythical ancestor of the Caribs created his offspring by sowing the soil with stones or with the fruit of the Mauritius palm, which sprouted forth into men and women,[1] while the Yurucares, much of whose mythology was perhaps borrowed from the Peruvians, clothed this crude tenet in a somewhat more poetic form, fabling that at the beginning the first of men were pegged, Ariel-like, in the knotty entrails of an enormous bole, until the god Tiri—a second Prospero—released them by cleaving it in twain.[2]

As in oriental legends the origin of man from the earth was veiled under the story that he was the progeny of some mountain fecundated by the embrace of Mithras or Jupiter, so the Indians often pointed to some height or some cavern, as the spot whence the first of men issued, adult and armed, from the womb of the All-mother Earth. The oldest name of the Alleghany Mountains is Pacmotinck or Pemolnick, an Algonkin word, the meaning of which is said to be " the origin of the Indians." [3]

---

[1] Müller, *Amer. Urrelig.*, pp. 109, 229.

[2] D'Orbigny, *Frag. d'une Voy. dans l'Amér. Mérid.*, p. 512. It is still a mooted point whence Shakspeare drew the plot of The Tempest. The coincidence mentioned in the text between some parts of it and South American mythology does not stand alone. Caliban, the savage and brutish native of the island, is undoubtedly the word Carib, often spelt Caribani, and Calibani in older writers ; and his " dam's god Setebos " was the supreme divinity of the Patagonians when first visited by Magellan. (Pigafetta, *Viaggio intorno al Globo*, Germ. Trans.: Gotha, 1801, p. 247.)

[3] Both Lederer and John Bartram assign it this meaning.

The Witchitas, who dwelt on the Red River among the mountains named after them, have a tradition that their progenitors issued from the rocks about their homes;[1] the Blackfoot legends point for the origin of their clans to Nina Stahu, " chief of mountains," a bold square-topped peak of the Rocky mountains near the great inland lake Omaxeen ; and many other tribes, the Takahlis, Navajos, Coyoteras, and the Haitians, for instance, set up this claim to be autochthones. Most writers have interpreted this simply to mean that they know nothing at all about their origin, or that they coined these fables merely to strengthen the title to the territory they inhabited when they saw the whites eagerly snatching it away on every pretext. No doubt there is some truth in this, but if they be carefully sifted, there is sometimes a deep historical significance in these myths, which has hitherto escaped the observation of students. An instance presents itself in our own country.

All those tribes, the Creeks, Seminoles, Choctaws, Chicasaws, and Natchez, who, according to tradition, were in remote times banded into one common confederacy, unanimously located their earliest ancestry near an artificial eminence in the valley of the Big Black River, in the Natchez country, whence they pretended to have emerged. Fortunately we have a description, though a brief one, of this interesting monument from the pen of an intelligent trav-

Gallatin gives in the Powhatan dialect the word for mountain as *pomottinke*, doubtless another form of the same.

[1] Marcy, *Exploration of the Red River*, p. 69.

eller. It is described as "an elevation of earth about half a mile square and fifteen or twenty feet high. From its northeast corner a wall of equal height extends for near half a mile to the high land." This was the Nunne Chaha or Nunne Hamgeh, the High Hill, or the Bending Hill (properly Nanih waiya, sloping hill), famous in Choctaw stories, and which Captain Gregg found they have not yet forgotten in their western home. The legend was that in its centre was a cave, the house of the Master of Breath. Here he made the first men from the clay around him, and as at that time the waters covered the earth, he raised the wall to dry them on. When the soft mud had hardened into elastic flesh and firm bone, he banished the waters to their channels and beds, and gave the dry land to his creatures.[1]

A parallel to this southern legend occurs among the Six Nations of the north. They with one consent, if we may credit the account of Cusic, looked to a mountain near the falls of the Oswego River in the State of New York, as the locality where their forefathers first saw the light of day, and that they had some such legend the name Oneida, people of the Stone, would seem to testify.

[1] Compare Romans, *Hist. of Florida*, pp. 58, 71; Adair, *Hist. of the North Am. Indians*, p. 195; and Gregg, *Commerce of the Pra'ries*, ii. p. 235. The description of the mound is by Major Heart, in the *Trans. of the Am. Philos. Soc.*, iii. p. 216. (1st series.) The Muskokees call this mountain *rvne-em-mekko*, King of mountains, and *ekvnvlwe-em-mekko*, King of the land or of the world. In its summit was located "the mouth of the earth," and from it "a great fire blazed upward and made a singing noise." See D. G. Brinton, *The National Legend of the Chahta Muskokee Tribes*, pp. 7, 10.

The cave of Pacari Tampu, the Lodgings of the Dawn, or the Place of Birth, was five leagues distant from Cuzco, surrounded by a sacred grove and inclosed with temples of great antiquity. From its hallowed recesses the mythical civilizers of Peru, the first of men, emerged, and in it during the time of the flood, the remnants of the race escaped the fury of the waves.[1] Viracocha himself is said to have dwelt there, though it hardly needed this evidence to render it certain that this consecrated cavern is but a localization of the general myth of the dawn rising from the deep. It refers us for its prototype to the Quichua allegory of the morning light flinging its beams like snow-white foam athwart the waves of Lake Titicaca.

An ancient legend of the Aztecs derived their nation from a place called Chicomoztoc, the Seven Caverns, located north of Mexico. Antiquaries have indulged in all sorts of speculations as to what this means. Sahagun explains it as a valley so named; Clavigero supposes it to have been a city ; Hamilton Smith, and after him Schoolcraft, construed caverns to be a figure of speech for the *boats* in which the early Americans paddled across from Asia (!) ; the Abbé Brasseur confounds it with Aztlan, and very many have discovered in it a distinct reference to the fabulous " seven cities of Cibola " and the Casas Grandes, ruins of large buildings of unburnt brick in the valley of the River Gila. From this story arose the supposed sevenfold division of the Nahuas, a division which never existed except in the imagina-

[1] Balboa, *Hist. du Pérou*, p. 4.

tion of Europeans. When Torquemada adds that *seven* hero gods ruled in Chicomoztoc and were the progenitors of all its inhabitants, when one of them turns out to be Xelhua, the giant who with six others escaped the flood by ascending the mountain of Tlaloc in the terrestrial paradise and afterwards built the pyramid of Cholula, and when we remember that in one of the flood-myths *seven* persons were said to have escaped the waters; further, when we find in Quiché legend the parallel story of Tulanzu, the Seven Caverns, from which proceeded the four primeval men, the four winds,[1] the whole narrative acquires a fabulous aspect that shuts it out from history, and brands it as one of those fictions of the origin of man from the earth so common to the race. Fictions, yet truths; for caverns and hollow trees were in fact the houses and temples of our first parents, and from them they went forth to conquer and adorn the world; and from the inorganic constituents of the soil acted on by Light, touched by Divine Force, vivified by the Spirit, did in reality the first of men proceed.

This cavern, which thus dimly lingered in the memories of nations, occasionally expanded to a nether world imagined to underlie this of ours, and still inhabited by beings of our kind, who have never been lucky enough to discover its exit. The Mandans and Minnetarees on the Missouri River supposed this exit was near a certain hill in their territory, and as it had been, as it were, the womb of the earth, the same power was attributed to it that in ancient times endowed various shrines with such charms; and thither

---

[1] Ximenes, *Or. de los Indios*, p. 186.

the barren wives of their nation made frequent pilgrimages when they would become mothers.[1] The Mandans added the somewhat puerile fable that the means of ascent had been a grapevine, by which many ascended and descended, until one day an immoderately fat old lady, anxious to get a look at the upper earth, broke it with her weight, and prevented any further communication.

Such tales of an under-world are very frequent among the Indians, and are a very natural outgrowth of the literal belief that the race is earth-born.

Man is indeed like the grass that springs up and soon withers away; but he is also more than this. The quintessence of dust, he is a son of the gods as well as a son of the soil. He is the direct product of the great creative power; therefore all the Athapascan tribes west of the Rocky Mountains—the Kenai, the Kolushes, and the Atnai—claim descent from a raven—from that same mighty cloud-bird who in the beginning of things seized the elements and brought the world from the abyss of the primitive ocean. Those of the same stock situate more eastwardly, the Dogribs, the Chepewyans, the Hare Indians, and also the west coast Eskimos, and the natives of the Aleutian Isles, all believe that they have sprung from a dog.[2] The latter animal, we have already seen, both in the old and new world was a frequent symbol of the water goddess. Therefore in these myths, which are found over so many thousand

[1] Long's *Expedition to the Rocky Mountains*, i. p. 274 ; Catlin's *Letters*, i. p. 178.

[2] Richardson, *Arctic Expedition*, pp. 239, 247; Klemm, *Culturgeschichte der Menschheit*, ii. p. 316.

square leagues, we cannot be in error in perceiving a reflex of their cosmogonical traditions already discussed, in which from the winds and the waters, represented here under their emblems of the bird and the dog, all animate life proceeded.

Without this symbolic coloring, a tribe to the south of them, a band of the Minnetarees, had the crude tradition that their first progenitor emerged from the waters, bearing in his hand an ear of maize,[1] very much as Viracocha and his companions rose from the sacred waves of Lake Titicaca, or as the Moxos imagined that they were descended from the lakes and rivers on whose banks their villages were situated.

These myths, and many others, hint of general conceptions of life and the world, wide-spread theories of ancient date, such as we are not accustomed to expect among savage nations, such as may very excusably excite a doubt as to their native origin, but a doubt infallibly dispelled by a careful comparison of the best authorities. Is it that hitherto, in the pride of intellectual culture, we have never done justice to the thinking faculty of those whom we call barbarians? Or shall we accept the only other alternative, that these are the unappreciated heirlooms bequeathed a rude race by a period of higher civilization, long since extinguished by constant wars and ceaseless fear? We are not yet ready to answer these questions. For a long time the latter was accepted as the true solution, but rather from the pre-

---

[1] Long, *Exped. to the Rocky Mountains*, i. p. 326. A more recent version is given by Dr. W. Matthews, *Hidatsa Grammar*, p. 17.

conceived theory of a state of primitive civilization from which man fell, than from ascertained facts.

It would, perhaps, be pushing symbolism too far to explain as an emblem of the primitive waters the coyote, which, according to the Root-Diggers of California, brought their ancestors into the world ; or the wolf, which the Lenni Lenape pretended released mankind from the dark bowels of the earth by scratching away the soil. They should rather be interpreted by the curious custom of the Toukaways, a wild people in Texas, of predatory and unruly disposition. They celebrate their origin by a grand annual dance. One of them, naked as he was born, is buried in the earth. The others, clothed in wolf-skins, walk over him, snuff around him, howl in lupine style, and finally dig him up with their nails. The leading wolf then solemnly places a bow and arrow in his hands, and to his inquiry as to what he must do for a living paternally advises him "to do as the wolves do —rob, kill, and murder, rove from place to place, and never cultivate the soil." [1] Most wise and fatherly counsel! But what is there new under the sun? Three thousand years ago the Hirpini, or Wolves, an ancient Sabine tribe, were wont to collect on Mount Soracte, and there go through certain rites in memory of an oracle which predicted their extinction when they ceased to gain their living as wolves by violence and plunder. Therefore they dressed in wolf-skins, ran with barks and howls over burning coals, and gnawed wolfishly whatever they could seize.[2]

[1] Schoolcraft, *Ind. Tribes,* v. p. 683.
[2] Schwarz, *Ursprung der Mythologie,* p. 121.

Though hasty writers have often said that the Indian tribes claim literal descent from different wild
beasts, probably in all other instances, as in these,
this will prove, on examination, to be an error rest-
ing on a misapprehension arising from the habit of
the natives of adopting as their totem or clan-mark
the figure and name of some animal, or else, in an
ignorance of the animate symbols employed with
such marked preference by the red race to express
abstract ideas. In some cases, doubtless, the natives
themselves came, in time, to confound the symbol
with the idea, by that familiar process of personification and consequent debasement exemplified in the
history of every religion; but I do not believe that
a single example could be found where an Indian
tribe had a tradition whose real purport was that
man came by natural process of descent from an
ancestor, a brute.

The reflecting mind will not be offended at the
contradictions in these different myths, for a myth is,
in one sense, a theory of natural phenomena expressed in the form of a narrative. Often several
explanations seem equally satisfactory for the same
fact, and the mind hesitates to choose, and rather
accepts them all than reject any. Then, again, an
expression current as a metaphor by-and-by crystal-
lizes into a dogma, and becomes the nucleus of a new
mythological growth. These are familiar processes
to one versed in such studies, and involve no logical
contradiction, because they are never required to be
reconciled.

CHAPTER IX.

THE SOUL AND ITS DESTINY.

Universality of the belief in a soul and a future state shown by the aboriginal tongues, by expressed opinions, and by sepulchral rites.—The future world never a place of rewards and punishments.—The house of the Sun the heaven of the red man.—The terrestrial paradise and the underworld.—Cupay.—Xibalba.—Mictlan.—Metempsychosis ?—Belief in a resurrection of the dead almost universal.

THE missionary Charlevoix wrote several excellent works on America toward the beginning of the last century, and he is often quoted by later authors; but probably no one of his sayings has been thus honored more frequently than this: " The belief the best established among our Americans is that of the immortality of the soul."[1] The tremendous stake that every one of us has on the truth of this dogma makes it quite a satisfaction to be persuaded that no man is willing to live wholly without it. Certainly exceptions are very rare, and most of those which materialistic philosophers have taken such pains to collect, rest on misunderstandings or superficial observation.

In the new world I know of only one well authenticated instance where all notion of a future state appears to have been entirely wanting, and this in quite a small clan, the Lower Pend d'Oreilles, of

[1] *Journal Historique*, p. 351: Paris, 1740.

Oregon. This people had no burial ceremonies, no notion of a life hereafter, no word for soul, spiritual existence, or vital principle. They thought that when they died, that was the last of them. The Catholic missionaries who undertook the unpromising task of converting them to Christianity, were at first obliged to depend upon the imperfect translations of half-breed interpreters. These " made the idea of soul intelligible to their hearers by telling them they had a gut which never rotted, and that this was their living principle!" Yet even they were not destitute of religious notions. No tribe was more addicted to the observance of charms, omens, dreams, and guardian spirits, and they believed that illness and bad luck generally were the effects of the anger of a fabulous old woman.[1] The aborigines of the Californian peninsula were as near beasts as men ever become. The missionaries likened them to " herds of swine, who neither worshipped the true and only God, nor adored false deities." Yet they must have had some vague notion of an after-world, for the writer who paints the darkest picture of their condition remarks, " I saw them frequently putting shoes on the feet of the dead, which seems to indicate that they entertain the idea of a journey after death."[2]

[1] *Rep. of the Commissioner of Ind. Affairs*, 1854, pp. 211, 212. The old woman is once more a personification of the water and the moon.

[2] Bægert, *Acc. of the Aborig. Tribes of the Californian Peninsula*, translated by Chas. Rau, in Ann. Rep. Smithson. Inst., 1866, p. 387. The custom recalls the *Todtenschuhe* which the ancient Germans placed on corpses " because they make a long journey." See Holtzmann, *Deutsche Mythologie*, s. 205.

Proof of Charlevoix's opinion may be derived from three independent sources. The aboriginal languages may be examined for terms corresponding to the word soul, the opinions of the Indians themselves may be quoted, and the significance of sepulchral rites as indicative of a belief in life after death may be determined.

The most satisfactory is the first of these. *We* call the soul a ghost or spirit, and often a shade. In these words, the *breath* and the *shadow* are the sensuous perceptions transferred to represent the immaterial object of our thought. Why the former was chosen, I have already explained ; and for the latter, that it is man's intangible image, his constant companion, and is of a nature akin to darkness, earth, and night, are sufficiently obvious reasons.

These same tropes recur in American languages in the same connection. The Choctaw belief was that each man has an outside shadow, *shilombish*, and an inside shadow, *shilup*, both of which survive his decease. The New England tribes called the soul *chemung*, the shadow, and in Quiché *natub*, in Eskimo *tarnak*, express both these ideas. In the several Costa-Rican dialects, the Brunka, the Bri-bri, the Cabecar and the Tiribi, the root of the words for ghost, shadow, spirit, is the same.[1] In Mohawk *atonritz* the soul, is from *atonrion*, to breathe, and other examples to the same purpose have already been given.[2]

---

[1] Gabb, Ind. Tribes, and Langs. of Costa Rica, p. 538.

[2] Of the Nicaraguans Oviedo says : " Ce n'est pas leur cœur qui va en haut, mais ce qui les faisait vivre ; c'est-à-dire, le souffle qui leur sort par la bouche, et que l'on nomme *Julio*"

Of course no one need demand that a strict immateriality be attached to these words. Such a colorless negative abstraction never existed for them, neither does it for us, though we delude ourselves into believing that it does. The soul was to them the invisible man, material as ever, but lost to the appreciation of the senses.

Nor let any one be astonished if its unity was doubted, and several supposed to reside in one body. This is nothing more than a somewhat gross form of a doctrine upheld by most creeds and most philosophies. It seems the readiest solution of certain psychological enigmas, and may, for aught we know, be an instinct of fact. The Rabbis taught a threefold division—*nephesh*, the animal, *ruah*, the human, and *neshamah*, the divine soul, which corresponds to that of Plato into *thumos*, *epithumia*, and *nous*. And even Saint Paul seems to have recognized such inherent plurality when he distinguishes between the bodily soul, the intellectual soul, and the spiritual gift, in his Epistle to the Romans. No such refinements of course as these are to be expected among the red men ; but it may be looked upon either as the rudiments of these teachings, or as a gradual debasement of them to gross and material expression, that an old and wide-spread notion was found among both Iroquois and Algonkins, that man has two souls, one of

(*Hist. du Nicaragua*, p. 36). The word should be *yulia*, kindred with *yoli*, to live. (Buschmann, *Uber die Aztekischen Ortsnamen*, p. 765.) In the Aztec and cognate languages we have already seen that *ehecatl* means both *wind*, *soul*, and *shadow* (Buschmann, *Spuren der Aztek. Spr. in Nördlichen Mexico*, p. 74).

a vegetative character, which gives bod
remains with the corpse after death, unt
to enter another body; another of more etherear ....
ure, which in life can depart from the body in sleep
or trance, and wander over the world, and at death
goes directly to the land of Spirits.[1]

The Sioux extended it to Plato's number, and are
said to have looked forward to one going to a cold
place, another to a warm and comfortable country,
while the third was to watch the body. Certainly a
most impartial distribution of rewards and punishments.[2] Some other Dakota tribes shared their views
on this point, but more commonly, doubtless, owing
to the sacredness of the number, imagined *four* souls,
with separate destinies, one to wander about the
world, one to watch the body, the third to hover
around the village, and the highest to go to the spirit
land.[3] Even this number is multiplied by certain
Oregon tribes, who imagine one in every member;
and by the Caribs of Martinique, who, wherever they
could detect a pulsation, located a spirit, all subordinate, however, to a supreme one throned in the
heart, which alone would be transported to the
skies at death.[4] For the heart that so constantly
sympathizes with our emotions and actions is, in
most languages and most nations, regarded as the
seat of life; and when the priests of bloody religions

---

[1] *Rel. de la Nouv. France,* An. 1636, p. 104; " Keating's *Narrative,*" i. pp. 232, 410.

[2] French, *Hist. Colls. of Louisiana,* iii. p. 26.

[3] Mrs. Eastman, *Legends of the Sioux,* p. 129.

[4] *Voy. à la Louisiane fait en* 1720, p. 155: Paris, 1768.

tore out the heart of the victim and offered it to the
idol, it was an emblem of the life that was thus torn
from the field of this world and consecrated to the
rulers of the next.   In many of the native tongues
the compound words formed with its name indicate
that various emotions and feelings were supposed to
arise from its conditions.[1]

The seat of the soul was variously located, however.   The Costa-Ricans place to this day the powers of thought and memory in the liver;[2] and a
Thlinkeet legend, quoted by Mr. Bancroft, who com-
ments on its obscurity,[3] relates that the first of all
men came into being " when the liver came out from
below," showing that this tribe also regarded that
gland as the seat of life.   Most usually the head
was regarded as the vital member.   Roger Williams
remarks of the New England Indians: " In the
braine their opinion is that the soule keeps her chiefe
seate and residence." [4] By an easy metonymy, exemplified in all the classical languages, the head represents
the man, and in this meaning appears in the picture
writing, in the usage of preserving heads and
skulls, and in the custom of scalping which was
encountered by the early explorers in both North and
South America.

Various motives impel the living to treat with
respect the body from which life has departed.
Lowest of them is a superstitious dread of death and

---

[1] See for example Matthews' *Hidatsa Dict.* s. v. *d'ati;* Baraga,
Otchipwe Dict. s. v. *Heart.*

[2] Gabb, *Ind. Tribes and Langs. of Costa Rica*, p. 538.

[3] *Native Races of the Pacific States*, vol. iii, p. 102.

[4] *Key into the Langs. of Am.*, p. 77.

the dead. The stoicism of the Indian, especially the northern tribes, in the face of death, has often been the topic of poets, and has often been interpreted to be a fearlessness of that event. This is by no means true. Savages have an awful horror of death ; it is to them the worst of ills ; and for this very reason was it that they thought to meet it without flinching was the highest proof of courage. Everything connected with the deceased was, in many tribes, shunned with superstitious terror. His name was not mentioned, his property left untouched, all reference to him was sedulously avoided. A Tupi tribe used to hurry the body at once to the nearest water, and toss it in ; the Arkanzas left it in the lodge and burned over it the dwelling and contents ; and the Algonkins carried it forth by a hole cut opposite the door, and beat the walls with sticks to fright away the lingering ghost. Burying places were always avoided, and every means taken to prevent the departed spirits exercising a malicious influence on those remaining behind.

These craven fears do but reveal the natural repugnance of the animal to a cessation of existence, and arise from the instinct of self-preservation essential to organic life. Other rites, undertaken avowedly for the behoof of the soul, prove and illustrate a simple but unshaken faith in its continued existence after the decay of the body.

None of these is more common or more natural than that which attributes to the emancipated spirit the same wants that it felt while on earth, and with loving foresight provides for their satisfaction. Clothing and utensils of war and the chase were, in

ancient times, uniformly placed by the body, under
the impression that they would be of service to the
departed in his new home. Some few tribes in the
far west still retain the custom, but most were
soon ridiculed into its neglect, or were forced
to omit it by the violation of tombs practised by
depraved whites in hope of gain. To these harmless
offerings the northern tribes often added a dog slain
on the grave; and doubtless the skeletons of these
animals in so many tombs in Mexico and Peru point
to similar customs there. It had no deeper meaning
than to give a companion to the spirit in its long
and lonesome journey to the far off land of shades.
The peculiar appropriateness of the dog arose not
only from the guardianship it exerts during life, but
further from the symbolic signification it so often
had as representative of the goddess of night and the
grave.

Where a despotic form of government reduced the
subject almost to the level of a slave and elevated
the ruler almost to that of a superior being, not
animals only, but men, women, and children were
frequently immolated at the tomb of the cacique.
The territory embraced in our own country was not
without examples of this custom. On the lower
Mississippi, the Natchez Indians practised it in all its
ghastliness. When a sun or chief died, one or several of his wives and his highest officers were knocked
on the head and buried with him, and at such times
the barbarous privilege was allowed to any of the
lowest caste to at once gain admittance to the highest
by the murder of their own children on the funeral
pyre—a privilege which respectable writers tell us

human beings were found base enough to take advantage of.[1]

Oviedo relates that in the province of Guataro, in Guatemala, an actual rivalry prevailed among the people to be slain at the death of their cacique, for they had been taught that only such as went with him would ever find their way to the paradise of the departed.[2] Theirs was therefore somewhat of a selfish motive, and only in certain parts of Peru, where polygamy prevailed, and the rule was that only one wife was to be sacrificed, does the deportment of husbands seem to have been so creditable that their widows disputed one with another for the pleasure of being buried alive with the dead body, and bearing their spouse company to the other world.[3] Wives who have found few parallels since the famous matron of Ephesus !

The fire built nightly on the grave was to light the spirit on its journey. By a coincidence to be explained by the universal sacredness of the number, both Algonkins and Mexicans maintained it for *four* nights consecutively. The former related the tradition that one of their ancestors returned from the spirit land and informed their nation that the journey thither consumed just *four* days, and that collecting fuel every night added much to the toil and fatigue the soul encountered, all of which could be spared

[1] Dupratz, *Hist. of Louisiana*, ii. p. 119; Dumont, *Mems. Hist. sur la Louisiane*, i. chap. 26.

[2] *Rel. de la Prov. de Cueba*, p. 140.

[3] Coreal, *Voiages aux Indes Occidentals*, ii. p. 94: Amsterdam, 1722.

it by the relatives kindling nightly a fire on the grave.
Or as Longfellow has told it :—

> " Four days is the spirit's journey
>   To the land of ghosts and shadows,
>   Four its lonely night encampments.
>   Therefore when the dead are buried,
>   Let a fire as night approaches
>   Four times on the grave be kindled,
>   That the soul upon its journey
>   May not grope about in darkness."

The same length of time, say the Navajos, does the
departed soul wander over a gloomy marsh ere it can
discover the ladder leading to the world below, where
are the homes of the setting and the rising sun, a
land of luxuriant plenty, stocked with game and
covered with corn. To that land, say they, sink all
lost seeds and germs which fall on the earth and do
not sprout. There below they take root, bud, and
ripen their fruit.[1]

After four days, once more, in the superstitions of
the Greenland Eskimos, does the soul, for that term
after death confined in the body, at last break from
its prison-house and either rise in the sky to dance
in the aurora borealis or descend into the pleasant
land beneath the earth, according to the manner of
death.[2] Certain of the Aztecs taught that four years
elapsed ere the wandering ghost reached its rest.[3]

That there are logical contradictions in this belief
and these ceremonies, that the fire is always in the
same spot, that the weapons and utensils are not

---

[1] *Senate Rep. on the Ind. Tribes*, p. 358 : Wash. 1867.
[2] Egede, *Nachrichten von Grönland*, p. 145
[3] *Codex Telleriano Remensis*, p. 191.

carried away by the departed, and that the food placed
for his sustenance remains untouched, is very true.
But those who would therefore argue that they were
not intended for the benefit of the soul, and seek
some more recondite meaning in them as " unconscious emblems of struggling faith or expressions of
inward emotions," [1] are led astray by the very sim-
plicity of their real intention. Where is the faith,
where the science, that does not involve logical contradictions just as gross as these? They are tolerable
to us merely because we are used to them. What
value has the evidence of the senses anywhere against
a religious belief? None whatever. A stumbling
block though this be to the materialist, it is universally true and must be accepted as an experimental
fact.

The preconceived opinions that saw in the meteorological myths of the Indian a conflict between the
Spirit of Good and the Spirit of Evil, have with like
unconscious error falsified his doctrine of a future
life, and almost without an exception drawn it more
or less in the likeness of the Christian heaven, hell,
and purgatory. Very faint traces of any such belief
except where derived from the missionaries are visible
in the New World. Nowhere was any well-defined
doctrine that moral turpitude was judged and punished in the next world. No contrast is discoverable
between a place of torments and a realm of joy, at
the worst but a negative castigation awaited the liar,
the coward, or the niggard. The typical belief of the
tribes of the United States was well expressed in the

[1] Alger, *Hist. of the D ctrine of a Fut're Lif*, p. 76.

reply of Esau Hajo, great medal chief and speaker for the Creek nation in the National Council, to the question, Do the red people believe in a future state of rewards and punishments ? " We have an opinion that those who have behaved well are taken under the care of Esaugetuh Emissee, and assisted ; and that those who have behaved ill are left to shift for themselves; and that there is no other punishment." [1]

Neither the delights of a heaven on the one hand, nor the terrors of a hell on the other, were ever held out by priests or sages as an incentive to well-doing or a warning to the evil-disposed. Different fates, indeed, awaited the departed souls, but these rarely, if ever, were decided by their conduct while in the flesh, but by the manner of death, the punctuality with which certain sepulchral rites were fulfilled by relatives, or other similar arbitrary circumstance beyond the power of the individual to control. This view, which I am well aware is directly at variance with that of all previous writers, may be shown to be that natural to the uncultivated intellect everywhere, and the real interpretation of the creeds of America. Whether these arbitrary circumstances were not construed to signify the decision of the Divine Mind on the life of the man, is a deeper question, which there is no means at hand to solve.

---

[1] Hawkins, *Sketch of the Creek Country*, p. 80. Of the Choctaws the Rev. Alfred Wright writes : " They believe that the soul survives the body, but they do not appear to think that its condition is at all affected by the conduct in this life." *Missionary Herald*, vol. xxiv. p. 178. sqq. Abundant evidence could be furnished to show that this is the typical doctrine of the red race, and indeed of primitive man generally.

Those who have complained of the hopeless confusion of American religions have but proven the insufficiency of their own means of analyzing them. The uniformity which they display in so many points is nowhere more fully illustrated than in the unanimity with which they all point to the *sun* as the land of the happy souls, the realm of the blessed, the scene of the joyous hunting-grounds of the hereafter. Its perennial glory, its comfortable warmth, its daily analogy to the life of man, marked its abode as the pleasantest spot in the universe. It matters not whether the eastern Algonkins pointed to the south, others of their nation, with the Iroquois and Creeks, to the west, or many tribes to the east, as 'the direction taken by the spirit; all these myths but mean that its bourn is the home of the sun, which is perhaps in the Orient whence he comes forth, in the Occident where he makes his bed, or in the South whither he retires in the chilling winter. Where the sun lives, they informed the earliest foreign visitors, were the villages of the deceased, and the milky way which nightly spans the arch of heaven was in their opinion the road that led thither, and was called the path of the souls (*le chemin des ames*).[1] To *hueyu ku*, the mansion of the sun, said the Caribs, the soul passes when death overtakes the body.[2] Toward the warm southwest, to the great manito, who sends the mild sunny days, the corn and the beans, said the New England natives to Roger Williams, will all souls go.[3] Our knowledge is scanty of the doctrines

[1] *Rel. de la Nouv. France*, 1634, pp. 17, 18.
[2] Müller, *Amer. Urreligionen*, p. 229.
[3] *Key into the Langs. of Am.*, p. 148.

taught by the Incas concerning the soul, but this much we do know, that they looked to the sun, their recognized lord and protector, as he who would care at death, and admit them to his palaces. There—not, indeed, exquisite joys—but a life of unruffled placidity, void of labor, vacant of strong emotions, a sort of material Nirvana, awaited them.[1] For these reasons, they, with most other American nations, interred the corpse lying east and west, and not as the traveller Meyen has suggested,[2] from the reminiscences of some ancient migration. Beyond the Cordilleras, quite to the coast of Brazil, the innumerable hordes who wandered through the sombre tropical forests of that immense territory also pointed to the west, to the region beyond the mountains, as the land where the souls of their ancestors lived in undisturbed serenity ; or, in the more brilliant imaginations of the later generations, in a state of perennial inebriety, surrounded by infinite casks of rum, and with no white man to dole it out to them.[3] The natives of the extreme south, of the Pampas and Patagonia suppose the stars are the souls of the departed. At night they wander about the sky, but the moment the sun rises they hasten to the cheerful light, and are seen no more until it disappears in the west. So the Eskimo of the distant north, in the long winter nights when the aurora bridges the sky with its changing hues and arrowy shafts of light,

---

[1] La Vega, *Hist. des Incas,* lib. ii. cap. 7.

[2] *Ueber die Ureinwohner von Peru* p. 41.

[3] Coreal, *Voy. aux Indes Occident.*, i. p. 224; Müller, *Amer. Urrelig.*, p. 289.

believes he sees the spirits of his ancestors clothed in celestial raiment, disporting themselves in the absence of the sun, and calls the phenomena *the dance of the dead.*

The home of the sun was *the heaven of the red man;* but to this joyous abode not every one without distinction, no miscellaneous crowd, could gain admittance. The conditions were as various as the national temperaments. As the fierce gods of the Northmen would admit no soul to the banquets of Walhalla but such as had met the " spear-death " in the bloody play of war, and shut out pitilessly all those who feebly breathed their last in the " straw death " on the couch of sickness, so the warlike Aztec race in Nicaragua held that the shades of those who died in their beds went downward and to naught; but of those who fell in battle for their country to the east, " to the place whence comes the sun." [1] In ancient Mexico not only the warriors who were thus sacrificed on the altar of their country, but with a delicate and poetical sense of justice that speaks well for the refinement of the race, also those women who perished in child-birth, were admitted to the home of the sun. For are not they also heroines in the battle of life? Are they not also its victims? And do they not lay down their lives for country and kindred? Every morning, it was imagined, the heroes came forth in battle array, and with shout and song and the ring of weapons, accompanied the sun to the zenith, where at every noon the souls of the mothers, the Cihuapipilti, received him with dances, music,

[1] Oviedo, *Il'st. du Nicaragua,* p. 22.

and flowers, and bore him company to his western couch.[1] Except these, none—unless, it may be, the victims sacrificed to the gods, and this is doubtful— was deemed worthy of the highest heaven.

A mild and unwarlike tribe of Guatemala, on the other hand, were persuaded that to die by any other than a natural death was to forfeit all hope of life hereafter, and therefore left the bodies of the slain to the beasts and vultures.

The Mexicans had another place of happiness for departed souls, not promising perpetual life as the home of the sun, but unalloyed pleasure for a certain term of years. This was Tlalocan, the realm of the god of rains and waters, the terrestrial paradise, whence flowed all the rivers of the earth, and all the nourishment of the race. The diseases of which persons died marked this destination. Such as were drowned, or struck by lightning, or succumbed to humoral complaints, as dropsies and leprosy, were by these tokens known to be chosen as the subjects of Tlaloc. To such, said the natives, "death is the commencement of another life, it is as waking from a dream, and the soul is no more human but divine (*teot*)." Therefore they addressed their dying in terms like these: "Sir, or lady, awake, awake; already does the dawn appear; even now is the light approaching; already do the birds of yellow plumage begin their songs to greet thee; already are the gayly-tinted butterflies flitting around thee."[2]

[1] Torquemada, *Monarquia Indiana*, lib. vi. cap. 27.
[2] Sahagun, *Hist. de la Nueva España*, lib. x. cap. 29.

Before proceeding to the more gloomy portion of the subject, to the destiny of those souls who were not chosen for the better part, I must advert to a curious coincidence in the religious reveries of many nations which finds its explanation in the belief that the house of the sun is the home of the blessed, and proves that this was the first conception of most natural religions. It is seen in the events and obstacles of the journey to the happy land. We everywhere hear of a water which the soul must cross, and an opponent, either a dog or an evil spirit, which it has to contend with. We are all familiar with the dog Cerberus (called by Homer simply "the dog"), which disputed the passage of the river Styx, over which the souls must cross; and with the custom of the vikings, to be buried in a boat so that they might cross the waters of Ginunga-gap to the inviting strands of Godheim. Relics of this belief are found in the Koran, which describes the bridge *el Sirat*, thin as a hair and sharp as a scimetar, stretched in a single span from heaven to earth; in the bridge Bifrost, which, according to the Edda, stretches from earth to heaven; in the Persian legend, where the rainbow arch Chinevad is flung across the gloomy depths between this world and the home of the happy; and even in the current Christian allegory which represents the waters of the mythical Jordan rolling between us and the Celestial City.

How strange at first sight does it seem that the Hurons and Iroquois should have told the earliest missionaries that after death the soul must cross a deep and swift river on a bridge formed by a single

slender tree most lightly supported, where it had to
defend itself against the attacks of a dog ?[1]   If only
they had expressed this belief, it might have passed
for a coincidence merely.   But the Athapascas (Chepewyans) also told of a great water, which the soul
must cross in a stone canoe; the Algonkins and Dakotas, of a stream bridged by an enormous snake, or
a narrow and precipitous rock, and the Araucanians
of Chili of a sea in the west, in crossing which the
soul was required to pay toll to a malicious old woman.   Were it unluckily impecunious, she deprived it
of an eye.[2]   With the Aztecs, this water was called
Chicunoapa, the Nine Rivers.   It was guarded by a
dog and a green dragon, to conciliate which the dead
were furnished with slips of paper by way of toll.
The Greenland Eskimos thought that the waters
roared through an unfathomable abyss over which
there was no other bridge than a wheel slippery with
ice, forever revolving with fearful rapidity, or a path
narrow as a cord with nothing to hold on by.   On
the other side sits a horrid old woman gnashing her
teeth and tearing her hair with rage.   As each soul
approaches she burns a feather under its nose; if it
faints she seizes it for her prisoner, but if the soul's
guardian spirit can overcome her, it passes through
in safety.[3]

[1] *Rel de la Nouv. France*, 1636, p. 105.   The Algonkin Ottawas had this form of the legend (Nic Perrot, *Mem. sur l'Amérique*, *Sept.*(1665), p. 41).   The Otchipwe name for the bridge is
Kokokajogan.   Owl Bridge (Baraga,*Otchipwe Dict.* s. v.)

[2] Molina, *Hist. of Chili*, ii. p. 81, and others in Waitz, *Anthropologie.* iii. p. 197.

[3] *Nachrichten von Grönland aus dem Tagebuche vom Bischof
Paul Egede*, p. 104; Kopenhagen, 1790.

The similarity to the passage of the soul across the Styx, and the toll of the obolus to Charon is in the Aztec legend still more striking, when we remember that the Styx was the ninth head of Oceanus (omitting the Cocytus, often a branch of the Styx). The Nine Rivers probably refer to the nine Lords of the Night, ancient Aztec deities guarding the nocturnal hours, and introduced into their calendar. The Tupis and Caribs, the Mayas and Creeks, entertained very similar expectations.

We are to seek the explanation of these wide-spread theories of the soul's journey in the equally prevalent tenet that the sun is its destination, and that that luminary has his abode beyond the ocean stream, which in all primitive geographies rolls its waves around the habitable land. This ocean stream is the water which all have to attempt to pass, and woe to him whom the spirit of the waters, represented either as the old woman, the dragon, or the dog of Hecate, seizes and overcomes. In the lush fancy of the Orient, the spirit of the waters becomes the spirit of evil, the ocean stream the abyss of hell, and those who fail in the passage the damned, who are foredoomed to evil deeds and endless torture.

No such ethical bearing as this was ever assigned the myth by the red race before they were taught by Europeans. Father Brebeuf could only find that the souls of suicides and those killed in war were supposed to live apart from the others; "but as to the souls of scoundrels," he adds, "so far from being shut out, they are the welcome guests, though for that matter if it were not so, their paradise would be a total desert, as Huron and scoundrel (*Huron*

et larron) are one and the same." [1]   When the Minnetarees told Major Long and the Mannicicas of the
La Plata the Jesuits, [2] that the souls of the bad fell
into the waters and were swept away, this was,
beyond doubt, attributable either to a false interpretation, or to Christian instruction.   No such distinction is probable among savages.   The Brazilian natives divided the dead into classes, supposing that
the drowned, those killed by violence, and those
yielding to disease, lived in separate regions; but
no ethical reason whatever seems to have been connected with this. [3]   If the conception of a place of
moral retribution was known at all to the race, it
should be found easily recognizable in Mexico, Yucatan, or Peru.   But the so-called "hells" of their
religions have no such significance, and the spirits
of evil, who were identified by early writers with
Satan, no more deserve the name than does the Greek
Pluto.

Cupay or Supay, the Shadow, in Peru was supposed to rule the land of shades in the centre of the
earth.   To him went all souls not destined to be the
companions of the Sun.   This is all we know of his
attributes; and the assertion of Garcilasso de la Vega,
that he was the analogue of the Christian Devil, and
that his name was never pronounced without spitting
and muttering a curse on his head, may be invali-

[1] *Rel. de la Nouv. France*, 1636, p. 105.

[2] Long's *Expedition*, i. p. 280; Waitz, *Anthropologie*, iii. p.
531.   Dr. Matthews found no such moral distinction believed
in by the Minnetarees of the present day. (*Hidatsa Grammar*,
p. xxiii.)

[3] Müller, *Amér. Urreligionen*, p. 287.

dated by the testimony of an earlier and better authority on the religion of Peru, who calls him the god of rains, and adds that the famous Inca, Huayna Capac, was his high priest.[1]

" The devil," says Cogolludo of the Mayas, "is called by them Xibilha, which means he who disappears or vanishes."[2] In the legends of the Quichés, the name Xibalba is given as that of the under-world ruled by the grim lords One Death and Seven Deaths. The derivation of the name is from a root meaning to fear, from which comes the term in Maya dialects for a ghost or phantom.[3] Under the influence of a century of Christian catechizing, the Quiché legends portray this really as a place of torment, and its rulers as malignant and powerful; but as I have before pointed out, they do so protesting that such was not the ancient belief, and they let fall no word that shows that it was regarded as the destination of the morally bad. The original meaning of the name given by Cogolludo points unmistakably to the simple fact of disappearance from among men, and corresponds in harmlessness to the true sense of those

[1] Compare Garcilasso de la Vega, *Hist. des Incas.*, liv. ii. chap. ii., with *Lett. sur les Superstitions du Pérou*, p. 104. Cupay is undoubtedly a personal form from *Cupan*, a shadow. (See Holguin, *Vocab. de la Lengua Quichua*, p. 80: Cuzco, 1608.)

[2] " El que desparece ó desvanece," *Hist. de Yucathan*, lib. iv. cap. 7.

[3] Ximenes, *Vocab. Quiché*, p. 224. The attempt of the Abbé Brasseur to make of Xibalba an ancient kingdom of renown with Palenque as its capital, is so utterly unsupported and wildly hypothetical as to justify the humorous flings which have so often been cast at antiquaries.

words of fear, Scheol, Hades, Hell, all signifying hidden from sight, and only endowed with more grim associations by the imaginations of later generations.[1]

Mictlanteuctli, Lord of Mictlan, from a word meaning to die (*mic* death, *tlan* near), was the Mexican Pluto. Like Cupay, he dwelt in the subterranean regions, and his palace was named Tlalxicco, the navel of the earth. Yet he was also located in the far north, and that point of the compass and the north wind were named after him. Those who descended to him were oppressed by the darkness of his abode, but were subjected to no other trials ; nor were they sent thither as a punishment, but merely from having died of diseases unfitting them for Tlalocan. Mictlanteuctli was said to be the most powerful of the gods. For who is stronger than Death? And who dare defy the Grave? As the skald lets Odin say to Bragi: " Our lot is uncertain ; even on the hosts of the gods gazes the gray Fenris wolf." [2]

These various abodes to which the incorporeal man took flight were not always his everlasting home. It will be remembered that where a plurality of souls was believed, one of these, soon after death, entered another body to recommence life on earth. Acting under this persuasion, the Algonkin women who desired to become mothers, flocked to the couch of those about to die, in hope that the vital principle, as it passed from the body, would enter theirs, and ferti-

---

[1] Scheol is from a Hebrew word, signifying to dig, to hide in the earth. Hades signifies the *unseen* or *unseeing* world. Hell Jacob Grimm derives from *hilan*, to conceal in the earth ; it is cognate with *hole* and *hollow*.

[2] Pennock, *Religion of the Northmen*, p. 148.

lize their sterile wombs ; and when, among the Seminoles of Florida, a mother died in childbirth, the
infant was held over her face to receive her parting
spirit, and thus acquire strength and knowledge for
its future use.[1] So among the Takahlis, the priest
is accustomed to lay his hand on the head of the
nearest relative of the deceased, and to blow into him
the soul of the departed, which is supposed to come
to life in his next child.[2] Probably, with a reference
to the current tradition that ascribes the origin of
man to the earth, and likens his life to that of the
plant, the Mexicans were accustomed to say that at
one time all men have been stones, and that at last
they would all return to stones,[3] and, acting literally
on this conviction, they interred with the bones of
the dead a small green stone, which was called the
principle of life.

Whether any nations accepted the doctrine of
metempsychosis, and thought that " the souls of
their grandams might haply inhabit a partridge," we
are without the means of knowing. La Hontan denies
it positively of the Algonkins ; but the natives
of Popoyan refused to kill doves, says Coreal,[4]
because they believed them inspired by the souls
of the departed. And Father Ignatius Chomé relates that he heard a woman of the Chiriquanes in
Buenos Ayres say of a fox : " May that not be the

[1] La Hontan, *Voy. dans l'Am. Sept.* i.. p. 232 ; *Narrative of
Oceola Nikkanoche.* p. 75.

[2] Morse, *Rep. on the Ind. Tribes*, App. p. 345.

[3] Garcia, *Or. de los Indios*, lib. iv. cap. 26, p. 310.

[4] *Voiages aux Indes Oc.*, ii. p. 132.

spirit of my dead daughter?"[1] But before accepting such testimony as decisive, we must first enquire
whether these tribes believed in a multiplicity of
souls, whether these animals had a symbolical value,
and if not, whether the soul was not simply presumed
to put on this shape in its journey to the land of the
hereafter : inquiries which are unanswered. Leaving,
therefore, the question open, whether the sage of
Samos had any disciples in the new world, another
and more fruitful topic is presented by their well-
ascertained notions of the resurrection of the dead.

This seemingly extraordinary doctrine, which some
have asserted was entirely unknown and impossible to the American Indians,[2] was in fact one of
their most deeply-rooted and wide-spread convictions, especially among the tribes of the eastern
United States. It is indissolubly connected with
their highest theories of a future life, their burial
ceremonies, and their modes of expression. The Moravian Brethren give the grounds of this belief
with great clearness: " That they hold the soul to
be immortal, and perhaps think the body will rise
again, they give not unclearly to understand when
they say, ' We Indians shall not forever die ; even
the grains of corn we put under the earth grow up
and become living things.' They conceive that when
the soul has been a while with God, it can, if it
chooses, return to earth and be born again."[3] This
is the highest and typical creed of the aborigines. But

---

[1] *Lettres Edif. et Cur.*, v. p. 203.
[2] Alger, *Hist. of the Doctrine of a Future Life*, p. 72.
[3] Loskiel, *Ges. der Miss. der evang. Brüder*, p. 49.

instead of simply being born again in the ordinary
sense of the word, they thought the soul would return to the bones, that these would clothe themselves
with flesh, and that the man would rejoin his tribe.
That this was the real, though often doubtless the
dimly understood reason of the custom of preserving
the bones of the deceased, can be shown by various
arguments.

This practice was almost universal. East of the
Mississippi nearly every nation was accustomed, at
stated periods—usually once in eight or ten years—
to collect and clean the osseous remains of those of
its number who had died in the intervening time,
and inter them in one common sepulchre, lined with
choice furs, and marked with a mound of wood, stone,
and earth. Such is the origin of those immense
tumuli filled with the mortal remains of nations and
generations which the antiquary, with irreverent
curiosity, so frequently chances upon in all portions
of our territory. Throughout Central America the
same usage obtained in various localities, as early
writers and existing monuments abundantly testify.
Instead of interring the bones, were they those of
some distinguished chieftain, they were deposited in
the temples or the council-houses, usually in small
chests of canes or splints. Such were the charnel-
houses which the historians of De Soto's expedition
so often mention, and these are the "arks" which
Adair and other authors, who have sought to trace the
descent of the Indians from the Jews, have likened
to that which the ancient Israelites bore with them
on their migrations. A widow among the Tahkalis
was obliged to carry the bones of her deceased hus-

18

band wherever she went for four years, preserving them in such a casket handsomely decorated with feathers.[1] The Caribs of the mainland adopted the custom for all without exception. About a year after death the bones were cleaned, bleached, painted, wrapped in odorous balsams, placed in a wicker basket, and kept suspended from the door of their dwellings.[2] When the quantity of these heirlooms became burdensome, they were removed to some inaccessible cavern, and stowed away with reverential care. Such was the cave Ataruipe, a visit to which has been so eloquently described by Alexander von Humboldt in his "Views of Nature."

So great was the respect for these remains by the Indians, that on the Mississippi, in Peru, and elsewhere, no tyranny, no cruelty, so embittered the indigenes against the white explorers as the sacrilegious search for treasures perpetrated among the sepulchres of past generations. Unable to understand the meaning of such deep feeling, so foreign to the European who, without a second thought, turns a cemetery into a public square, or seeds it down in wheat, the Jesuit missionaries in Paraguay accuse the natives of worshipping the skeletons of their forefathers,[3] and the English in Virginia repeated it of the Powhatans.

I may here say a few words of ancestral worship in general. In origin, it is a branch of the religion of sex, for only when the ties of relationship are

---

[1] Richardson, *Arctic Expedition*, p. 260.

[2] Gumilla, *Hist. del Orinoco*, i. pp. 199, 202, 204.

[3] Ruis, *Conquista Espiritual del Paraguay*, p. 48, in Lafitau.

somewhat strongly felt, can it arise. In America it existed, but was not prominent. The Knisteneaux on Nelson river were accustomed to strangle their parents when old; yet each master of a family, the deed performed, kept by him a bunch of feathers tied with a string, called it his "father's head," and looked upon it with most superstitious reverence.[1] The Aztecs celebrated a feast to the dead once in each year, at which time they gazed to the north and called upon their ancestors to "come soon, for we await you." [2] The Tupis worshipped Tamoin and the Incas Pacarina, names which represented "the forefather of the clan idealized as the soul or essence of his descendants." [3] And this somewhat subtle explanation of an able writer, recondite as it may seem for a savage mind, was the prevailing form of ancestral worship in the New World.

The question has been debated and variously answered, whether the art of mummification was known and practised in America. Without entering into the discussion, it is certain that preservation of the corpse by a long and thorough process of exsiccation over a slow fire was nothing unusual, not only in Peru, Popoyan, the Carib countries, and Nicaragua,

---

[1] J. Robson, *Ac. of Res. in Hudson's Bay*, p. 48.

[2] *Codex Telleriano-Remensis*, p. 192.

[3] Clements R. Markham, *Jour. Roy. Geog. Soc.*, 1871, p. 291. Compare Ives d'Evreux, *Hist. de Maragnan*, pp. 91, 92. When Markham adds that the actual body of the ancestor was worshipped under the name *malqui*, I believe he is in error. This is not a true Quichua word, as M. Leonce Angrand points out in a note to Desjardins, *Ancien Pérou.* It is not in Holguin's *Diccionario.* In modern Quichua it means simply mummy.

but among many of the tribes north of the Gulf of Mexico, as I have elsewhere shown.[1] The object was essentially the same as when the bones alone were preserved ; and in the case of rulers, the same respect was often paid to their corpses as had been the due of their living bodies.

The opinion underlying all these customs was, that a part of the soul, or one of the souls, dwelt in the bones; that these were the seeds which, planted in the earth, or preserved unbroken in safe places, would, in time, put on once again a garb of flesh, and germinate into living human beings. Language illustrates this not unusual theory. The Iroquois word for bone is *esken*—for soul, *atisken*, literally that which is within the bone.[2] In an Athapascan dialect bone is *yani*, soul *i-yune*.[3] The Hebrew Rabbis taught that in the bone *lutz*, the coccyx, remained at death the germ of a second life, which, at the proper time, would develop into the purified body, as the plant from the seed.

But mythology and superstitions add more decisive testimony. One of the Aztec legends of the origin of man was, that after one of the destructions of the world the gods took counsel together how to renew the species. It was decided that one of their number, Xolotl, should descend to Mictlan, the realm of the dead, and bring thence a bone of the perished race. The fragments of this they sprinkled with blood, and on the fourth day it grew into a youth,

---

[1] *Notes on the Floridian Peninsula*, pp. 191 sqq.

[2] Bruyas, *Rad. Verborum Iroquæorum.*

[3] Buschmann, *Athapask. Sprachstamm*, pp. 182, 188.

the father of the present race.[1] The profound mystical significance of this legend is reflected in one told by the Quichés, in which the hero gods Hunahpu and Xblanque succumb to the rulers of Xibalba, the darksome powers of death. Their bodies are burned, but their bones are ground in a mill and thrown into the waters, lest they should come to life. Even this precaution is insufficient—" for these ashes did not go far; they sank to the bottom of the stream, where, in the twinkling of an eye, they were changed into handsome youths, and their very same features appeared anew. On the fifth day they displayed themselves anew, and were seen in the water by the people," [2] whence they emerged to overcome and destroy the powers of death and hell (Xibalba).

The strongest analogies to these myths are offered by the superstitious rites of distant tribes. Some of the Tupis of Brazil were wont on the death of a relative to dry and pulverize his bones and then mix them with their food, a nauseous practice they defended by asserting that the soul of the dead remained in the bones and lived again in the living.[3] Even the lower animals were supposed to follow the same law. Hardly any of the hunting tribes, before their original manners were vitiated by foreign influence, permitted the bones of game slain in the chase to be broken, or left carelessly about the encampment. They were collected in heaps, or thrown into the water. Mrs. Eastman observes that even yet the Dakotas deem it

---

[1] Torquemada, *Monarquia Indiana*, lib. vi. cap. 41.

[2] *Le Livre Sacré des Quichés*, pp. 175–177.

[3] Müller, *Amér. Urrelig.*, p. 290, after Spix.

an omen of ill luck in the hunt, if the dogs gnaw the
bones or a woman inadvertently steps over them ; and
the Chipeway interpreter, John Tanner, speaks of the
same fear among that tribe.   The Yurucares of Bo-
livia carried it to such an inconvenient extent that
they carefully put by even small fish bones, saying
that unless this is done the fish and game will dis-
appear from the country.[1] The traveller on our western prairies often notices the buffalo skulls, countless numbers of which bleach on those vast plains,
arranged in circles and symmetrical piles by the careful hands of the native hunters.   The explanation they
offer for this custom gives the key to the whole theory
and practice of preserving the osseous relics of the
dead, as well human as brute.   They say that, " the
bones contain the spirits of the slain animals, and that
some time in the future they will rise from the earth,
re-clothe themselves with flesh, and stock the prairies
anew." [2]   This explanation, which comes to us from
indisputable authority, sets forth in its true light the
belief of the red race in a resurrection.   It is not
possible to trace it out in the subtleties with which
theologians have surrounded it as a dogma.   The very
attempt would be absurd.   They never occurred to
the Indian.   He thought that the soul now enjoying
the delights of the happy hunting grounds would
some time return to the bones, take on flesh, and live
again.   Such is precisely the much discussed statement that Garcilasso de la Vega says he often heard
from the native Peruvians.   He adds that so careful

1 D'Orbigny, *Annuaire des Voyages*, 1845, p.77.
2 Long's *Expedition*, i. p. 278.

were they lest any of the body should be lost that they preserved even the parings of their nails and clippings of the hair.[1] In contradiction to this the writer Acosta has been quoted, who says that the Peruvians embalmed their dead because they " had no knowledge that the bodies should rise with the soul." [2] But, rightly understood, this is a confirmation of La Vega's account. Acosta means that the Christian doctrine of the body rising from the dust being unknown to the Peruvians (which is perfectly true), they preserve the body just as it was, so that the soul when it returned to earth, as all expected, might not be at a loss for a house of flesh.

The notions thus entertained by the red race on the resurrection are peculiar to it, and stand apart from those of any other. They did not look for the second life to be either better or worse than the present one; they regarded it neither as a reward nor a punishment to be sent back to the world of the living; nor is there satisfactory evidence that it was ever distinctly connected with a moral or physical theory of the destiny of the universe, or even with their prevalent expectation of recurrent epochs in the course of nature. It is true that a writer whose personal veracity is above all doubt, Mr. Adam Hodgson, relates an ancient tradition of the Choctaws, to the effect that the present world will be consumed by a conflagration, after which it will be reformed pleasanter than it is now, and that then the spirits of the dead will return to the bones in the bone mounds, flesh will knit

---

[1] *Hist. des Incas*, lib. iii. chap. 7.
[2] *Hist. of the New World*, bk. v. chap. 7.

together their loose joints, and they shall again inhabit their ancient territory.[1]

There was also a similar belief among the Eskimos.
They said that in the course of time the waters will
overwhelm the land, purify it of the blood of the
dead, melt the icebergs, and wash away the steep
rocks. A wind will then drive off the waters, and
the new land will be peopled by reindeers and young
seals. Then will He above blow once on the bones
of the men and twice on those of the women, whereupon they will at once start into life, and lead there-
after a joyous existence.[2]

But though there is nothing in these narratives
alien to the course of thought in the native mind, yet
as the date of the first is recent (1820), as they are
not supported (so far as I know) by similar traditions
elsewhere, and as they may have arisen from Christian doctrines of a millennium, I leave them for
future investigation.

What strikes us the most in this analysis of the
opinions entertained by the red race on a future
life is the clear and positive hope of a hereafter, in
such strong contrast to the feeble and vague notions
of the ancient Israelites, Greeks, and Romans, and
yet the entire inertness of this hope in leading them
to a purer moral life. It offers another proof that
the fulfilment of duty is in its nature nowise connected with or derived from a consideration of ultimate personal consequences. It is another evidence

---

[1] *Travels in North America,* p. 280.
[2] Egede, *Nachrichten von Grönland*, p. 156.

that the religious is wholly distinct from the moral sentiment, and that the origin of ethics is not to be sought in connection with the ideas of divinity and personal survival.

CHAPTER X.

THE NATIVE PRIESTHOOD.

Their titles.—Practitioners of the healing art by supernatural means.— Their power derived from natural magic and the exercise of the clairvoyant and mesmeric faculties.—Examples.—Epidemic hysteria.— Their social position.—Their duties as religious functionaries.—Terms of admission to the Priesthood.—Inner organization in various nations. —Their esoteric languages and secret societies.

THUS picking painfully amid the ruins of a race gone to wreck centuries ago, thus rejecting much foreign rubbish and scrutinizing each stone that lies around, if we still are unable to rebuild the edifice in its pristine symmetry, yet we can at least discern and trace the ground plan and outlines of the fane. Before leaving the field to the richer returns of more fortunate workmen, it will not be inappropriate to add a sketch of the ministers of these religions, the servants in this temple.

Shamans, conjurors, sorcerers, medicine men, wizards, and many another hard name have been given them, but I shall call them *priests*, for in their poor way, as well as any other priesthood, they set up to be the agents of the gods, and the interpreters of divinity. No tribe was so devoid of religious sentiment as to be without them. Their power was terrible, and their use of it unscrupulous. Neither men nor gods, death nor life, the winds nor the waves, were beyond their control. Like Old Men of the Sea, they have clung to the neck of their nations, throttling all attempts at progress, binding them to the thraldom of superstition and profligacy, dragging them down to wretchedness and death. Christianity and civilization meet in them their most determined, most implacable foes. But what is this but the story of priestcraft and intolerance everywhere, which Old Spain can repeat as well as New Spain, the white race as well as the red ? Blind leaders of the blind, dupers and duped fall into the ditch.

In their own languages they are variously called ; by the Algonkins and Dakotas, "those knowing divine things " and " dreamers of the gods " (*manitou-siou, wakanwacipi*) ; in Mexico, " masters or guardians of the divine things " (*teopixqui, teotecuhtli*) ; in Cherokee their title means, " possessed of the divine fire " (*atsilung kelawhi*) ; in Iroquois, " keepers of the faith " (*honundeunt*) ; in Quichua, " the learned " (*amauta*) ; in Maya, " the listeners " (*cocome*). The popular term in French and English of " medicine men" is not such a misnomer as might be supposed. The noble science of medicine is connected with divinity not only by the rudest savage but the profoundest philosopher, as has been already adverted to. When sickness is looked upon as the effect of the anger of a god, or as the malicious infliction of a sorcerer, it is natural to seek help from those who assume to control the unseen world, and influence the fiats of the Almighty. The recovery from disease is the kindliest exhibition of divine power. Therefore the earliest canons of medicine in India and Egypt are attributed to no less distinguished authors than the gods Brahma and Thoth;[1] therefore the earliest practitioners of the healing art are universally the ministers of religion.

But, however creditable this origin is to medicine, its partnership with theology was no particular advantage to it. These mystical doctors shared the disdain still so prevalent among ourselves for a treatment based on experiment and reason, and regarded the administration of emetics and purgatives, tonics and diuretics, with a contempt quite equal to that of the disciples of Hahnemann. The practitioners of the rational school formed a separate class among the Indians, and had nothing to do with amulets, powwows, or spirits.[2] They were of different name and standing, and though held in less estimation, such valuable additions to the pharmacopœia as guaiacum, cinchona, and ipecacuanha, were learned from them. The priesthood scorned such ignoble means. Were they summoned to a patient, they drowned his groans in a barbarous clangor of instruments in order to fright away the demon that possessed him; they sucked and blew upon the diseased organ; they sprinkled him with water, and catching it again threw it on the ground, thus drowning out the disease; they rubbed the part with their hands, and exhibiting a bone or splinter asserted that they drew it from the body, and that it had been the cause of the malady; they manufactured a little image to represent the spirit of sickness, and spitefully knocked it to pieces, thus vicariously destroying its prototype; they sang

---

[1] Haeser, *Geschichte der Medicin*, pp. 4, 7: Jena, 1845.

[2] Schoolcraft, *Ind. Tribes*, v. p. 440.

doleful and monotonous chants at the top of their voices, screwed their countenances into hideous grimaces, twisted their bodies into unheard of contortions, and by all accounts did their utmost to merit the honorarium they demanded for their services. A double motive spurred them to spare no pains. For if they failed, not only was their reputation gone, but the next expert called in was likely enough to hint, with that urbanity so traditional in the profession, that the illness was in fact caused or much increased by the antagonistic nature of the remedies previously employed, whereupon the chances were that the doctor's life fell into greater jeopardy than that of his quondam patient.

Considering the probable result of this treatment, we may be allowed to doubt whether it redounded on the whole very much to the honor of the fraternity. Their strong points are rather to be looked for in the real knowledge gained by a solitary and reflective life, by an earnest study of the appearances of nature, and of those hints and forest signs which are wholly lost on the white man and beyond the ordinary insight of a native. Travellers often tell of changes of the weather predicted by them with astonishing foresight and of information of singular accuracy and extent gleaned from most meagre materials. There is nothing in this to shock our sense of probability—much to elevate our opinion of the native sagacity. They were also adepts in tricks of sleight of hand, and had no mean acquaintance with what is called natural magic. They would allow themselves to be tied hand and foot with knots innumerable, and at a sign would shake them loose as so many wisps of straw;

they would spit fire and swallow hot coals, pick glowing stones from the flames, walk naked over burning brush, and plunge their arms to the shoulder in kettles of boiling water with apparent impunity.[1] Nor was this all. With a skill not inferior to that of the jugglers of India, they could plunge knives into vital parts, vomit blood, or kill one another out and out to all appearances, and yet in a few minutes be as well as ever; they could set fire to articles of clothing and even houses, and by a touch of their magic restore them instantly as perfect as before.[2] If it were not within our power to see most of these miracles performed any night in our great cities by a well dressed professional, we would at once deny their possibility. As it is, they astonish us but little.

One of the most characteristic exhibitions of their power was to summon a spirit to answer inquiries concerning the future and the absent. A great similarity marked this proceeding in all northern tribes from the Eskimos to the Mexicans. A circular or conical lodge of stout poles four or eight in number planted firmly in the ground, was covered with skins or mats, a small aperture only being left for the seer to enter. Once in, he carefully closed the hole and commenced his incantations. Soon the lodge trembles, the strong poles shake and bend as with the united strength of a dozen men, and strange, unearthly sounds, now far aloft in the air,

[1] Carver, *Travels in North America*, p. 73; Boston, 1802; *Narrative of John Tanner*, p. 135.

[2] Sahagun, *Hist. de la Nueva España*, lib. x. cap. 20; *Le Livre Sacré des Quichés*, p. 177; *Lett. sur les Superstit. du Pérou*, pp. 89, 91.

now deep in the ground, anon approaching near and
nearer, reach the ears of the spectators   At length
the priest announces that the spirit is present, and
is prepared to answer questions.   An indispensable
preliminary to any inquiry is to insert a handful of
tobacco, or a string of beads, or some such douceur
under the skins, ostensibly for the behoof of the
celestial visitor, who would seem not to be above
earthly wants and vanities.   The replies received,
though occasionally singularly clear and correct, are
usually of that ambiguous purport which leaves the
inquirer little wiser than he was before.   For all
this, ventriloquism, trickery, and shrewd knavery
are sufficient explanations.   Nor does it materially
interfere with this view, that converted Indians, on
whose veracity we can rely, have repeatedly averred
that in performing this rite they themselves did not
move the medicine lodge ; for nothing is easier than
in the state of nervous excitement they were then in
to be self-deceived, as the now familiar phenomenon
of table-turning illustrates.

But there is something more than these vulgar
arts now and then to be perceived.   There are
statements supported by unquestionable testimony,
which ought not to be passed over in silence, and
yet I cannot but approach them with hesitation.
They are so revolting to the laws of exact science,
so alien, I had almost said, to the experience of our
lives.   Yet is this true, or are such experiences
only ignored and put aside without serious consideration ?   Are there not in the history of each of us
passages which strike our retrospective thought with
awe, almost with terror?   Are there not in nearly

every community individuals who possess a mysterious power, concerning whose origin, mode of action,
and limits, we and they are alike in the dark? I
refer to such organic forces as are popularly summed
up under the words clairvoyance, mesmerism, rhab-
domancy, animal magnetism, physical spiritualism.
Civilized thousands stake their faith and hope here
and hereafter on the truth of these manifestations ;
rational medicine recognizes their existence, and
while she attributes them to morbid and exceptional
influences, confesses her want of more exact knowledge, and refrains from barren theorizing. Let us
follow her example, and hold it enough to show that
such powers, whatever they are, were known to the
native priesthood as well as the modern spiritualists
and the miracle mongers of the Middle Ages.

Their highest development is what our ancestors
called " second sight." That under certain conditions knowledge can pass from one mind to another
otherwise than through the ordinary channels of the
senses, is claimed to be shown by the examples of
persons *en rapport*. The limit to this we do not know,
but it is not unlikely that clairvoyance or second
sight is based upon it. In his autobiography, the
celebrated Sac chief Black Hawk, relates that his
great grandfather " was inspired by a belief that at the
end of four years he should see a white man, who
would be to him a father." Under the direction of
this vision he travelled eastward to a certain spot,
and there, as he was forewarned, met a Frenchman,
through whom the nation was brought into alliance
with France.[1] No one at all versed in the Indian

_____
[1] *Life of Black Hawk*, p. 13.

character will doubt the implicit faith with which this legend was told and heard. But we may be pardoned our skepticism, seeing there are so many chances of error. It is not so with an anecdote related by Captain Jonathan Carver, a cool-headed English trader, whose little book of travels is a good authority. In 1767 he was among the Killistenoes at a time when they were in great straits for food, and depending upon the arrival of the traders to rescue them from starvation. They persuaded the chief priest to consult the divinities as to when the relief would arrive. After the usual preliminaries, this magnate announced that next day, precisely when the sun reached the zenith, a canoe would arrive with further tidings. At the appointed hour the whole village, together with the incredulous Englishman, was on the beach, and sure enough, at the minute specified, a canoe swung round a distant point of land, and rapidly approaching the shore brought the expected news.[1]

Charlevoix is nearly as trustworthy a writer as Carver. Yet he deliberately relates an equally singular instance.[2]

But these examples are surpassed by one described in the *Atlantic Monthly* of July, 1866, the author of which, Gen. John Mason Brown, has assured me of its accuracy in every particular. Some years since, at the head of a party of voyageurs, he set forth in search of a band of Indians somewhere on the vast plains along the tributaries of the Copper-mine and

[1] *Travs. in North America*, p. 74.
[2] *Journal Historique*, p. 362.

Mackenzie rivers.   Danger, disappointment, and the fatigues of the road, induced one after another to turn back, until of the original ten only three remained.   They also were on the point of giving up the apparently hopeless quest, when they were met by some warriors of the very band they were seeking. These had been sent out by one of their medicine men to find three whites, whose horses, arms, attire, and personal appearance he minutely described, which description was repeated to Gen. Brown by the warriors before they saw his two companions.   When afterwards, the priest, a frank and simple-minded man, was asked to explain this extraordinary occurrence, he could offer no other explanation than that " he saw them coming, and heard them talk on their journey."[1]

Many tales such as these have been recorded by travellers, and however much they may shock our sense of probability, as well-authenticated exhibitions of a power which sways the Indian mind, and which has ever prejudiced it so unchangeably against Christianity and civilization, they cannot be disregarded. Whether they too are but specimens of refined knavery, or whether they are instigations of the Devil, or whether they must be classed with other facts as illustrating certain obscure and curious men-

---

[1] Sometimes facts like this can be explained by the quickness of perception acquired by constant exposure to danger.   The mind takes cognizance unconsciously of trifling incidents, the sum of which leads it to a conviction which the individual regards almost as an inspiration.   This is the explanation of *presentiments.*

tal faculties, each may decide as the bent of his mind inclines him, for science makes no decision.

Those nervous conditions associated with the name of Mesmer were nothing new to the Indian magicians. Rubbing and stroking the sick, and the laying on of hands, were common parts of their clinical procedures, and at the initiations to their societies they were frequently exhibited. Observers have related that among the Nez Percés of Oregon, the novice was put to sleep by songs, incantations, and "certain passes of the hand," and that with the Dakotas he would be struck lightly on the breast at a preconcerted moment, and instantly "would drop prostrate on his face, his muscles rigid and quivering in every fibre."[1]

There is no occasion to suppose deceit in this. It finds its parallel in every race and every age, and rests on a characteristic trait of certain epochs and certain men, which leads them to seek the divine, not in contemplation on the laws of the universe and the facts of self consciousness, but in an immolation of the latter, a sinking of their own individuality in that of the spirits whose alliance they seek. This is an outgrowth of that ignoring of the universality of Law which belongs to the lower stages of enlightenment.[2] And as this is never done with impunity, but with certainty brings a punishment with it, the study of the mental conditions thus evoked, and the

[1] Schoolcraft, *Indian Tribes*, iii. p. 287; v. p. 652.

[2] "The progress from deepest ignorance to enlightenment," remarks Herbert Spencer in his *Social Statics*, "is a progress from entire unconsciousness of law, to the conviction that law is universal and inevitable."

results which follow them, offers a salutary subject of reflection to the theologian as well as the physician. For these examples of nervous pathology are identical in kind, and alike in consequences, whether witnessed in the primitive forests of the New World, among the convulsionists of St. Medard, or in the scenes of a religious revival in one of our own churches.

Sleeplessness and abstemiousness, carried to the verge of endurance—seclusion, and the pertinacious fixing of the mind on one subject—obstinate gloating on some morbid fancy, rarely failed to bring about hallucinations with all the garb of reality. Physicians are well aware that the more frequently these diseased conditions of the mind are sought, the more readily they are found. Then, again, they were often induced by intoxicating and narcotic herbs. Tobacco, the maguey, coca; in California the chucuaco; among the Mexicans the snake plant, ollinhiqui or coaxihuitl; and among the southern tribes of our own country the cassine yupon and iris versicolor,[1] were used;

---

[1] The Creeks had, according to Hawkins, not less than seven sacred plants; chief of them were the cassine yupon, called by botanists *Ilex vomitoria*, or *Ilex cassina*, of the natural order Aquifoliaceæ; and the blue flag, *Iris versicolor*, natural order Iridaceæ. The former is a powerful diuretic and mild emetic, and grows only near the sea. The latter is an active emeto-cathartic, and is abundant on swampy grounds throughout the Southern States. From it was formed the celebrated "black drink," with which they opened their councils, and which served them in place of spirits. Two of the others were *Eryngium aquaticum* and *Salix candida*. For further concerning them see my *National Legend of the Chahta-Muskokee Tribes*, pp. 8, 11.

and, it is even said, were cultivated for this purpose. The seer must work himself up to a prophetic fury, or speechless, lie in apparent death, before the mind of the gods would be opened to him. Trance and ecstasy were the two avenues he knew to divinity; fasting and seclusion the means employed to discover them. His ideal was of a prophet who dwelt far from men, without need of food, in constant communion with divinity. Such a one, in the legends of the Tupis, resided on a mountain glittering with gold and silver, near the river Uaupe, his only companion a dog, his only occupation dreaming of the gods. When, however, an eclipse was near, his dog would bark; and then, taking the form of a bird, he would fly over the villages, and learn the changes that had taken place.[1]

But man cannot trample with impunity on the laws of his physical life, and the consequences of these deprivations and morbid excitements of the brain show themselves in terrible pictures. Not unfrequently they were carried to the pitch of raving mania, reminding one of the worst forms of the Berserker fury of the Scandinavians, or the Bacchic rage of Greece. The enthusiast, maddened with the fancies of a disordered intellect, would start forth from his seclusion in an access of frenzy. Then woe to the dog, the child, the slave, or the woman who crossed his path; for nothing but blood could satisfy his craving, and they fell instant victims to his madness. But were it a strong man, he bared his arm, and let the frenzied hermit bury his teeth in the

[1] Martius, *Von dem Rechtzustande unter den Ureinwohnern Brasiliens,* p. 32.

flesh.   Such is a scene at this day not uncommon on
the northwest coast, and few of the natives around
Milbank Sound are without the scars the result of
this custom.[1]

This frenzy, terrible enough in individuals, had
its most disastrous effects when with that facility
of contagion which marks hysterical maladies, it
swept through whole villages, transforming them
into bedlams filled with unrestrained madmen·
Those who have studied the strange mental epi-
demics that visited Europe in the middle ages, such
as the tarantula dance of Apulia,the chorea German-
orum, and the great St. Vitus' dance, will be prepared
to appreciate the nature of a scene at a Huron village, described by Father le Jeune in 1639.   A
festival of three days and three nights had been in
progress to relieve a woman who, from the description, seems to have been suffering from some obscure
nervous complaint.   Toward the close of this vigil,
which throughout was marked by all sorts of de-
baucheries and excesses, all the participants seemed
suddenly seized by ten thousand devils.   They ran
howling and shrieking through the town, breaking
everything destructible in the cabins, killing dogs,
beating the women and children, tearing their garments, and scattering the fires in every direction with
bare hands and feet.   Some of them dropped senseless, to remain long or permanently insane, but the
others continued until worn out with exhaustion.
The Father learned that during these orgies not
unfrequently whole villages were consumed, and the

<hr/>

[1] Mr. Anderson, in the *Am. Hist. Mag.*, vii. p. 79.

total extirpation of some families had resulted. No wonder that he saw in them the workings of the prince of evil, but the physician is rather inclined to class them with cases of epidemic hysteria, the common products of violent and ill-directed mental stimuli.[1]

These various considerations prove that the authority of the priesthood did by no means rest exclusively on deception. They indorse and explain the assertions of converted natives, that their power as prophets was something real, and inexplicable to themselves. And they make it understood how those missionaries failed who attempted to persuade them that all this boasted power was false. More correct views than these ought to have been suggested by the facts themselves, for these magicians did not hesitate at times to test their strength on each other. In these strange duels *à outrance*, one would be seated opposite his antangonist, surrounded with the mysterious emblems of his craft, and call upon his gods one after another to strike his enemy dead.

---

[1] Such spectacles were nothing uncommon. They are frequently mentioned in the Jesuit Relations, and they were the chief obstacles to missionary labor. In the debauches and excesses that excited these temporary manias, in the recklessness of life and property they fostered, and in their disastrous effects on mind and body, are depicted more than in any other one trait the thorough depravity of the race and its tendency to ruin. In the quaint words of one of the Catholic fathers, "If the old proverb is true that every man has a grain of madness in his composition, it must be confessed that this is a people where each has at least half an ounce " (De Quen, *Rel. de la Nouv. France*, 1656, p. 27). For the instance in the text see *Rel. de la Nouv. France*, An 1639, pp. 88–94.

Sometimes one, " gathering his medicine," as it was termed, feeling within himself that force of will which makes itself acknowledged even without words, would rise in his might, and in a loud and severe voice command his opponent to die! Straightway the latter would drop dead, or yielding in craven fear to a superior volition, forsake the implements of his art, and with an awful terror at his heart creep to his lodge, refuse all nourishment, and presently perish. Still more despotic was the tyranny they exerted on the minds of the masses. Let an Indian once be possessed of the idea that he is bewitched, and he will probably reject all food, and sink under the phantoms of his own fancy.

How deep the veneration of these men has struck its roots in the soul of the Indian, it is difficult for civilized minds to conceive. Their sway is currently supposed to be without any bounds, " extending to the raising of the dead and the control of all laws of nature." [1] The grave offers no escape from their omnipotent arms. The Sacs and Foxes, Algonkin tribes, think that the soul cannot leave the corpse until set free by the medicine men at their great annual feast ; [2] and the Puelches of Buenos Ayres guard a profound silence as they pass by the tomb of some redoubted necromancer, lest they should disturb his repose, and suffer from his malignant skill. [3]

While thus investigating their real and supposed empire over the physical and mental world, their

[1] Schoolcraft, *Indian Tribes*, v. p. 423.

[2] J. M. Stanley, in the *Smithsonian Miscellaneous Contributions*, ii. p. 38.

[3] D'Orbigny, *L'Homme Américain*, ii. p. 81.

strictly priestly functions, as performers of the rites
of religion, have not been touched upon. Among
the hunting tribes these, indeed, were of the most
rudimentary character. Sacrifices, chiefly in the
form of feasts, where every one crammed to his utmost, dances, often winding up with scenes of licentiousness, the repetition of long and monotonous
chants, the making of the new fire, these are the
ceremonies that satisfy the religious wants of savages.
The priest finds a further sphere for his activity in
manufacturing and consecrating amulets to keep off
ill luck, in interpreting dreams, and especially in
lifting the veil of the future. In Peru, for example,
they were divided into classes, who made the various means of divination specialties. Some caused
the idols to speak, others derived their foreknowledge
from words spoken by the dead, others predicted by
leaves of tobacco or the grains and juice of cocoa,
while to still other classes the shapes of grains of
maize taken at random, the appearance of animal
excrement, the forms assumed by the smoke rising
from burning victims, the entrails and viscera of animals, the course taken by a certain species of spider,
the visions seen in drunkenness, the flights of birds,
and the directions in which fruits would fall, all
offered so many separate fields of prognostication,
the professors of which were distinguished by different ranks and titles.[1]

As the intellectual force of the nation was chiefly
centred in this class, they became the acknowledged
depositaries of its sacred legends, the instructors in

---

[1] See Balboa, *Hist. de Pérou*, pp. 28–30.

the art of preserving thought; and from their duty to regulate festivals, sprang the observation of the motions of the heavenly bodies, the adjustment of the calendars, and the pseudo-science of judicial astrology. The latter was carried to as subtle a pitch of refinement in Mexico as in the old world; and large portions of the ancient writers are taken up with explaining the method adopted by the native astrologers to cast the horoscope, and reckon the nativity of the newly-born infant.

How was this superior power obtained? What were the terms of admission to this privileged class? In the ruder communities the power was strictly personal. It was revealed to its possessor by the character of the visions he perceived at the ordeal he passed through on arriving at puberty, and by the northern nations was said to be the manifestation of a more potent personal spirit than ordinary. Thus it is said of the New England Indians that when one of them dreamed that his personal spirit appeared to him in the form of a serpent, he forthwith called a feast and became a *pow-wow*.[1] It was not a faculty, but an inspiration; not an inborn strength, but a spiritual gift. The curious theory of the Dakotas, as recorded by the Rev. Mr. Pond, was that the necromant first wakes to consciousness as a winged seed, wafted hither and thither by the intelligent action of the Four Winds. In this form he visits the homes of the different classes of divinities, and learns the chants, feasts, and dances, which it is proper for the

[1] *The Day Breaking of the Gospel with the Indians in New England:* London, 1647, p. 27.

human race to observe, the art of omnipresence or clairvoyance, the means of inflicting and healing diseases, and the occult secrets of nature, man, and divinity. This is called " dreaming of the gods." When this instruction 'is completed, the seed enters one about to become a mother, assumes human form, and in due time manifests his powers. *Four* such incarnations await it, each of increasing might, and then the spirit returns to its original nothingness. The same necessity of death and resurrection was entertained by the Eskimos. To become of the highest order of priests, it was supposed requisite, says Bishop Egede, that an ordinary mortal should be drowned and eaten by sea monsters. Then, when his bones, one after another, were all washed ashore, his spirit, which meanwhile had been learning the secrets of the invisible world, would return to them, and, clothed in flesh, he would go back to his tribe. At other times a vague longing seizes a young person, a morbid appetite possesses him, or he falls a prey to restlessness, and melancholy. These signs the old priests recognize as the expression of a personal spirit of the higher order. They take charge of the youth, and educate him to the mysteries of their craft. For months or years he is condemned to seclusion, receiving no visits but from the brethren of his order. At length he is initiated with ceremonies of more or less pomp into the brotherhood, and from that time assumes that gravity of demeanor, sententious style of expression, and general air of mystery and importance, everywhere deemed becoming in a doctor and a priest. A peculiarity of the Moxos was, that they thought none designated

for the office but such as had escaped from the claws
of the South American tiger,[1] which must have effect-
ually limited the guild.

Occasionally, in very uncultivated tribes, some
family or totem claimed a monopoly of the priesthood. Thus, among the Nez Percés of Oregon, it
was transmitted in one family from father to son and
daughter, but always with the proviso that the children at the proper age reported dreams of a satisfactory character.[2] Perhaps alone of the Algonkin
tribes the Shawnees confined it to one totem, but it
is remarkable that the greatest of their prophets,
Elskataway, brother of Tecumseh, was not a member
of this clan. From the most remote times, the Cherokees have had one family set apart for the priestly
office. This was when first known to the whites that
of the Nicotani, but its members, puffed up with
pride, abused their birthright so shamefully, and pros-
tituted it so flagrantly to their own advantage, that
with savage justice they were massacred to the last
man. Another was appointed in their place which
to this day officiates in all religious rites. They have,
however, the superstition, possibly borrowed from
Europeans, that the *seventh* son is a natural born
prophet, with the gift of healing by touch.[3] Adair
states that their former neighbors, the Choctaws,
permitted the office of high priest, or Great Beloved
Man, to remain in one family, passing from father to
eldest son, and the very influential *piaches* of the

---

[1] D'Orbigny, *L'Homme Américain*, ii. p. 235.

[2] Schoolcraft, *Ind. Tribes*, v. p. 652.

[3] Dr. MacGowan, in the *Amer. Hist. Mag.*, x. p. 139; Whipple, *Rep. on the Ind. Tribes*, p. 35.

Carib tribes very generally transmitted their rank and position to their children.

In ancient Anahuac the prelacy was as systematic and its rules as well defined, as in the Church of Rome. Except those in the service of Huitzilopochtli, and perhaps a few other gods, none obtained the priestly office by right of descent, but were dedicated to it from early childhood. Their education was completed at the *Calmecac*, a sort of ecclesiastical college, where instruction was given in all the wisdom of the ancients, and the esoteric lore of their craft. The art of mixing colors and tracing designs, the ideographic writing and phonetic hieroglyphs, the songs and prayers used in public worship, the national traditions, and the principles of astrology, the hidden meaning of symbols and the use of musical instruments, all formed parts of the really extensive course of instruction they there received. When they manifested a satisfactory acquaintance with this curriculum, they were appointed by their superiors to such positions as their natural talents and the use they had made of them qualified them for, some to instruct children, others to the service of the temples, and others again to take charge of what we may call country parishes. Implicit subordination of all to the high priest of Huitzilopochtli, hereditary *pontifex maximus*, chastity, or at least temperate indulgence in pleasure, gravity of carriage and strict attention to duty, were laws laid upon all.

The state religion of Peru was conducted under the supervison of a high priest of the Inca family, and its ministers, as in Mexico, could be of either sex, and hold office either by inheritance, education, or election.   For political reasons, the most important posts were usually enjoyed by relatives of the ruler, but this was usage, not law.   It is stated by Garcilasso de la Vega[1] that they served in the temples by turns, each being on duty the fourth of a lunar month at a time.   Were this substantiated it would offer the only example of the regulation of public life by a week of seven days to be found in the New World.

In every country there is perceptible a desire in this class of men to surround themselves with mystery, and to concentrate and increase their power by forming an alliance among themselves.   They affected singularity in dress and a professional costume. Bartram describes the junior priests of the Creeks as dressed in white robes and carrying on their head or arm " a great owlskin, stuffed very ingeniously, as an insignia of wisdom and divination.   These bachelors are also distinguishable from the other people by their taciturnity, grave and solemn countenance, dignified step, and singing to themselves songs or hymns, in a low sweet voice, as they stroll about the towns." [2]   The priests of the civilized nations adopted various modes of dress to typify the divinity which they served, and their appearance was often in the highest degree unprepossessing.

To add to their self-importance they pretended to converse in a tongue different from that used in ordinary life, and the chants containing the prayers and legends were often in this esoteric dialect.   Fragments of one or two of these have floated down to

1 *Hist. des Incas*, lib. iii. ch. 22.
2 Travels in the Carolinas, p. 504.

us from the Aztec priesthood. The travellers Balboa and Coreal mention that the temple services of Peru were conducted in a language not understood by the masses,[1] and the incantations of the priests of Powhatan were not in ordinary Algonkin, but some obscure jargon.[2] The same peculiarity has been observed among the Dakotas and Eskimos, and in these nations, fortunately, it fell under the notice of competent linguistic scholars, who have submitted it to a searching examination. The results of their labors prove that certainly in these two instances the supposed foreign tongues were nothing more than the

---

[1] *Hist. de Pérou*, p. 128; *Voiages aux Indes Occidentales*, ii. p. 97.

[2] Beverly, *Hist. de la Virginie*, p. 266. The dialect he specifies is "celle d' Occaniches," and on page 252 he says, "On dit que la langue universelle des Indiens de ces Quartiers est celle des *Occaniches*, quoiqu'ils ne soient qu'une petite Nation, depuis que les Anglois connoissent ce Pais ; mais je ne sais pas la différence qui'l y a entre cette langue et celle des Algonkins." (French trans., Orleans, 1707.) This is undoubtedly the same people that Johannes Lederer, a German traveller, visited in 1670, and calls *Akenatzi*. They dwelt on an island, in a branch of the Chowan River, the Sapona, or Deep River (Lederer's *Discovery of North America*, in Harris, Voyages, p. 20). Thirty years later the English surveyor, Lawson, found them in the same spot, and speaks of them as the *Acanechos* (see *Am. Hist. Mag.*, i. p. 163). Their totem was that of the serpent, and their name is not altogether unlike the Tuscarora name of this animal *usquauhne*. As the serpent was so widely a sacred animal, this gives Beverly's remarks an unusual significance. It by no means follows from this name that they were of Iroquois descent. Lederer travelled with a Tuscarora (Iroquois) interpreter, who gave them their name in his own tongue. On the contrary, it is extremely probable that they were an Algonkin totem, which had the exclusive right to the priesthood.

ordinary dialects of the country modified by an affected accentuation, by the introduction of a few cabalistic terms, and by the use of circumlocutions and figurative words in place of ordinary expressions, a slang, in short, such as rascals and pedants are very apt to coin.[1]

All these stratagems were intended to shroud with impenetràble secrecy the mysteries of the brotherhood. With the same motive, the priests formed societies of different grades of illumination, only to be entered by those willing to undergo trying ordeals, whose secrets were not to be revealed ʻunder the severest penalties. The Algonkins had three such grades, the *waubeno*, the *meda*, and the *jossakeed*, the last being the highest. To this no white man was ever admitted. All tribes appear to have been controlled by these secret societies. Alexander von Humboldt mentions one, called that of the Botuto or Holy Trumpet, among the Indians of the Orinoco, whose members must vow celibacy and submit to severe scourgings and fasts. The Collahuayas of Peru were a guild of itinerant quacks and magicians, who never remained permanently in one spot.

Withal, there was no class of persons who so widely influenced the culture and shaped the destiny of the Indian tribes as their priests. In attempting to gain a true conception of the race's capacities and history, there is no one element of their social life

---

[1] Riggs, *Gram. and Dict. of the Dakota*, p. 9 ; Kane, *Second Grinnell Expedition*, ii. p. 127. Paul Egede gives a number of words and expressions in the dialect of the sorcerers, *Nachrichten von Grönland*, p. 122.

which demands closer attention than the power of
these teachers. Hitherto, they have been spoken of
with a contempt which I hope this chapter shows is
unjustifiable. However much we may deplore the
use they made of their skill, we must estimate it fairly,
and grant it its due weight in measuring the influence of the religious sentiment on the history of man.

20

CHAPTER XI.

THE INFLUENCE OF THE NATIVE RELIGIONS ON THE MORAL AND SOCIAL LIFE OF THE RACE.

Natural religions hitherto considered of Evil rather than of Good.—Distinctions to be drawn.—Morality not derived from religion.—The positive side of natural religions in incarnations of divinity.—Examples.—Prayers as indices of religious progress.—Religion and social advancement.—Conclusion.

DRAWING toward the conclusion of my essay, I am sensible that the vast field of American mythology remains for the most part untouched—that I have but proved that it is not an absolute wilderness, pathless as the tropical jungles which now conceal the temples of the race; but that, go where we will, certain landmarks and guide-posts are visible, revealing uniformity of design and purpose, and refuting, by their presence, the oft-repeated charge of incoherence and aimlessness. It remains to examine the subjective power of the native religions, their influence on those who held them, and the place they deserve in the history of the race. What are their merits, if merits they have? what their demerits? Did they purify the life and enlighten the mind, or the contrary? Are they in short of evil or of good? The problem is complex—its solution most difficult. An author who studied profoundly the savage races of the globe, expressed the discouraging conviction: "Their religions have not acted as levers to raise them to civilization; they have rather worked, and that powerfully, to impede every step in advance, in the first place by ascribing everything unintelligible in nature to spiritual agency, and then by making the fate of man dependent on mysterious and capricious forces, not on his own skill and foresight." [1]

It would ill accord with the theory of mythology which I have all along maintained if this verdict were final. But in fact these false doctrines brought with them their own antidotes, at least to some extent, and while we give full weight to their evil, let us also acknowledge their good. By substituting direct divine interference for law, belief for knowledge, a dogma for a fact, the highest stimulus to mental endeavor was taken away. Nature, to the heathen, is no harmonious whole swayed by eternal principles, but a chaos of causeless effects, the meaningless play of capricious ghosts. He investigates not, because he doubts not. All events are to him miracles. Therefore his faith knows no bounds, and those who teach that doubt is sinful must contemplate him with admiration. The damsels of Nicaragua destined to be thrown into the craters of volcanoes, went to their fate, says Pascual de Andagoya, "happy as if they were going to be saved," [2] and doubtless believing so. The subjects of a Central American chieftain, remarks Oviedo, "look upon it as the crown of favors to be permitted to die with their cacique, and thus to acquire immortality." [3]

[1] Waitz, *Anthropologie der Naturvoelker*, i. p. 459.

[2] Navarrete, *Viages*, iii. p. 415.

[3] *Relation de Cueba*, p. 140. Ed. Ternaux-Compans.

The power exerted by the priests rested, as they themselves often saw, largely on the implicit acceptance of their dicta.

In some respects the contrast here offered to enlightened nations is not in favor of the latter. Borrowing the antithesis of the poet, one might exclaim—

> "This is all
> The gain we reap from all the wisdom sown
> Through ages: Nothing doubted those first sons
> Of Time, while we, the schooled of centuries,
> Nothing believe."

But the complaint is unfounded. Faith is dearly bought at the cost of knowledge; nor in a better sense has it gone from among us. Far more sublime than any known to the barbarian is the faith of the astronomer, who spends the nights in marking the seemingly wayward motions of the stars, or of the anatomist, who studies with unwearied zeal the minute fibres of the organism, each upheld by the unshaken conviction that from least to greatest throughout this universe, purpose and order everywhere prevail.

Natural religions rarely offer more than this negative opposition to reason. They are tolerant to a degree. The savage, void of any clear conception of a supreme deity, sets up no claim that his is the only true church. If he is conquered in battle, he imagines that it is owing to the inferiority of his own gods to those of his victor, and he rarely therefore requires any other reasons to make him a convert. Acting on this principle, the Incas, when they overcame a strange province, sent its most venerated idol for a time to the temple of the Sun at Cuzco, thus proving its inferiority to their own divinity, but took no more violent steps to propagate their creeds.[1] So in the city of Mexico there was a temple appropriated to the idols of conquered nations in which they were shut up, both to prove their weakness and prevent them from doing mischief. A nation, like an individual, was not inclined to patronize a deity who had manifested his incompetence by allowing his charge to be worn away by disaster. As far as can now be seen, in matters intellectual, the religions of ancient Mexico and Peru were far more liberal than that introduced by the Spanish conquerors, which, claiming the monopoly of truth, sought to enforce its claim by inquisitions and censorships.

In this view of the relative powers of deities lay a potent corrective to the doctrine that the fate of man was dependent on the caprices of the gods. For no belief was more universal than that which assigned to each individual a guardian spirit. This invisible monitor was an ever present help in trouble. He suggested expedients, gave advice and warning in dreams, protected in danger, and stood ready to foil the machinations of enemies, divine or human. With unlimited faith in this protector, attributing to him the fortunate chances of life and the devices suggested by his own quick wits, the savage escaped the oppressive thought that he was the slave of demoniac forces, and dared the dangers of the forest and the war path without anxiety.

By far the darkest side of such a religion is that which it presents to morality. The religious sense

---

[1] La Vega, *Hist. des Incas*, liv. v. cap. 12.

is by no means the voice of conscience. The
Takahli Indian when sick makes a full confession of
sins, but a murder, however unnatural and unpro-
voked, he does not mention, not counting it a crime.[1]
Scenes of licentiousness were approved and sustained
throughout the continent as acts of worship ; maiden-
hood was in many parts offered up or claimed by the
priests as a right ; in Central America twins were
slain for religious motives ; human sacrifice was
common throughout the tropics, and was not unusual
in higher latitudes; cannibalism was often enjoined ;
and in Peru, Florida, and Central America it was
not uncommon for parents to slay their own children
at the behest of a priest.[2] The philosophical moralist,
contemplating such spectacles, has thought to recognize in them one consoling trait. All history, it has
been said, shows man living under an irritated God,
and seeking to appease him by sacrifice of blood ; the
essence of all religion, it has been added, lies in that
of which sacrifice is the symbol, namely, in the offering up of self, in the rendering up of our will to
the will of God.[3] But sacrifice, when not a token of

[1] Morse, *Rep. on the Ind. Tribes,* App. p. 345.

[2] Ximenes, *Origen de los Indios de Guatemala,* p. 192 ; Acosta,
Hist. of the New World, lib. v. chap. 18.

[3] Joseph de Maistre, *Eclaircissement sur les Sacrifices;* Trench,
Hulsean Lectures, p. 180.   The famed Abbé Lammennais and
Professor Sepp, of Munich, with these two writers, may be
taken as the chief exponents of a school of mythologists, all of
whom start from the theories first laid down by Count de
Maistre in his *Soirées de St. Petersbourg.* To them the strongest
proof of Christianity lies in the traditions and observances of
heathendom.   For these show the wants of the religious sense,
and Christianity, they maintain, purifies and satisfies them all.

gratitude, cannot be thus explained. It is not a rendering up, but a *substitution* of our will for God's will. A deity is angered by neglect of his dues; he will revenge, certainly, terribly, we know not how or when. But as punishment is all he desires, if we punish ourselves he will be satisfied; and far better is such self-inflicted torture than a fearful looking for of judgment to come. Craven fear, not without some dim sense of the implacability of nature's laws, is at its root. Looking only at this side of religion, the ancient philosopher averred that the gods existed solely in the apprehensions of their votaries, and the moderns have asserted that "fear is the father of religion, love her late-born daughter;"[1] that "the first form of religious belief is nothing else but a horror of the unknown;" and that "no natural religion appears to have been able to develop from a germ within itself anything whatever of real advantage to civilization."[2]

Far be it from me to excuse the enormities thus committed under the garb of religion, or to ignore their disastrous consequences on human progress.

The rites, symbols, and legends of every natural religion, they say, are true, and not false; all that is required is to assign them their proper places and their real meaning. Therefore the strange resemblances in heathen myths to what is revealed in the Scriptures, as well as the ethical anticipations which have been found in ancient philosophies, all so far from proving that Christianity is a natural product of the human mind, in fact, are confirmations of it, unconscious prophecies, and presentiments of the truth.

[1] Alfred Maury, *La Magie et l'Astrologie dans l'Antiquité et au Moyen Age*, p. 8: Paris, 1860.

[2] Waitz, *Anthropologie*, i. pp. 325, 465.

Yet this question is a fair one—if the natural religious belief has in it no germ of anything better, whence comes the manifest and undeniable improvement occasionally witnessed—as, for example, among the Toltecs, the Peruvians, and the Mayas? The reply is by the influence of great men, who cultivated within themselves a purer faith, lived it in their lives, preached it successfully to their fellows, and, at their death, still survived in the memory of their nation unforgotten models of noble qualties.[1] Where, in America, is any record of such men? We are pointed, in answer, to Quetzalcoatl, Viracocha, Zamna, and their congeners. But these august figures I have shown to be wholly mythical, creations of the religious fancy, parts and parcels of the earliest religion itself. The entire theory falls to nothing, therefore, and we discover a positive side to natural religions—one that conceals a germ of endless progress, which vindicates their lofty origin, and proves that He " is not far from every one of us."

I have already analyzed these figures under their physical aspect. Let it be observed in what antithesis they stand to most other mythological creations. Let it be remembered that they primarily correspond to the stable, the regular, the cosmical phenomena, that they are always conceived under human form, not as giants, fairies, or strange beasts ; that they were said at one time to have been visible leaders of their nations, that they did not suffer death, and that, though absent, they are ever present, favoring those who remain mindful of their

---

[1] So says Dr. Waitz, *Anthropologie, i.* p. 465.

precepts. I touched but incidentally
aspects. This was likewise in contra
ity of inferior deities. The worship o
a tribute extorted by fear. The Indian deposits
tobacco on the rocks of a rapid, that the spirit of the
swift waters may not swallow his canoe; in a
storm he throws overboard a dog to appease the
siren of the angry waves. He used to tear the hearts
from his captives to gain the favor of the god of war.
He provides himself with talismans to bind hostile deities. He fees the conjurer to exorcise the demon of
disease. He loves none of them; he respects none of
them; he only fears their wayward tempers. They
are to him mysterious, invisible, capricious goblins.
But, in his highest divinity, he recognized a Father
and a Preserver, a benign Intelligence, who provided
for him the comforts of life—man, like himself, yet
a god—God of All. "Go and do good," was the
parting injunction of his father to Michabo in Algonkin legend;[1] and in their ancient and uncorrupted
stories such is ever his object. "The worship of
Tamu," the culture hero of the Guaranis, says the
traveller D'Orbigny, "is one of reverence, not of
fear."[2] They were ideals, summing up in themselves the best traits, the most approved virtues of
whole nations, and were adored in a very different
spirit from other divinities.

None of them has more humane and elevated traits
than Quetzalcoatl. He was represented of majestic
stature and dignified demeanor. In his train came
skilled artificers and men of learning. He was chaste

[1] Schoolcraft, *Algic Researches*, i. p. 143.
[2] *L'Homme Américain*, ii. p. 319.

and temperate in life, wise in council, generous of gifts, conquering rather by arts of peace than of war; delighting in music, flowers, and brilliant colors, and so averse to human sacrifices that he shut his ears with both hands when they were even mentioned.[1] Such was the ideal man and supreme god of a people who even a Spanish monk of the sixteeth century felt constrained to confess were " a good people, attached to virtue, urbane and simple in social intercourse, shunning lies, skillful in arts, pious towards their gods."[2] Is it likely, is it possible, that with such a model as this before their minds, they received no benefit from it? Was not this a lever, and a mighty one, lifting the race toward civilization and a purer faith.

Transfer the field of observation to Yucatan, and we find in Zamna, to New Granada and in Nemqueteba, to Peru and in Viracocha, or his reflex Manco Capac, the lineaments of Quetzalcoatl—modified, indeed, by difference of blood and temperament, but each combining in himself all the qualities most esteemed by their several nations. Were one or all of these proved to be historical personages, still the fact remains that the primitive religious sentiment, investing them with the best attributes of humanity, dwelling on them as its models, worshipping them as gods, contained a kernel of truth potent to encourage moral excellence. But if they were mythical, then this truth was of spontaneous growth, self-developed by the growing distinctness of the idea of God, a

---

[1] Brasseur, *Hist. de Mexique*, liv. iii. chaps. 1 and 2.
[2] Sahagun, *Hist. de la Nueva España*, lib. x. cap. 29.

living witness that the religious sense, like every
other faculty, has within itself a power of endless
evolution.

If we inquire the secret of the happier influence of
such an ideal in worship, it is all contained in one
word—its *humanity.* " The Ideal of Morality," says
the contemplative Novalis, " has no more dangerous
rival than the Ideal of the Greatest Strength, of the
most vigorous life, the Brute Ideal " (*das Thier-
Ideal*).[1] Culture advances in proportion as man recognizes what faculties are peculiar to him *as man*,
and devotes himself to their education. The moral
value of religions can be very precisely estimated by
the human or the brutal character of their gods. The
worship of Quetzalcoatl in the city of Mexico was
subordinate to that of lower conceptions, and consequently the more sanguinary and immoral were the
rites there practised. The Algonkins, who knew no
other meaning for Michabo than the Great Hare, had
lost, by a false etymology, the best part of their religion.

Looking around for other standards wherewith to
measure the progress of the knowledge of divinity in
the New World, *prayer* suggests itself as one of the
least deceptive. " Prayer," to quote again the words
of Novalis,[2] " is in religion what thought is in philosophy. The religious sense prays, as the reason thinks."
Guizot, carrying the analysis farther, thinks that it is
prompted by a painful conviction of the inability of
our will to conform to the dictates of reason.[3] Origin-

---

[1] Novalis, *Schriften*, i. p. 244 : Berlin, 1837.

[2] Ibid., p. 267.

[3] *Hist. de la Civilisation en France*, i. pp. 122, 130.

ally it was connected with the belief that divine caprice, not divine law, governs the universe, and that material benefits rather than spiritual gifts are to be desired. The gradual recognition of its limitations and proper objects marks religious advancement. The Lord's Prayer contains seven petitions, only one of which may perhaps be for a temporal advantage, and it the least that can be asked for. What immeasurable interval between it and the prayer of the Nootka Indian on preparing for war!—

"Great Quahootze, let me live, not be sick, find the enemy, not fear him, find him asleep, and kill a great many of him." [1]

Or again, between it and the petition of a Huron to a local god, heard by Father Brebeuf:—

"Oki, thou who livest in this spot, I offer thee tobacco. Help us, save us from shipwreck, defend us from our enemies, give us a good trade, and bring us back safe and sound to our villages." [2]

This is a fair specimen of the supplications of the lowest religion. Another equally authentic is given by Father Allouez.[3] In 1670 he penetrated to an outlying Algonkin village, never before visited by a white man. The inhabitants, startled by his pale face and long black gown, took him for a divinity. They invited him to the council lodge, a circle of old men gathered around him, and one of them, approaching him with a double handful of

---

[1] *Narrative of J. R. Jewett among the Savages of Nootka Sound*, p. 121.

[2] *Rel. de la Nouv. France*, An 1636, p. 109.

[3] Ibid., An 1670, p. 99.

tobacco, thus addressed him, the others grunting approval :—

" This, indeed, is well, Blackrobe, that thou dost visit us. Have mercy upon us. Thou art a Manito. We give thee to smoke.

" The Naudowessies and Iroquois are devouring us. Have mercy upon us.

" We are often sick; our children die; we are hungry. Have mercy upon us. Hear me, O Manito, I give thee to smoke.

" Let the earth yield us corn; the rivers give us fish; sickness not slay us; nor hunger so torment us. Hear us, O Manito, we give thee to smoke."

In this rude but touching petition, wrung from the heart of a miserable people, nothing but their wretchedness is visible. Not the faintest trace of an aspiration for spiritual enlightenment cheers the eye of the philanthropist, not the remotest conception that through suffering we are purified can be detected.

By the side of these examples we may place the prayers of Peru and Mexico, forms composed by the priests, written out, committed to memory, and repeated at certain seasons. They are not less authentic, having been collected and translated in the first generation after the conquest. One to Viracocha Pachacamac, was as follows :—

" O Pachacamac, thou who hast existed from the beginning and shalt exist unto the end, powerful and pitiful; who createdst man by saying, let man be; who defendest us from evil and preservest our life and health; art thou in the sky or in the earth, in the clouds or in the depths? Hear the voice of him who

implores thee, and grant him his petitions. Give us
life everlasting, preserve us, and accept this our sacrifice." [1]

In the voluminous specimens of Aztec prayers
preserved by Sahagun, moral improvement, the
" spiritual gift," is very rarely if at all the object
desired. Health, harvests, propitious rains, release
from pain, preservation from dangers, illness, and
defeat, these are the almost unvarying themes. But
here and there we catch a glimpse of something better, some dim sense of the beauty of suffering, some
glimmering of the truth so nobly expressed by the
poet :—

> aus des Busens Tiefe strömt Gedeihn
> Der festen Duldung und entschlossner That.
> Nicht Schmerz ist Unglück, Glück nicht immer Freude;
> Wer sein Geschick erfüllt, dem lächeln beide.

" Is it possible," says one of them, " that this
scourge, this affliction, is sent to us not for our cor-
rection and improvement, but for our destruction
and annihilation? O Merciful Lord, let this chas-
tisement with which thou hast visited us, thy people,
be as those which a father or mother inflicts on a
child, not out of anger, but to the end that he may
be free from follies and vices." Another formula,
used when a chief was elected to some important

---

[1] Geronimo de Ore, *Symbolo Catholico Indiano*, chap. ix., quoted by Ternaux-Compans. De Ore was a native of Peru and
held the position of Professor of Theology in Cuzco in the latter half of the sixteenth century. He was a man of great
erudition, and there need be no hesitation in accepting this extraordinary prayer as genuine. For his life and writings see
Nic. Antonio, *Bib. Hisp. Nova*, tom. ii. p. 43.

position, reads: " O Lord, open his eyes and give him light, sharpen his ears and give him understanding, not that he may use them to his own advantage, but for the good of the people he rules. Lead him to know and to do thy will, let him be as a trumpet which sounds thy words. Keep him from the commission of injustice and oppression." [1]

At first, good and evil are identical with pleasure and pain, luck and ill-luck. " The good are good warriors and hunters," said a Pawnee chief,[2] which would also be the opinion of a wolf, if he could express it. Gradually the eyes of the mind are opened, and it is perceived that " whom He loveth, He chastiseth," and physical give place to moral ideas of good and evil. Finally, as the idea of God rises more distinctly before the soul, as " the One by whom, in whom, and through whom all things are," evil is seen to be the negation, not the opposite of good, and itself "a porch oft opening on the sun."

The influence of these religions on art, science, and social life, must also be weighed in estimating their value.

Very many of the remains of American plastic art, sculpture, and painting, were designed for religious purposes. Idols of stone, wood, or baked clay, were found in every Indian tribe, without exception, so far as I can judge ; and in only a few directions do these arts seem to have been applied to secular purposes. The most ambitious attempts of

1 Sahagun, *Hist. de la Nueva España*, lib. vi. caps. 1, 4.

2 Morse, *Rep. on the Ind. Tribes*, App. p. 250.

architecture, it is plain, were inspired by religious fervor. The great pyramid of Cholula, the enormous mounds of the Mississippi valley, the elaborate edifices on artificial hills in Yucatan, were miniature representations of the mountains hallowed by tradition, the "Hill of Heaven," the peak on which their ancestors escaped in the flood, or that in the terrestrial paradise from which flow the rains.   Their construction took men away from war and the chase, encouraged agriculture, peace, and a settled disposition, and fostered the love of property, of country, and of the gods.   The priests were also close observers of nature, and were the first to discover its simpler laws.   The Aztec sages were as devoted star-gazers as the Chaldeans, and their calendar bears unmistakable marks of native growth, and of its original purpose to fix the annual festivals.   Writing by means of pictures and symbols was cultivated chiefly for religious ends, and the word *hieroglyph* is a witness that the phonetic alphabet was discovered under the stimulus of the religious sentiment.   Most of the aboriginal literature was composed and taught by the priests, and most of it refers to matters connected with their superstitions.   As the gifts of votaries and the erection of temples enriched the sacerdotal order individually and collectively, the terrors of religion were lent to the secular arm to enforce the rights of property.   Music, poetic, scenic, and historical recitations, formed parts of the ceremonies of the more civilized nations, and national unity was strengthened by a common shrine.   An active barter in amulets, lucky stones, and charms, existed all over the continent, to a much greater extent than we might think. As experience demonstrates that nothing so efficiently promotes civilization as the free and peaceful intercourse of man with man, I lay particular stress on the common custom of making pilgrimages.

The temple on the island of Cozumel in Yucatan was visited every year by such multitudes from all parts of the peninsula, that roads, paved with cut stones, had been constructed from the neighboring shore to the principal cities of the interior.[1] Each village of the Muyscas is said to have had a beaten path to Lake Guatavita, so numerous were the devotees who journeyed to the shrine there located.[2] In Peru the temples of Pachacamà, Rimac, and other famous gods, were repaired to by countless numbers from all parts of the realm, and from other provinces within a radius of three hundred leagues around. Houses of entertainment were established on all the principal roads, and near the temples, for their accommodation; and when they made known the object of their journey, they were allowed a safe passage even through an enemy's territory.[3]

The more carefully we study history, the more important in our eyes will become the religious sentiment. It is almost the only faculty peculiar to man. It concerns him nearer than aught else. It is the

---

[1] Cogolludo, *Hist. de Yucathan*, lib. iv. cap. 9. Compare Stephens, *Travs. in Yucatan*, ii. p. 122, who describes the remains of these roads as they now exist.

[2] Rivero and Tschudi, *Antiqs. of Peru*, p. 162.

[3] La Vega, *Hist. des Incas*, lib. vi. chap. 30; Xeres, *Rel. de la Conq. du Pérou*, p. 151; *Let. sur les Superstit. du Pérou*, p. 98, and others.

key to his origin and destiny. As such it merits in all its developments the most earnest attention, an attention we shall find well repaid by the clearer conceptions we thus obtain of the forces which control the actions and fates of individuals and nations.

THE END.

INDICES.

I.—AUTHORS.

II.—SUBJECTS.

Steinerbooks

ISBN Prefix: 0-8334

The Spiritual Sciences in quality paperback format, 4¼" × 7" racksize, unless otherwise noted.

ALCHEMY/MYSTICISM/ROSICRUCIANISM

1704-5	**Alchemists Through the Ages**	Waite/$2.75
3505-1	**Christian Rosenkreutz Anthology** (7×10)	Allen/$15.00
1721-5	**Eleven European Mystics**	Steiner/$2.50
1720-7	**Lamps of Western Mysticism**	Waite/$2.75
1738-X	**Real History of the Rosicrucians** (5¼×8¼)	Waite/$6.50

ATLANTIS/EGYPTOLOGY/SPIRITUAL HISTORY

1717-7	**Atlantis/Europe:** Secret of the West	Merejkowski/$3.50
1758-6	**Atlantis in Ireland:** Round Towers of Ireland (5¼×8¼)	O'Brien/$6.50
1724-X	**Atlantis:** The Antediluvian World	Donnelly/$3.95
1716-9	**Cosmic Memory:** Atlantis & Lemuria	Steiner/$2.50
1705-3	**From Sphinx to Christ**	Schure/$2.50
1735-5	**Great Pyramid:** Miracle in Stone	Seiss/$2.50
1729-0	**Maya/Atlantis:** Queen Moo & the Egyptian Sphinx	LePlongeon/$2.95
1727-4	**Mysteries of Egypt:** Secret Rites of the Nile	Spence/$2.50
3503-5	**Our Inheritance in the Great Pyramid** (7×10)	Smyth/$12.95
1718-5	**Ragnarok:** The Destruction of Atlantis	Donnelly/$3.25

APPLIED SPIRITUAL SCIENCE

1707-X	**Education As An Art**	Steiner/$1.95
1715-0	**Gardening For Health:** The Organic Way	Philbrick/$1.50
1701-0	**Meditations on the Signs of the Zodiac**	Jocelyn/$2.50

COMPARATIVE & ESOTERIC RELIGIONS

1708-8	**Ancient Mysteries of the East:** Rama-Krishna	Schure/$1.75
1719-3	**Christianity and the Occult Mysteries of Antiquity**	Steiner/$2.50
1731-2	**Commentaries on the Bhagavad Gita**	Sri Chinmoy/$1.95
1751-3	**Great Initiates** (5¼×8¼)	Schure/$6.50
1759-6	**Qabbalah** (5¼×8¼)	Myer/$6.50

METAPHYSICS/PHILOSOPHY

1728-2	**Pictorial Key to the Tarot**	Waite/$2.50
1703-7	**Unknown Philosopher:** de Saint-Martin	Waite/$3.95

MYTHOLOGY/FOLKLORE/SYMBOLISM

1745-2	**Myths & Legends of North American Indian** (5¼×8¼)	Spence/$5.50
1742-8	**Myths of the New World Indians** (5¼×8¼)	Brinton/$5.50
1762-3	**Myths & Legends of Ancient Egypt** (5¼×8¼)	Spence/$5.50
1746-0	**Myths of China & Japan** (5¼×8¼)	Mackenzie/$5.50
1764-9	**Myths of Greece & Rome** (5¼×8¼)	Guerber/$5.50
1726-6	**Golem:** Mystical Tales of the Ghetto	Bloch/$2.25

PSYCHIC & OCCULT PHENOMENA

1730-4	**ESPecially Irene:** A Guide to Psychic Awareness	Hughes/$1.95
1739-8	**Occult and Curative Powers of Precious Stones**	Fernie/$3.95
3502-7	**Secret Societies of All Ages & Countries** (7×10)	Heckethorn/$15.00